7/00

The Limits of Idealism

When Good Intentions Go Bad

CLINICAL SOCIOLOGY
Research and Practice

SERIES EDITOR:

John G. Bruhn, *Pennsylvania State University/Harrisburg*
Middletown, Pennsylvania

CLINICAL SOCIOLOGY: An Agenda for Action
John G. Bruhn and Howard M. Rebach

THE LIMITS OF IDEALISM: When Good Intentions Go Bad
Melvyn L. Fein

THE PARTNERSHIP MODEL IN HUMAN SERVICES: Sociological
Foundations and Practices
Rosalyn Benjamin Darling

A Continuation Order Plan is available for this series. A continuation order will bring delivery of each
new volume immediately upon publication. Volumes are billed only upon actual shipment. For further
information please contact the publisher.

The Limits of Idealism
When Good Intentions Go Bad

Melvyn L. Fein
Kennesaw State University
Kennesaw, Georgia

Kluwer Academic / Plenum Publishers
New York, Boston, Dordrecht, London, Moscow

Library of Congress Cataloging-in-Publication Data

Fein, Melvyn L.
    The limits of idealism : when good intentions go bad / Melvyn L.
Fein.
        p.   cm. -- (Clinical sociology)
    Includes bibliographical references and index.
    ISBN 0-306-46211-7
    1. Radicalism--History--20th century. 2. Radicalism--United
States--History--20th century. 3. Idealism--History--20th century.
I. Title. II. Series.
HN17.5.F44 1999
303.48'4--dc21   99-42793
                                                                  CIP

ISBN 0-306-46211-7

©1999 Kluwer Academic/Plenum Publishers, New York
233 Spring Street, New York, N.Y. 10013

10 9 8 7 6 5 4 3 2 1

A C.I.P. record for this book is available from the Library of Congress

Printed in the United States of America

In memory of my uncle,
Milton Tarriff,
the best human being I have personally known.

No period in history has ever been great or ever can be that does not act on some sort of high, idealistic motives, and idealism in our time has been shoved aside, and we are paying the penalty for it.

Alfred North Whitehead, January 13, 1944

By these intellectual maneuvers, radicals have been able to resurrect the utopian vision and the destructive enterprise it engenders. The perfect future is once again invoked to condemn the imperfect present. Nietzsche observed, 'Idealism kills.' Without the noble utopian idea, the evil practice would not exist.

David Horowitz, *The Politics of Bad Faith*, 1998

Before we praise radical egalitarians for their noble if unrealizable ideals, we do well to remember that noble ideals can themselves be the source of ignoble actions. ... It is not enough to declare an idea noble and one's hands clean; one needs to ask what will happen to that uplifting ideal when people behave not like angels but like fallible, biased human beings.

Richard J. Ellis, *The Dark Side of the Left*, 1998

Many have dreamed up republics and principalities that have never in truth been known to exist: the gap between how one should live and how one does live is so wide that a man who neglects what is actually done for what should be done learns the way to self destruction rather than self preservation.

Niccolo Machiaveli, *The Prince*, 1514

Fanaticism consists in redoubling your efforts when you have forgotten your aim.

George Santayana, *The Life of Reason*, 1905–1906

Preface

If the truth be known, I am only a partially reformed idealist. In the secret depths of my soul, I still wish to make the world a better place and sometimes fantasize about heroically eradicating its faults. When I encounter its limitations, it is consequently with deep regret and continued surprise. How, I ask myself, is it possible that that which seems so right can be a chimera? And why, I wonder, aren't people as courageous, smart, or nice as I would like? The pain of realizing these things is sometimes so intense that I want to close my eyes and lose myself in the kinds of daydreams that comforted me as a youngster.

One thing is clear, my need to come to grips with my idealism had its origin in a lifetime of naiveté. From the beginning, I wanted to be a "good" person. Often when life was most treacherous, I retreated into a corner from whence I escaped into reveries of moral glory. When I was very young, my faith was in religion. In Hebrew school, I took my lessons seriously and tried to apply them at home. By my teen years, this had been replaced by an allegiance to socialism. In the Brooklyn where I grew up, my teachers and relatives made this seem the natural course. When I reached my twenties, however, and was obliged to confront a series of personal deficiencies, psychotherapy shouldered its way to the fore. Just getting through some days required a confidence in its efficacy. Subsequently becoming a clinical sociologist and a college professor did not decisively alter this propensity; my faith was merely transferred to social science and its ability to remedy our ills.

Along the way I also discovered that others too were pursuing doctrinaire ideals. Thus when I worked as a clinician, my clients would implore me for help in becoming the kind of person whom they admired. The trouble was that they were usually unsure of what qualities this sort of person possessed. When I became a college professor, my students were generally more certain of what was ideal. Where I was bedeviled by questions about personal responsibility and social mobility, they confidently assumed that androgyny and a classless society were best. I also came to realize that in the political arena, people were promoting unexamined ideals. Whether from the Right or the Left, social activists lobbied for intemperate policies that struck me as foolishly romantic. Even groups such as the libertarians, with which I was in sympathy, took their ideas to extremes and slid off into a kind of intellectual nihilism.

Worse yet, it became plain to me that people were often trapped by their ideals. Even when these did not work out, letting them go seemed to entail huge amounts of discomfort. Idealism, I came to recognize, could be both misleading and dangerously seductive. Yet in the right hands it was clearly a blessing. When an awareness of its limitations prevented it from going too far, it seemed to expand people's horizons. This was exemplified, for me, by a favorite uncle. Milton Tarriff was unequivocally the best human being I have personally known. Throughout his life he was an ardent socialist, but this did not prevent us debating—and chuckling over—our many disagreements. Although serious about his beliefs, his humanity came first, and therefore so did the dignity he accorded others.

In his teen years, Milton attended meetings of the Communist Party hoping to find a path out of the Great Depression. Later, after serving under General Patton during World War II, he sought a civil service job in his native New York City. This was almost denied because of his earlier infatuation. Nonetheless, he held no grudges. When my cousin Michael and I suggested that his continued belief in governmental interventions was out of date, he smiled broadly, looked to the skies, and muttered something like, "Where did I go wrong?" We would all then laugh and continue our discussion. But more than this, as a humane person, he believed that the humanity of others came first. Aware of his limitations, he was prepared to accept those of others as a matter of course. Too many idealists, unfortunately, are ideologues whose commitments leave them frustrated by the frailties of adversaries who refuse to adopt their perspective. My Uncle Milton was unusual in that he considered the concrete needs of individuals more valid than the theoretical benefits of his personal convictions.

Given all these considerations, in the end I found writing this book to be one of the more agonizing experiences of my life. Despite how much I thought I knew, I was forced to confront my ongoing illusions. As I reviewed other people's foibles, my own came into greater relief. No longer could I excuse them as a sign of inner goodness. Nor could I rationalize failures as due to the imperfections of others. In retrospect, I now recognize that it is accomplishing the world's mundane tasks that deserves the most respect; it is this day to day labor that takes the greatest courage.

Acknowledgments

When I began investigating the deceptive nature of idealism, among those who furnished me assistance were my immediate colleagues at Kennesaw State University. Usually, in a Preface, one acknowledges those who provided intellectual, research, and editorial assistance, and I especially wish to thank Mary Platt, Deborah Malone, Nuru Akenyemi, John Bruhn, and Marti Boyd for having done so—but I also wish to applaud others who have provided moral inspiration. Best discovered through example, genuine integrity can be confirmed only in action. Ironically, a series of professional setbacks enabled me to learn what makes some people tick. Several of these were good enough to provide support even at the risk of their own careers. Specifically, Vasilli Economopoulos, Barbara Karcher, Lana Wachniak, William Wallace, and Wayne Van Horne have demonstrated an internal fortitude that separates genuine decency from the counterfeit variety. My hat is off to them. I must likewise express my gratitude to several members of my immediate family. Through the decades, in good times and bad, my sister Carol Schwartz, my brother Joel Fein, and my cousin Michael Tarriff have generously offered their assistance and a model of perseverance that I could not have done without.

Finally, I must mention the many ordinary students in my sociology classes at Kennesaw State. The discomfort they expressed with purely conceptual accounts of social issues made it imperative that I find a more effective way to proceed. Ultimately what worked best was storytelling. Because examples drawn from my personal experience so captivated them, this encouraged their utilization in a work intended for broader consumption.

Contents

Chapter 1

Idealism on Trial

SCENE I: NEW YORK CITY DURING THE MID-1960S

The St. Nicholas Welfare Center stood in the heart of Harlem. Located in a multistory brick office building on 125th Street, it had a well-worn, kind of grimy atmosphere, with grey metal desks and institutional green walls. Inside, it was not a place of joy; on one floor, plodding and perpetually glum caseworkers sat mostly bent over piles of case folders, and on another milling and quarrelsome clients impatiently awaited their turn to be interviewed. The sounds and sights outside were those of a poor section of the city. Most of 125th Street was a shopping strip where inexpensive furniture stores jostled for limited business with shoe outlets and small-scale groceries. On the surrounding side streets solid tenements were crowded with large families and grim-faced transients. In front of them, brownstone stoops led down to asphalt roadways lined with automobiles and sidewalks that hosted a sporadic pedestrian traffic.

I am not sure if this is what I had expected. The place was, after all, Harlem. But it was not the Harlem of the Black Renaissance, for it was no longer a mythical playground for white partygoers seeking entertainment from the world's best jazz musicians. Still, it remained the nation's premier Negro neighborhood. This was a time before African-Americans were called African-American and even before the designation "black" came into favor. It was, however, a time when heroin was firmly established in the community. Even car-bound passersby on their way toward the Bronx could spot the addicts sprawled in the doorways. For better or worse, the district possessed a long-established, and richly earned, reputation as a dangerous slum.

For me, it represented the place where I would hold one of my first real jobs. I had been hired as a full-time caseworker by the City of New York. Although my college degree was in Philosophy, I found that, as my father had warned, not many positions were available for a professional philosopher. Fortunately, my test-taking abilities had served me well, and after scoring near the top in a citywide examination, I had, with zero fanfare, been assigned a caseload in this community I had never before visited. My mother, of course, was worried. Would her sheltered eldest son be able to survive in a sea of hoodlums? I had told her that part of my job would entail visits with clients to determine if they were following departmental regulations. Would this, she wondered, leave me exposed to ambush by savage thugs bent on pummeling a nice Jewish boy? She was not sure; neither was I.

Yet I was unworried. Harlem quickly became for me a real place, with real people, who were perhaps louder and more abrasive than those I was used to, but people nevertheless—not the caricatured gangsters of my mother's fears. Besides, my supervisors and co-workers assured me that the job was safe. At the time caseworkers carried small black loose-leaf books in which they recorded the results of their home visits. I was told that when carried in the open, these were readily identifiable and served as an informal safe-conduct pass. If people saw you carrying one, they supposedly left you alone because they did not want to interfere with the delivery of money to their friends and neighbors. Later on the rules of this game changed, but during my tenure the situation was as described.

I was also protected by my lofty ideals. Although I had backed into this position, it was one I took up proudly. I really did want to help those I perceived as poor and downtrodden. What was the point of being a "good" person, or a college-educated one, if I could not join in making the world a better place? After all, this was the mid-1960s. While it is true that I had been on the periphery of the Civil Rights movement, my Brooklyn roots tilted me toward the left. I had not gone on freedom rides through the South, or picketed segregated lunch counters, but had been active in the peace movement, at one point even leading a delegation to the Soviet UN Embassy to persuade them to renounce the atomic bomb. Consequently, when I went to listen to speeches by Malcolm X, I did so sympathetically. I knew that someday all men would be brothers, if, that is, people like me would risk reaching out to the less fortunate.

It was with this attitude that I ventured into an urban landscape that had recently been crossed by the shadow of civic riots. Even so, my primary concern was with doing my job and guaranteeing that people received the assistance to which they were entitled. Some months into this task, having learned the ropes and, as it were, acquired my sea legs, I visited a client whose apartment I had not previously seen. When I entered, I was struck by how neat it was. This was evidently a person concerned with her surroundings and with maintaining her personal dignity. After welcoming me with a broad smile, the lady of the house, a single mother, ostentatiously conducted me to the living room sofa. It was flanked by two overstuffed armchairs into one of which she settled while waving me into the other. Graciously she offered me something to drink, which I declined, and we moved on to discussing her financial situation. We matter-of-factly established that she was a good money manager and obviously eligible for public assistance. As I was getting ready to leave, she, with some apprehension, indicated that there was something else she wished to discuss. With a wide sweep of her hand she called my attention to her furniture. "Look at this," she moaned, "Isn't it pitiful? I can't live like this. You need to get me new stuff."

At first I was incredulous. As she elaborated in detail the defects of each item, I reflected on how her furnishings compared with my own. Hers were, as she insisted, getting old, but they were clean and serviceable. Besides the larger pieces, there were tables, lamps and pictures that added up to a complete and coordinated living room suite. In contrast, my smaller apartment was sparsely appointed with odds and ends collected as best I could. When I mentioned that what she had seemed adequate, she became indignant and passionately proclaimed that no human being should be allowed to live in such squalor. She then demanded that I provide her with the funds to purchase something decent. When I stammered that I couldn't because she already had what she needed, she became more angry and upbraided me for the insensitivity of the system. By now I was getting confused and could only think to put her off by telling her that I would consult my supervisor. I then took my leave while she hectored me all the way to the hall.

I later discussed this incident with my supervisor and he assured me that I had done the right thing. We were not in the business of purchasing furniture for people just because they were unhappy with what they had. I then put the matter out of my mind and went on with other things. Several weeks later while visiting other clients, I happened to pass by the woman's home. There, piled in a heap a few feet from the front steps, were a couch, chairs, and tables that I thought I recognized. I had to make sure and proceeded upstairs, knocked on the door, and when it opened, my suspicions were confirmed. In front of me stood my client with a huge smile on her face. "You see," she said, "I don't have furniture anymore. Now you have to get me stuff." To my astonishment, she asserted that welfare regulations required me to provide her with a minimum number of items. If I didn't live up to this obligation, she would force me to do so.

Once I returned to the office, I quickly apprised my supervisor of the situation. I could tell from the look on his face that it was an unusual one. It was also clear that he was both bemused and puzzled as to what should be done. He then told me that he would consult with his supervisor. Several days passed before a response came, and it took me by surprise. I had assumed that intentionally throwing away one's furniture in order to get new things was a form of extortion and could not be tolerated by a bureaucracy with clear operating instructions. This turned out to be wrong. As my supervisor explained, the issue had not only gone to his supervisor, but to hers, and hers too. In the end it was decided to give the client what she wanted rather than provoke trouble. Mayor Lindsay had decreed that as long as he was on duty, there would be no "long hot summer" and we, therefore, were to give bothersome people what they demanded, regardless of the law or the equities of the situation.[1] At this, I quietly initiated the paperwork. It was approved within the hour.

SCENE II: NEW YORK CITY DURING THE MID-1970S

Call him Kevin. He was nineteen years old, soon to turn twenty. A heroin addict, he was my client at a city-run methadone clinic. The newly opened clinic was aboard a ferry boat—the *Gold Star Mother*—docked at a pier in the Hudson River just off Greenwich Village. It was an ordinary ferry boat with no special provisions for its latest assignment except for several dozen ramshackle desks placed at strategic intervals between wooden benches originally designed to seat commuters bound from Staten Island to Manhattan. It was at one of these that Kevin and I got acquainted.

Kevin was of multi-racial ancestry. That one of his parents was white and the other black could almost be read from his physiognomy. Although his features had an African cast, his skin color was pink and his eyes blue. His visage was also very round and smooth, and struck most people as baby faced. Still his lips were thick, his hair kinky, and his body incongruously narrow and fragile, all of which made him look different. And that is how he was regarded. Today he might be called of mixed race, but at the time he was considered a black person who was not quite black. As a result, people did not know what to make of him; to whites he was a strange looking exotic who was not their problem; to blacks he was one of them, but one who did not fit. Nor did Kevin know what to do with himself. Because he felt alien wherever he went, he was not comfortable anywhere.

As his counselor, I soon noted that Kevin was consumed with self-loathing. His pain seeped from every pore, as did his youth. He was so callow, so alone, so inexperienced, and so lost, I almost wanted to embrace him and raise him as my own child. But Kevin would allow no such thing. In an effort to establish contact, I steered him into taking long walks around the open deck, sometimes talking, sometimes watching the sea birds, sometimes spying on the midshipmen on the high school ship berthed along side. Nonetheless, despite my reaching out, he resisted, always keeping our conversation light and impersonal.

The depth of Kevin's self-hatred was intermittently on graphic display when he would overdose. Methadone, which he was given every day, was specifically designed to keep heroin cravings at bay.[2] A narcotic, it theoretically kept the addiction satisfied while ensuring that the addict did not get high. Someone who could not free himself from bondage to his habit could take it as a substitute—for a lifetime if necessary—and still live a relatively normal life. For Kevin this had not happened. Every now and then he went out and got high, very high. He would consume so much heroin that he later came staggering up the steps leading to the ferry landing. He would then pass out with his thin body bent over backwards, his eyes open, glazed, and looking toward the rear. Usually he would vomit as well, with the discharge covering his face, chest, and the surrounding deck. As Kevin lay there, sometimes writhing to make his distress more visible, the clinic's other clients would step gingerly around him, trying to pretend he wasn't there. Eventually someone would alert the clinic physician, who would come out to assess the damage. Invariably she looked heavenward in disgust and slowly returned to her office shaking her head resignedly. Soon an ambulance arrived to take Kevin to the hospital for detoxification. A week or two later he returned, only to repeat the cycle later.

As Kevin's counselor, it was my job to interrupt this pattern. What is more, I desperately wanted to. I had been reading books that assured me that when a person acted this self-destructively, it was a call for help that needed to be heeded. I was certain that I was doing this, but I didn't know what else to do. My only plan was to help Kevin recognize that I was there for him. This, I was convinced, would encourage him to share his pain, after which we would be able to work together to deal with it. Yet Kevin would not cooperate. Instead, he disappeared again, this time returning, not in a heroin-induced stupor, but with the lower half of his face wired up to hold a broken jaw in place.

The story, as Kevin related it, was that he had been minding his business when a stranger walked up, and, totally without provocation, punched him. Later, someone else confided that this was not quite all. It seemed that while Kevin was hanging around not far from his home—as usual taking drugs and making a nuisance of himself—he confronted a drug dealer, backing him against a wall and insulting him by saying something like "your mama." At this point the other guy—whom, I was told, was much larger than Kevin—let loose and struck him. According to the witnesses, Kevin was lucky that he had not been treated more roughly.

From my point of view, this was yet another indication of self-loathing and a further plea for help that spurred me to redouble my efforts to break through his armor. Although I was an inexperienced counselor, I was a good listener with a warm and understanding manner. With these tools, and I hoped a keen intelligence, I pressured Kevin to tell me his story—the whole of it. Reluctantly, and almost unintelligibly, because of the broken jaw, he began to fill in some of the missing pieces. It seemed that his white mother had been a prostitute to whom he had been an inconvenience; hence within a year of his birth she had abandoned him to his black father. But he had not wanted the boy either, so several years later he too walked out, this time bequeathing Kevin to an uncle who lived in a tiny apartment in Harlem. The uncle was a caring person, but he had neither the time, the resources, nor the skills to raise a young child, which left Kevin to raise himself—on the streets and without much success.

All this came out slowly and with much anguish. At times I felt that I was intensifying Kevin's pain, but if the authorities were correct, this would provide a catharsis that would eventually strengthen him. I was therefore encouraged. My supervisor, on the other hand, was less so. From his perspective Kevin was an irritation. Instead of being a cooperative client, he was a troublemaker who presented a bad example for others. Why, my supervisor asked, didn't I just transfer him? A new methadone clinic opening in Harlem was seeking clients, so it would be easy to unload him. I, of course, was appalled. How could he suggest abandoning this needy person with whom I was just beginning to make progress? Besides, we had established a relationship and it would be unfair to violate his trust. It would be tantamount to rejecting him in the same way as had everyone else.

My supervisor ultimately relented and I continued my discussions with Kevin until his jaw healed, which I hoped would enable him to talk more freely. But Kevin disappeared again. Within a week he was back with his jaw once again wired shut. It seemed that he had again confronted a person who was bigger and badder than he, again in a hallway, and as before had been punched in the mouth. With some embarrassment, he admitted that he had gone too far, but he did not seem to recognize the extent to which he was responsible for his own predicament. As might be expected, I perceived these events as a reaffirmation of his plea for help. By now I knew enough about his situation to believe that he desperately craved love and, in an oddly Freudian way, often provoked others to reject him in the hope that they would not. If this were the case, I could not afford to join those who discarded him. Even though I was only his counselor and he was making my life difficult, I would stick by him, making certain that he knew I cared. In this way I would help him discover that love was possible.

Unfortunately, my supervisor did not share this view. To him, this latest episode was proof that Kevin was intractable. When I tried to explain the dynamics of his apparently senseless behavior, he brushed this aside. Why didn't I see how much easier it would be to initiate a transfer? Then, about two months later, I took a week's vacation. When I returned, my caseload was as I had left it, except for Kevin. My supervisor had taken the opportunity to arrange the transfer he had been advocating. There was nothing I could do. No matter how much I might protest, the deed was done. It was something I had to accept, for too much of a disapproval would interfere with my ability to work with my other clients. Never again would I see Kevin. He did not come downtown to visit and I did not go uptown to check on his progress. Those who knew him told me that he was going about his business as he always had.

Within a few months, however, these accounts changed. To my great sorrow, word came that Kevin was dead. Those who lived in his neighborhood reported that, as was his wont, he continued to interact with, and to insult, those who were meaner than himself. Again, he had confronted a dealer in a hallway. But this time, he was not punched out; this time the other guy pulled out a knife and stabbed him in the chest. Kevin bled to death on the spot. No one was there to help. Perhaps no one could have been. It may even have been that Kevin would not have wanted assistance—merely a release from his travail.

SCENE III: ROCHESTER, NEW YORK DURING THE EARLY 1980S

The name over the door read *Medical & Surgical Building*, but it was neither medical nor surgical. Years earlier, when this, the hospital's main building, had been erected, there had been thoughts of using portions of its ample space to perform psychosurgery. In the interim, however, prefrontal lobotomies, insulin shock treatments, and even electroshock therapy had gone out of favor. Instead the Rochester Psychiatric Center (RPC) used this multistory, red brick tower primarily as a dormitory for the almost thousand patients in its care. Although the building contained offices and workshops, most of its floors were devoted to wards on which men and women, young and old, severely psychotic or only moderately neurotic, resided and presumably received psychiatric interventions.

My office was not in the M&S Building, but in the nearby Rehabilitation Building. Indeed, technically I did not work for the hospital, but for a state vocational rehabilitation agency (OVR). I was merely outstationed at RPC for the convenience of my clients. Though I was a guest, the space I occupied was comfortable, as the structure was new, mostly concrete and glass, and the disruptions limited because patients stopped by only for specific purposes. Inasmuch as I sometimes needed to visit on a ward, I was provided with a huge skeleton key. It opened the metallic doors that sealed off the inpatient living areas. Entering these was, in fact, an experience. In many ways it reminded me of visiting a prison. A friend of mine, who worked as a teacher at the nearby Attica Correctional Facility, had recently given me a tour of the penitentiary, and while walking through remarked that the clanking of the metal doors gave him the willies. The same sense of confinement was present at RPC, the primary difference being that once through a portal, instead of depending on a guard to relock it, I had to do so myself.

That this procedure left the patients feeling trapped was evident from the few who always hung out on the off chance a staffer would carelessly fail to seal an exit. Once past these expectant yet vacant-looking sentries, one walked down a long, depressing corridor. It was painted the same institutional green with which I had become familiar at Welfare and lined with counselor offices and patient sleeping rooms. The latter tended to be small and barren, furnished with a metallic bed and wooden chest, and graced by a single, cheerless window. Further down its length, the hall was intersected by another corridor that also was lined with patient rooms, but featured a communal bathroom and a nurse's station for dispensing medications. These too were dreary, with peeling metal grates separating the nurses from the patients. Nothing whatever screened off the shared commodes. At the terminus of the central passageway was a large common room where most of the patients could be found lounging. Typically they sat around on overstuffed chairs, lay about on leather couches, or sprawled on the vinyl-tiled floor. For the most part they did nothing. Some watched TV soap operas, but the majority stared into space. Even the appearance of a visitor did not disturb their reveries. Those who recognized an intruder or needed a favor might feel roused to pester her for a cigarette, but the others hardly moved.

I came to the hospital after completing the course work for my Ph.D. in sociology. This subject had appealed to me, rather than the more usual psychology, on the assumption that to help people in distress it was necessary to understand the social pressures operating on them. My experiences in methadone treatment and welfare had convinced me that good intentions were not enough; insights into what lay behind client actions were also essential. I had not been disappointed in this. My professors and my independent researches had convinced me that there were both structural and cultural reasons why few things went as advertised. I was likewise persuaded that this knowledge could be translated into power—that properly assimilated, it would point the way toward interventions that worked.

Among the works that most influenced my thinking was Erving Goffman's *Asylums*.[3] Based on his personal observations, it characterized psychiatric hospitals as "total institutions," that is, as organizations dedicated to controlling every aspect of their residents' lives. As I looked about me, this seemed true. Goffman also suggested that many of the measures employed served the needs of the controllers, not those of the clients. This too seemed accurate. In fact, a casual glance around the common room confirmed it. The dozing patients were not there by choice, but by institutional mandate. They had been locked out of their rooms. After they arose, washed, and dressed, they were literally forbidden to return to their beds until the evening. If they wanted to nap, they had to find another place. Although sometimes it was claimed that this kept them active, the real purpose was to make it easier to maintain surveillance. Certainly most patients did not become more lively as a result of this policy, nor was there much evidence it was therapeutic.

When I broached the possibility of modifying these arrangements, my fellow staffers seemed oddly indifferent. It was as if the subject bored them. Rather than investigate new procedures that enabled clients to assume greater control over their lives, they changed the topic. Nor were supervisory personnel more receptive. After I finished my spiel, they patiently explained that I didn't understand why things were as they were, then went about their business. If I persisted, they became annoyed. Obviously, no one had been awaiting my sociological insights so that they could proceed with a thoroughgoing reform. It even occurred to me that there might be institutional imperatives militating against change. After all, if the arguments of someone such as Goffman had not persuaded intelligent people to alter their course, perhaps they were constrained by stressors I did not comprehend.

As it happened, during this same period external pressures to dismantle the psychiatric hospitals were also rising. For their separate reasons, liberal and conservative critics had arrived at a consensus that the "asylums" were really "snake pits"[4] that could not be revived and had to be eliminated. Under the banner of "deinstitutionalization,"[5] they had even crafted legislation to close their doors. Patients were to be released to their families or to the guardianship of small-scale institutions such as group homes, day hospitals, and community mental health centers. The confluence of several scientific advances made this project feasible. The most important was the development of psychoactive drugs that offered the prospect of containing serious psychoses without walls or guards. If a medication could remove symptoms such as hallucinations and delusions, even schizophrenic individuals might participate in society. It would be possible for them to live comfortably with their families and receive psychotherapy as outpatients. In the end, this would make them indistinguishable from everyone else. Moreover, the theories of R.D. Laing[6] had assured the public that schizophrenics were fundamentally normal. If they seemed different, it was only because they were more sensitive than most others. They had simply preserved the virtues of childhood into adulthood; hence if we permitted them to circulate unfettered, we would all profit from their perceptiveness.

Those less romantically inclined viewed the closing of the psychiatric hospitals as a financial boon. Providing medical services to thousands of patients within huge impersonal institutions had been intended to be efficient, but was clearly more expensive than medicating them at home. In the end, both freedom and fiscal prudence coalesced to argue for the termination of institutions that refused to modify themselves. As a result, the staff members at RPC were instructed to release patients to community-based facilities as quickly as possible. Psychologists, social workers, and nurses who ordinarily functioned as counselors became the primary agents in developing their exit strategies. In consultation with the patients, their relatives, and cooperating agencies, they were to decide the best ways to effect the transition.

The problem was that these usually didn't work. Too often the patients did not know what they wanted, their families were unreceptive to their coming home, and the community facilities that were supposed to monitor them did not exist. Thus a psychologist might consult with a family only to discover that its frictions contributed to the patient's original confinement and would probably drive him or her onto the street were he or she forced back. Similarly, the proprietor of a boarding house might express a willingness to accept psychiatric residents, but an investigation would reveal a tendency to quarrelsomeness that previous referrals had found intolerable. On more than one occasion those responsible for creating the discharge plans expressed their frustrations to me. They bemoaned the fact that no good options existed; nevertheless they had to pretend they did. Often they would sigh and admit that they knew a particular formula would unravel within months.

As time dragged by, and the process of releasing patients into the community proceeded more glacially than the architects of the policy had predicted, the legislators and state administrators grew restless. Eventually a decision was made to force the issue. A command came from Albany that a specified number of patients would be discharged by a certain date—no excuses tolerated. A collective groan went up from RPC personnel, but there was nothing they could do. Heads shook in disbelief, but treatment plans confidently forecast to flounder went forward anyway. When the cutoff date arrived, the required target was achieved and those in charge proclaimed victory. They even trumpeted the accomplishment in the local newspapers. Within weeks, however, the expected failures began to accumulate. Patients came knocking at the hospital door seeking readmission, but, as per policy, were refused. Many others stopped going to the clinics for medication. With a thundering lack of publicity, they left parental homes, had fights with co-residents at boarding houses, and refused to visit counselors. Months later stories began to appear in the Rochester papers of derelicts living under the Genesee River bridges. As amazing as it seemed, homelessness had come to their prosperous city. Nobody understood why. Some experts suggested that this was part of a nationwide trend precipitated by a poor economy and insufficient public housing.[7] The solution was obviously further government spending to create additional jobs and living quarters.

SCENE IV: ROCHESTER, NEW YORK DURING THE MID-1980S

Greg (not his real name) had been referred to me for vocational counseling. He was attending a day treatment center attached to a different hospital, but had begun working with me while still an inpatient at RPC. A smallish man of about thirty-five, with a sharp-featured face and anxious eyes, his situation was unusual in that he had been a professional social worker before his breakdown. Although Greg possessed an MSW, and had functioned for years as a counselor of psychiatric clients, he experienced an emotional overload that made it impossible for him to bear further interaction with people in as much pain as himself.

Because Greg was officially attached to a different facility, I had to coordinate my activities with its staffers. My contact was an occupational therapist, a young woman in her mid-twenties. From our first meeting over the phone, I liked her. She was warm, earnest, and possessed a tough-minded common sense I found refreshing. As importantly, she had taken the time to get to know Greg. Not content to read his records, she engaged in long conversations with him in which she listened to what he said. The two even discussed his hopes and dreams, which made it possible to talk with her about his vocational plans.

At first Greg was reluctant to think about employment. His collapse at social work had been so complete he did not wish to risk a repetition. After some months, however, he became bored. The day hospital had lost its luster and he began to contemplate other possibilities. Initially he was uncertain about what would be appropriate. He knew that he was emotionally fragile and that under pressure his depression and anxiety might recur, but he also realized he needed an intellectual challenge to feel fulfilled. Because we were not making progress in discovering something suitable, I asked the OT if they could do some brainstorming. Both agreed. After a short interval, Greg came to me with an idea. Would it be possible for him to take a college course in computer programming? When I asked why he wanted to pursue this, he responded that it offered the prospect of financial success and personal prestige. He further explained that with people-work now out of the question, working with data was a reasonable alternative. At first blush I agreed, but wondered if the demands of college might be too stressful. He was not certain, but we concluded that it made sense to test the waters. If he became overwhelmed, he could withdraw. When I later checked with the OT, she too found this reasonable.[8]

Some weeks afterwards the OT called me to say that the psychiatrist in charge of Greg's case wanted to set up a meeting. She was not sure what he had in mind, but asked if I could come to their place at a specified time. I agreed. When the appointed day arrived, I entered a medium-sized office and found a circle of chairs occupied mostly by persons I did not know. Greg was there, as was the OT, but the first participant to introduce himself was the psychiatrist. A large, rumpled man, he was a stranger to me. We had never previously interacted, not even over the phone. Also present were two professional-looking women, one of whom may have been a nurse. The psychiatrist began by announcing that we were gathered to discuss Greg's vocational plans. This was my first official notice regarding the agenda. He next affirmed how important planning was and how we all intended to do the right thing. At this he paused, cleared his throat, and rather deliberately asserted that he had reservations about the direction things had taken. Turning to me, he pointedly asked why I believed college work was appropriate for Greg. I enumerated my reasons, but did so uneasily for the psychiatrist had started shaking his head. When I concluded, he indicated that he strongly disagreed and was convinced that Greg could not manage the program. At this, the two unknown persons nodded in approval. They did not, however, offer justifications for their reaction.

I tried to respond, but the psychiatrist was adamant. At this point the OT attempted to express her opinion. Somewhat hesitantly she suggested that a college course might work, but the psychiatrist abruptly reasserted himself and she backed off. Now the psychiatrist looked toward Greg and asked if he thought he could handle the schooling. Greg, who seemed intimidated by the doctor's manner, stammered that he believed he could. Before he had concluded his explanation, however, the psychiatrist contradicted him and asked the rest of us to notice how anxious Greg was becoming. How, he pointedly inquired, could anyone so fear-ridden be expected to succeed in higher education?

Although this was not the sort of interchange I had anticipated, at first I tried to persuade the psychiatrist that there was no harm in giving the idea a chance. But in what quickly degenerated into a debate, he retorted that he would not allow it, that it would risk precipitating a suicide attempt when Greg failed. I responded that there was more reason to expect this reaction if we arbitrarily denied him the opportunity. This merely provoked the psychiatrist's wrath and he flatly declared that he could not countenance it. To this I replied that I did not work for his hospital and he did not have the authority to forbid me from doing what I thought best. By now things were getting out of hand. As a physician, the psychiatrist clearly believed that his M.D. trumped my Ph.D. and that, in consequence, I had no right to contradict him. "You," he said, staring me in the eye and pointing a finger at my face, "are guilty of malpractice," and he reiterated his determination not to tolerate the plan. At this he stood up and stomped out.

With the psychiatrist gone, the meeting quickly adjourned. As I walked down the hallway to return to my office, the OT intercepted me. "I'm sorry I didn't say more," she whispered, "but my job was on the line. After all, he's my boss." Once she left, several yards further along, Greg stopped me. In equally hushed tones he thanked me for being "on his side." No one else, he said, had exhibited the courage to come to his defense. Then he too hastily departed. Later that afternoon, back at my own desk, I alerted my supervisor that we might be in for a spell of trouble. I related what had happened and we agreed to await developments. The next day the psychiatrist made his move. He called my supervisor to demand that the college course be vetoed. It was, he declared, medically contraindicated and he suggested that I did not understand the gravity of the situation. Furthermore, he insisted, his professional expertise must determine the nature of what was appropriate. According to my supervisor, he had himself responded noncommittally, promising only to look into the matter. The conversation terminated with the psychiatrist once again demanding that the plan be denied.

By the next day, things had changed. When again I spoke to my supervisor, I found myself on the defensive. Why, I was asked, did I believe my judgment was superior to a psychiatrist's? Did I really imagine that I knew more about medicine than he? And didn't I understand that I was creating irreparable frictions between our respective organizations? Besides, what was the big deal? Why not just say no? As luck would have it, our time to work this through was limited by my supervisor's urgent need to attend another meeting and my previously scheduled vacation, which was to begin the next day. Having been through a similar situation years before, I asked him to promise that no action would be taken until I returned. He assented. We shook hands, both of us smiling, and we went our separate ways.

Upon resuming my duties two weeks later, I looked for Greg's file and found it on my supervisor's desk. Opening it up, I discovered that in my absence he had written up, and approved, a new plan that explicitly forbid the college course. A spasm of anger passed through my body. How could so clear-cut a promise have been so flatly broken? How could he have so flagrantly ignored my wishes or the needs of the client? When I confronted him with these questions, trying my best to be diplomatic, he responded that he was doing what he thought necessary. The discussion was closed and the case would be transferred to someone else. About four months further along I received word that Greg had attempted suicide. I do not know what happened afterwards, because he moved to another city. As for the relationship between me and my supervisor, it deteriorated rapidly. Within a year, I was transferred from RPC to the agency's central office. This put me several doors away from him, where it was easier to keep tabs on me.[9]

DISILLUSIONMENT

Life is awash with surprises. Far from being predictable, it often fails to live up to our expectations. Things we were certain were true turn out to be imaginary, while those we believed vital to our happiness never transpire, or if they do, disappoint. As a result, many of us become frustrated idealists. We continue to strive for improvements, but roadblocks invariably crop up and we are diverted down unforeseen channels. Sometimes we give up, but more often keep going on the off-chance that the "good guys" will win and things will develop as they "should." Surprisingly, frustrated idealism is an inevitable part of growing up. As the columnist George Will[10] has pointed out, "disillusionment is the beginning of wisdom." Before we can learn what the world is about, we must first relinquish the simplified dreams left over from childhood. Most of us, for instance, come to understand that Santa Claus, though a wonderful character, is not a real person. We may in the beginning resist this notion, but sooner or later accept the fact that it was our parents who purchased the presents delivered in his name. Were we unable to do so, we could not become competent adults.

Disillusionment is, in fact, a lengthy process. My experiences at Welfare and the Rochester Psychiatric Center were merely part of a series of unwelcome shocks that combined to disabuse me of my immature ideals. But the progression had began much earlier—as it does with everyone.

Think of how it felt to discover that one's parents did not know everything; that their omniscience was an illusion. Infants must depend upon their parents to supply their needs without being asked. At first mother and father may even seem to be mind-readers, but this does not last long. Older children must learn to specify what they want. They may desire clairvoyance, but when frustrated by an inability to articulate their yearnings, have to acknowledge this limitation and try to overcome it—or do without. The fantasy that big people can understand everything is abandoned despite the disappointment of doing so.

Think too of the blunders parents make when they attempt to enforce justice. Children, being children, get into fights that they expect adults to referee. Theirs is an implicit faith that grown-ups perceive who did what to whom and know how to set things aright. Yet recall the sinking feeling when a Johnny-come-lately mother mistakenly punished the victim of a fight and/or rewarded the transgressor. The fracturing of our assumption that she knew what had happened hurt more than the chastisement. Worst of all was the realization that this sort of error could not be eliminated. No matter how articulate the child, or how often iniquities were actually corrected, the normal opacity to events guaranteed that some injustices would persist.

Nor do such lessons end with adulthood. Many people imagine that after they are grown, they will be able to understand everything and control everything. They also contemplate complete equity. When eventually they enter the business world, they expect to be rewarded by superiors who are truly pleased with the exceptional performances they will no doubt render. Life, they imagine, will resemble a well-ordered elementary school with dedicated teacher/bosses passing out gold stars upon the completion of assigned tasks. Many, especially those who excel academically, believe the world to be rational—that its lessons are fully enumerated, the right and wrong answers firmly established, and benevolent arbiters always on hand to reward the diligent. Only gradually does it dawn on them that those who get A's are not always the best or the most conscientious. Even worse, those who determine the correct answers are not infallible. Most unbelievable of all, it is sometimes the cheaters who rush to the front of the room to take over the class.

The consternation this precipitates is evident in the popularity of the comic strip "Dilbert." Its inventory of self-serving, dithering bosses, who don't understand the businesses they run—bosses who care about nothing except remaining in charge—has struck a responsive chord with millions of Americans. Scott Adams'[11] perpetually put-upon hero is an everyman whose pompous superior, after proudly proclaiming some imaginary accomplishment, asks his subordinates why they never bring him bad news. When one of them makes the mistake of responding that it is because he punishes people for doing so, the miscreant is promptly punished. The prevalence of this sort of contradictory, small-minded leadership is not the way things were supposed to be. Most of us once believed that authority was based on real achievements, not a capacity to inflate one's contributions. Yet, to our chagrin, it is this latter we encounter when we enter the workplace.

But people hate being disillusioned. They desperately want their ideals to be authenticated. They want this so badly they will go to the extreme of denying reality. Thus, should a boss turn out to be a dimwitted misanthrope, his underlings will believe that somewhere there must exist good bosses in whom it is possible to repose faith. This need is so great that people regularly try to reproduce the certitude of their ideals in the games they play. Baseball, for instance, is designed to run on merit. Its rules are such that the criteria for winning are precise. Scoring one more run that the other team decides the matter, whereas sending a fair ball one inch over the outfield wall equals a homer. This crispness is further enhanced by calculating batting averages, earned run percentages, and team standings. Umpires are even employed to keep the contest honest. As neutral third parties, they are delegated to call balls and strikes and to decide who is safe or out. This theoretically ensures a game uncontaminated by sham or error, and that once a winner is determined, it is because the victor has earned it. In stark contrast are pastimes such as stickball where the rules are made up by the players as they go along—but these, as we shall see, are closer to real life.

As a youngster, I was certainly one of those who expected precision. When my father told me that life isn't played that way, that it was really a "dog eat dog" affair, I dismissed this as evidence of his bitterness. He was obviously a burned-out old man who had projected his failures onto others. Had he been able to achieve the vocational triumphs of which he once dreamt, he would not have had to blame innocent people for his limitations. Being a child of the sixties, this was reaffirmed by my peers who attested that one should never trust anyone over thirty. Only we who had not been corrupted by the Great Depression, the Second World War, or even the Viet Nam fiasco, had the courage to stand up for what was right. Only we had the youthful exuberance necessary to rescue the world from itself.

It is, therefore, with considerable irony that I today confront idealistic college students who view me, a professor of sociology, as a bitter old man. Many of the eighteen- and nineteen-year-olds who fill my introductory courses are certain that I am wrong when I tell them life has limitations. When I assign policy papers in which they are asked to recommend means for solving contemporary social problems, they typically become moralistic and confidently assert that if people become more loving, we can rid ourselves of homelessness or that if sex education is introduced into elementary schools, we can eliminate teenage pregnancies.[12]   There is nevertheless a deep schism between them and their non-traditional classmates. The former tend to be wide-eyed romantics, whereas the latter, having endured many unexpected events, show the wear. As a consequence, when I explain why people indulge in falsifications or why social class disparities are intractable, the older heads nod in approval. Decades of struggling to resolve their own frustrated ideals leave them grateful to have their skepticism confirmed. The teenagers are nonetheless disturbed. They suspect that I am trying to persuade them to relinquish their dreams and they resent it.

Usually I try to explicate this difficulty by discussing the contrasting theories of Thomas Hobbes[13] and Jean-Jacques Rousseau.[14]   Hobbes, a witness to the English political disorders of the seventeenth century, was pessimistic about human nature. He believed that people are selfish, dangerous creatures who need to be protected from themselves by an agency more powerful than they, in his case, by a legitimate King who commanded the reverence of his subjects. A century later in France, Rousseau conceived of mankind as basically kind and loving. He argued that in a state of nature we are all essentially noble savages; that it is the temptations of civilization that corrupt us. Even so, he believed that a loving education[15] can turn children into loving adults. I then ask my students which version comes closer to the truth. Generally the younger ones prefer Rousseau, while the older ones lean toward Hobbes. Even more instructively, the human service students favor Rousseau, whereas the criminal justice types pride themselves on a Hobbesian realism.

When I continue by describing how Rousseau kept a mistress lodged in a Parisian back street lest an awareness of her existence interfere with his pursuit of conventional success, and that when they had children, he used his poverty to justify sending them to foundling hospitals[16]—this in an era when the majority of such children died—the younger students are mortified. They do not change their opinions, but they are disappointed. Their older classmates, however, with more time to have been buffeted by the winds of fortune, are not as astonished. They too have had experiences in which powerful persons have protected their prerogatives rather than do something that would have benefited others.

Those who train helping professionals often speak of "reality shock." In doing this, they refer to the typical reaction of uninitiated social workers to their first paid jobs. Although these educators wish their pupils to be sensitive and caring clinicians, they do not want them overwhelmed by the obstacles they will surely encounter when working with real people. They know all too well that most human problems are not solved quickly or completely, and that even when progress is made, clients tend not to be grateful. The textbooks[17] may present case studies with unambiguous principles and happy endings, but having been out in the field, they realize these are the exceptions. In any event, they are careful to caution their students that things will be different than they anticipate. Nonetheless, tyro helpers are routinely amazed by what they later undergo. Apparently they, as do all of us, have a deep-seated need to hold on to our ideals and refuse to believe crass warnings. We may intellectually realize that our hopes are inflated, but desperately want them fulfilled anyway. This may even be advantageous if it provides the strength to cope with obdurate facts.

THE LAST BEST HOPE

During his second annual Congressional address, Abraham Lincoln expressed an opinion that neatly encapsulates a sentiment shared by most Americans. While urging the legislators not to shirk from fighting to save the Union, he reminded them that it was in their power to "nobly save or meanly lose the last, best hope of earth."[18] Like most of his fellow citizens, Lincoln firmly believed that their shared institutions were special, and that he, as their President, shouldered a unique responsibility; one that only he, and they, could bring to fruition.

Americans are unquenchable optimists. The heirs of one of the few political revolutions to have succeeded and of courageous immigrants who crossed oceans in search of freedom and riches, they are not about to abandon what they collectively designate the American Dream. The details of this vision may vary with the individual, but its power to inspire is incontrovertible. Americans, as Seymour Martin Lipset[19] has richly documented in his *American Exceptionalism*, believe that they differ from, and are better than, the citizens of other nations. Conjointly, they subscribe to what he calls the American Creed. As Lipset explains, a belief in liberty, equality, individualism, populism, and laissez-faire government animate their actions. These ideals, in turn, have helped produce a tolerance of and a disdain for authority, that, as Alexis de Tocqueville[20] ascertained, is unique in the world. They have also helped produce a patriotism and a faith in opportunity that enables them to share their good fortune with others not as blessed, including those they once oppressed. Whether or not these aspirations fully reflect the reality of the American experience, they have contributed to anchoring the country's democratic institutions and furnishing a panoply of shared goals that encourage, if not guarantee, a widespread sense of charity.[21] People continue to emigrate to the United States hoping to find a better life and, by and large, they do. The road they traverse may be uneven, but surrounded, as they will be, by legions of unreconstructed idealists, they too are given a chance to achieve their ideals.

One of the current expressions of this American faith in a benign future is the slogan "If you can dream it, you can achieve it." This may sound reasonable, but it is hopelessly naive. Most dreams surely do not come true. Many cannot, no matter how earnestly they are sought. Closer to reality is Dirty Harry's incantation that "a man's got to know his limitations." Ever since Sun-tzu,[22] military strategists have advised those in quest of victory to assess honestly what is possible. They have counseled an accurate and fearless appraisal of one's strengths and weaknesses relative to those of one's opponents and recognized that those willing to accept any challenge, irrespective of the odds, while they may get off to a good start, eventually find themselves confronted by a superior foe to whom they inevitably succumb. No one, they suggest, is so strong that he can triumph in every contest on any field.

Another expression of this unbounded American idealism was popularized by the late Senator Robert Kennedy. As his admirers are fond of recalling, when on the campaign trail he often declared that: "Some people look at what is and ask, 'Why?' But I dream things that never were and ask why not?" They perceive this to be a solemn pledge (albeit lifted from George Bernard Shaw[23]) to seek fresh solutions to old dilemmas, and they glory in his hopefulness. The difficulty with this is that they do not take the last clause in his statement seriously. Instead of literally asking "Why not?," they tend to assume that whatever proposal they favor is feasible. In their imaginations, they believe that because their intentions are honorable, and their minds sharp, what they consider best, is. To genuinely ask "Why not?" would, however, include the possibility that some things are not, and never can be, true. It would assume an understanding that even visions of perfection are capable of disconfirmation by unanticipated facts.

When I was in graduate school, one of my professors was the noted feminist Cynthia Fuchs Epstein.[24] In her best known work, *Woman's Place*, she discussed the historic limitations placed on women's vocational choices. These, she argued, were not necessary, and could, had people been so inclined, have been reversed. Moreover, just because some things have never transpired does not mean they never will. As an example, just because no woman has ever been elected President does not mean no woman ever will. This conclusion, most people would agree, is almost self evident. After all, not long ago a majority of pundits predicted that human beings would never fly and that moving pictures could not be transmitted through space. Nonetheless, it should also be evident that because some things never were, does not ensure that they will be. Some things truly are impossible. Although modern advances have made it possible to fly with the aid of airplanes, we still cannot soar with our bare arms. It may be difficult to tell which things are possible, but a failure to entertain the prospect that some are not is fatuous.

The upshot is that ideals, as inspiring as they may be, can go too far. When held too tightly or promiscuously, they fail to make the necessary adjustments. At such moments, they may justify actions that, rather than being beneficial, are injurious. Sadly, extravagantly rosy scenarios are routinely subverted by an obdurate universe and by our own tendency to overdo. Remarkably, because of, and not despite, our best natures, we blithely stumble off innumerable cliffs, sometimes rushing headlong over their edges to our own destruction. This must not, however, be taken as a blanket put-down of idealism. An overidealized commitment to being nonidealistic is itself a significant error. In some ways towering ideals are the calling card of a vibrant life force. Entailing, as they do, a future orientation and the promise of a better destiny, they betoken a healthy willingness to take risks. Nevertheless an uncritical idealism is a disaster waiting to happen. Those who will not allow reality to modify their aspirations are headed for real surprises. They are so dazzled by their dreams that they do not learn from the facts. One can say of them, as Samuel Johnson[25] rather ungallantly remarked of a man who remarried immediately after his wife's death, that theirs is "the triumph of hope over experience."

Yet the tendency to be seduced by ideals seems universal and remarkably durable. A hallmark of American public life, it is also encountered worldwide, both today and in the past. Almost every people from the ancient Greeks to communism-intoxicated Russians have, at one time or another, been ruined by their dreams. Conservative and liberal, religious and agnostic, optimist and pessimist alike, in their eagerness to construct a better world, they became unrealistic, extreme, and, in the end, lost their bearings. More specifically, for almost four hundred years now, many Americans have lurched from one idealistic binge to another, seemingly unable to prevent themselves careening from one fanciful world-saving scheme to another. Whether it is today's political correctness and environmental crusades, or yesterday's prohibition and fundamentalist Great Awakenings, those who have been beguiled by these chimera could not seem to imagine their being deficient and have adhered to them as to an inebriating elixir.

Lamentably, the War on Poverty, McCarthyism, the temperance movement, Wilson's War to End All Wars, abolitionism, the Know Nothings, isolationism, hippie lovefests, and the New Deal all have a terrible secret in common. While some have produced negative outcomes, and others beneficial ones, each has been prey to an emotional contagion that has interfered with its proponents' abilities to engage in rational problem-solving. With the truth of their presumptions trumped by their zeal, rather than carefully evaluate what was being conjured up, they have plunged ahead—sometimes to founder very badly. Instead of examining the likely ramifications of a policy such as Prohibition, they have assumed its benefits and later been shocked by the unanticipated side effects.

But why, one must ask, is this so? How can intelligent human beings repeatedly be fooled by their hopes? Why are the dreams we collectively and individually defend more real to us than are our daily routines? Perhaps there is something in human nature that makes us vulnerable to moralistic excess. Perhaps too there is a reason why we refuse to take the measure of those standards by which we evaluate our other aspirations. For better or worse, these tendencies seem to be universal. Even a casual perusal of events reveals that in an attempt to be moral, people habitually go overboard and do things that make no sense. Like lovers in the grip of a grand passion, they overvalue the loved object,[26] becoming so enthralled by what seems best that they misperceive what even children are capable of seeing. With eyes firmly closed, they march forward toward a glorious millennium that exists only in their imaginations.

But again, why is this so? Why do so many of us persist in folly? In the next few chapters we examine how the nature of morality undermines our rationality. Surely one of the greatest paradoxes of human existence is that in the pursuit of virtue good people precipitate wholesale mayhem. Ironically, evil and frivolous individuals have no monopoly on outrageous mistakes. With the best of intentions, normal human beings eagerly subscribe to agendas as wretched as Nazism, then justify them as indispensable to their salvation. Even more implausibly, people often take fairminded objectives, such as feminism and civil rights, to extremes that allow them to jubilantly undermine the lives of millions of their compatriots.

Sometimes we imagine that only the unhinged are capable of being seduced by the pernicious. When we hear of the members of Heaven's Gate swallowing poison because they believe this will liberate their souls to rendezvous with a space ship behind the Hale-Bopp comet, we cringe. Surely they were not like us. Even more unlike us are those who were weak enough to be beguiled by a Jim Jones or a David Koresh. Yet even science has been perverted in the name of unexamined ideals. Though we tend to ignore it, the great Isaac Newton was a convinced alchemist and the eugenics movement once had the blessings of mainstream biologists. In what follows, some of our more revered orthodoxies are inspected to see what lies at their core. In doing so, we will learn that values, however resolutely held, are not always what they seem and that even our best intentions can be turned against us.

Chapter 2

In the Name of Morality

AN ADULT GAME

"Why would you want to write about that? Everybody knows that stuff." Such was my mother's response when I told her that I had embarked on a book about morality. From her perspective, the subject was transparent. There was simply nothing that could be said that was not already common knowledge. Some years later I had a conversation with Alan Wolfe, the distinguished social critic, during which he casually remarked that many of his colleagues were puzzled when he first broached the idea of conducting a study of middle-class values. Why, they wondered, would he want to do that? Wasn't his time too valuable to squander on such well trod territory? He went ahead nonetheless because, as he explained, he decided that it was the right thing to do.

Many people seem to believe that the topic of morality is not worth the candle. Rather than take the time to explore it, they assume that there is nothing meriting examination. For them, it is a nonsubject that elicits yawns. I experienced this firsthand when I tried to interest publishers in a book about morality. More than one replied that while the topic was important, it was something that would not sell. As one wrote, "Unfortunately, while questions of morality are intriguing, I have trouble envisioning a strong general audience." At first I found this surprising, since all about me I observed people engaged in nonstop moralizing. Questions such as those about the O.J. Simpson case or President Clinton's romantic entanglements evidently gripped the public imagination with sufficient tenacity to keep cable TV networks in business. Besides, were we not in the midst of a Culture War, with politicians of both the left and the right heatedly denouncing each other's contemptible foibles? And hadn't society also been divided by competing therapeutic and fundamentalist revolutions? Indeed, hadn't I, while working as a clinician, regularly been implored to help clients decide what was the "right" course of action? And wasn't I, as a sociologist, when teaching Social Problems courses, routinely called upon to define what was a problem by first assessing what was moral?

Yet the more closely I contemplated the situation, the more I decided the publishers were correct. Although people habitually made moral judgments, they hardly ever explored their origins, preferring to seek answers rather than explanations. Moralizing, it seemed, was very different from trying to understand morality. The former possessed the piquancy of hot chili peppers, while the latter had the soporific effect of a blank television screen. The best way to comprehend this, I decided, was through a sports analogy. If morality were thought of as similar to tennis, it was evident that because people loved to play the game did not mean they would enjoy analyzing it. Anyone who has dabbled in tennis can attest that being in the middle of a match is quite stimulating. There is scarcely a moment of boredom between the instant one determines where an opponent's shot will land and the need to be physically present to return it. Listening to a lecture about the kinesthetics of the wrist muscles is, however, another matter. Only experts in sports physiology seem to care; most others simply want to know how to improve their backhands. Nor do people like being lectured to. Though they more than occasionally take pleasure in doing the lecturing, given a choice, they elect not to have their own deficiencies pointed out—not even implicitly.

Nonetheless, a knowledge of how morality operates is of vital importance. Without a passing acquaintance with its particulars, we are vulnerable to dreadful errors. We may fool ourselves into thinking we know enough to get by, whereas in reality we understand just enough to risk getting ourselves in serious trouble. Most of us make the elementary mistake of assuming that the topic is easily grasped by anyone, including children. We believe that every well brought up five-year-old is drilled in its do's and don'ts and that these remain constant to serve as beacons for ethically minded grownups. Just as Robert Fulghum[1] convinced millions of his readers that all they needed to know, they had already learned in kindergarten, most of us believe that moral basics are laid down early in life, with rules about lying and respecting the rights of others instilled even before we are taught to share cookies with classmates or to clean up after fingerpainting.

Yet far from being a child's game, morality is one of the most complex of all adult endeavors. One of today's best kept secrets is just how complicated and difficult it is in practice. Indeed, most people fail even to realize that it is a social process.[2] Instead they hold firm to a series of simplified myths carried over from infancy. It does not so much as occur to them that many of rules they confidently proclaim to be self evident are logically incompatible. Nor do they imagine that scores of these propositions are fairy tales. Morality is, in short, not what it seems. Surprisingly, much of what most people assume to be true is but comforting illusion. For example, many people believe that morality is a search for a unique kind of knowledge;[3] the quest for an, as it were, circumscribed set of facts about good and evil that when discovered must be embraced with the greatest tenacity. Whether these are regarded as "natural laws," "non-natural qualities," or "mystical essences," they are deemed to possess an undeniable reality. Indeed, their truth is considered so absolute that once they are mastered, they are expected to anchor a person's worldview forever—the equivalent of immutable signposts that if honored, will always produce the best results.

A second simple, yet equally mistaken, way of conceiving of morality is as a distinctive "mental sense."[4] Whether this is believed to be a genetic disposition, an emotional faculty, or a peculiar form of reasoning, it is imagined to be a privileged mode of understanding that automatically validates what it apprehends. In recent years, one of the most popular guises this has taken has been as a specifically moral kind of judging.[5] When this aptitude operates correctly, it is believed to enable people to draw authoritative conclusions from intuitively understood principles. As a result, it is presumed that all mentally normal people must eventually arrive at the same conclusions. Another widely accepted and closely related mental faculty has been proposed by evolutionary psychologists.[6] This posits a genetically transmitted inclination toward altruism that allegedly shapes our moral conduct. In other words, what people determine to be good derives from a genetic desire to help others who share the same biological heritage as themselves.

Rather than go into the details of these theories, I shall concentrate on several specific misunderstandings regarding morality. Because abstractions can become disassociated from reality, spending large amounts of time with them might actually increase our confusions. But even on a concrete level, morality is a kaleidoscopic wonderland where time can run backwards and rabbits spout poetry. Still, we have no choice but to jump into the rabbit hole and delve into how morality works. Idealism simply cannot be understood without doing so. The extremes inherent in it are totally inexplicable without plumbing these very strange depths. For one thing, as answers to pressing moral questions, ideals are something in which people want to believe. This does not mean, however, that they are always good answers. Indeed, the less well people comprehend what they are doing, the more likely they will not be. It thus behooves us to investigate the nature of the morality game; especially its limitations. The penalty for doing otherwise is to convert our shining hopes into dangerous fantasies. Though an uncomfortable disillusionment may proceed from this exercise, the resulting frustrations are better than idealism run amok.

THE TWELVE COMMANDMENTS

One sort of moral "fact" in which we Westerners tend to invest ourselves is found in the Ten Commandments. This familiar set of injunctions is firmly implanted in the psyches of everyone influenced by the Judeo-Christian tradition. As a result, its component rules appear not only to have been decreed by God, but also to be laws of nature. Ostensibly clear, explicit, and unequivocally correct, to doubt them is considered evidence of a mental disorder or a moral defect. It is regarded as an admission of moral incompetence. Nevertheless, the Ten Commandments are not what they seem. People believe they understand them when they usually do not. Even if they can recite them—which incidentally most cannot—they fail to realize their implications. This was driven home to me when one day I decided to look them up in *The New Columbia Encyclopedia*.[7] The entry began by describing these mandates as "the summary of divine law given by God to Moses on Mt. Sinai." So far so good, but later in the same paragraph there appeared the following statement: "The Decalogue is in fact divisible into twelve commandments, since the first of the ten actually consists of three passages." How was that again? The Ten Commandments—of which there are really twelve? Nobody taught me this when I was in Sunday School, nor was it brought to my attention in any synagogue or church I ever attended.

The article went on to explain that the Eastern Orthodox and most Protestant churches tend to divide the commandments one way, while Roman Catholics, Lutherans, and Jews enumerate them differently. Thus, the former separate the injunctions to have no God before God and not to worship graven images into two distinct rules, whereas the latter combine them into one. Likewise, where the latter detect discrete prohibitions against coveting one's neighbor's wife and one's neighbor's property, the former blend these into a single number ten. Remarkably, even though both traditions utilize the same Bible to make their calculations, they come to contradictory conclusions.

This prompted me to consult my own Bible[8] to see what it said. At the bottom of a list I had read many times—but evidently not very carefully—was the following: "Thou shalt not covet thy neighbor's home, thou shalt not covet thy neighbor's wife, nor his man-servant, nor his maid-servant, nor his ox, nor his ass, nor anything that is thy neighbor's." Once more I did a double-take. My familiarity with history made me aware that in Biblical times man-servants and maid-servants were typically bondsmen; that is, they were slaves. Was I reading this right? Was one of the Ten Commandments actually enjoining people to respect the institution of slavery? I was positive that opinions had to be divided about this one, which made it intriguing to see how William Bennett[9] would handle the problem in his *Book of Virtues*. Under commandment number ten I found the declarative sentence: "Thou shalt not covet." There was nothing else; nothing about homes, oxen, asses, or maid-servants. Bennett apparently had the good sense to finesse a potentially explosive question.

But this was not all; moving up to commandment number nine, I encountered a further surprise. If asked to list the Ten Commandments, most people confidently include "Thou shalt not lie." The Bible, and Bennett, however, did not. They recorded it as: "Thou shalt not bear false witness against thy neighbor." This rang a bell for it was what I recalled my Rabbi having taught me when I was studying for my Bar Mitzvah. But I also realized that this was not the same as a blanket prohibition against lying. Strictly constructed, it suggested that God might not be distressed by people who faxed false receipts to the Internal Revenue Service or who, in writing advertising copy, made claims they knew to be exaggerated.

But even this was not all. I went back and revisited the injunction against graven images. Whether it is counted as part of commandment number one or two, it reads as follows: "Thou shalt not make unto thee any graven image, or any likeness that is in heaven above, or that is in the earth beneath, or that is in the water under the earth; thou shalt not bow down thyself to them, nor serve them; for I the Lord thy God am a jealous God, visiting the iniquity of the fathers upon the children unto the third and fourth generation of them that hate me; and showing mercy unto thousands of them that love me, and keep my commandments." This is strong stuff, much stronger than the rule against lying. Not only are a broad variety of images explicitly forbidden, but the punishment for violating the injunction is severe, applying even to those who have not literally infringed upon it.

Even so, there is disagreement about what this commandment proscribes. When I was a boy, my Rabbi asserted that he had no doubts. As he explained, the passages in which Jehovah declared that his chosen people were not to make graven images meant what they said. Didn't they forbid any likeness whatsoever, whether of what is in heaven, on earth, or under water? To do otherwise was plainly to be an idolater; it was to bow down before a God other than the one true God. When Roman Catholics knelt down before representations of Christ or the Virgin Mary, they consequently revealed themselves to be pagans. We Jews, in contrast, were faithful to God's word, as could be seen by looking around our synagogues. There were no paintings of Jehovah, no statues of Moses, no stained glass windows depicting King David. Yes, the ark in which the Torah was stored was richly sculpted, and the sacred scrolls were ornamented in brocades and silver, but there were no sacrilegious images to deflect from the glory of the Lord.

Needless to say, my Catholic friends did not concur with this assessment. They admitted that their churches were replete with statuary, paintings, and stained glass, but were adamant that these were not idols, and hence not violations of the letter of God's law. In our streetside conversations, they patiently explained that they believed in a Trinity and it was to this Trinity that they prayed. These other accruals were only aids in professing their faith. While they might be venerated, they were not confused with God and decidedly not worshipped in His stead. They merely created a psychological atmosphere that stimulated the appropriate attitude. Had my friends been more conversant with the history of their church, they might also have cited Popes Gregory II and Adrian I for support.

Moslems, had any lived on our block, would, of course, have been scandalized by this line of argument. As fellow believers in the Bible, they too revered the Ten Commandments, but they interpreted them as disallowing any human images whatsoever. In their mosques, they strove to celebrate the glory of Allah without any hint of representational figures. Instead they decorated their walls with elaborate calligraphy. Quotes from the Koran were rendered in intricate Arabic script for the instruction and admiration of the faithful. A full figure likeness of Mohammed not only would be considered gauche; it would be condemned as blatant idolatry. Mohammed was, after all, a prophet and not God.

Within Christianity, the issue has been less clearly delineated, with numerous schisms at times dividing believers into hostile, and sometimes warring, camps. Beginning as early as the synod of Elvira in 305 AD, church fathers warned against placing images on church walls lest these be worshipped. This became an ongoing point of contention in the Eastern Orthodox Church which experienced a stop-and-go iconoclastic movement[10] that sought to smash all representational images. Culminating in eighth and ninth century Byzantium, this ended only after blood had been shed, at which time a compromise was finally reached which persists to this day. Ultimately it was decided that some images were acceptable, if, that is, they are stylized. The result has been a tradition of paintings and mosaics usually identified as "icons." Although unquestionably human in their subject matter—often depicting Christ or a Madonna and Child—they possess an unreal, almost ethereal, quality that is intended to convey their sanctity of purpose.

In Western Christianity, there has been less of a consensus and a greater division into mutually antagonistic sects. New England, for instance, was initially colonized by settlers characterized as Puritan. Calvinist in their theology, they were appalled by idolatrous art; hence when they built their churches, sought to keep them simple and pure. On their altars were found crosses, but not crucifixes to which an image of Christ had been affixed. To their south, however, Anglicanism continued to flourish. In America, its communicants congregated in places such as Virginia where eventually they became known as Episcopalians. In their cathedrals, for example, St. John the Divine in New York City, representational art remains as prevalent as in any Catholic cathedral. The splendor of these adornments can literally take one's breath away. Indeed, the light streaming through multihued windows depicting the lives of saints can feel other-worldly. Most other Protestant denominations fall somewhere in between.[11] It is hard to be precise because attitudes toward graven images remain in flux. With new churches continuously springing into being, and others merging by settling their doctrinal differences, it is impossible to provide a definitive account of what all believe. What is clear is that the first—or is it the second—commandment is subject to interpretation. As transparent as its language may appear, its meaning has been, and continues to be, in dispute.

Also surprisingly open to interpretation are rules about more familiar activities such as lying. Regardless of the exact wording of the ninth commandment, even small children learn that not all lies are equally serious. Though they may be instructed never to tell a lie, even before they enter grammar school they are aware of "white" lies. Falsehoods that do not possess hurtful consequences, especially when they have beneficial ones, are not only acceptable but also can be mandatory. One kind of lie actually has a name: we call it "tact." To be tactful is to shade the truth so that it does not trample on the sensitivities of others. It may entail avoiding saying something factual because another might find it offensive or stating a truth in euphemistic language so as to conceal one's real intent. Just when, or where, one is allowed to do this is, as might be suspected, subject to debate. It was, after all, not long ago that most doctors felt obligated to hide the terminal nature of a disease from their patients. Today it is more likely to be race and gender that make people feel uncomfortable. Despite all of the public declarations extolling candor, when these subjects come up, the rules of political correctness make it expedient for the average person to be less than forthright.

Lying,[12] of course, lends itself to equivocation. Words have a plasticity that virtually invites manipulation. Murder, in contrast, would seem less open to interpretation. If the meaning of a prohibition against murder isn't clear, then what is? And yet it is not. If we return to the Bible, we see that the language it uses is: "Thou shalt not kill." How could anyone confuse this? With only four unambiguous words, there would seem to be no room for imprecision. Yet we all know that not all killing is prohibited. Taking the life of another in self-defense, or in wartime, is almost universally condoned. As a result most people reinterpret the sixth (or is it the fifth?) commandment to read, "Thou shalt not murder," where murder is defined as "wrongful" killing. Since self-defense is not wrongful, it is not considered murder, and is therefore not forbidden.

This is simple enough, but if we examine the fine print, everything goes out of focus. Let us consider the making of war. Although soldiers are everywhere encouraged to deprive their enemies of their lives, there turn out to be many conditions limiting this authorization, which, in addition, change with startling rapidity. It was little more than one hundred years ago, during the Zulu Wars[13]—1878 to be exact, that British arms achieved one of its most celebrated victories. Within hours after having inflicted a crushing defeat on a British column at Isandalwana, an Impe of the Zulu army descended on the isolated post of Rorke's Drift. A converted mission station, it was manned by fewer than 150 Tommies assigned to supply duty. Arrayed against them were several thousand dedicated warriors, invigorated by a history of successful aggression against neighboring tribes, and determined to make a name for themselves. These attacked in disciplined waves hoping to impale their enemies on their short spears, the infamous assagais. To this the British responded with equal discipline and vigor. In the end, their breach loading rifles provided the difference, with perhaps as many as a thousand of their attackers falling before the rest retreated.

After the battle, the victors went out among the vanquished to assess their accomplishment. Along the way they dispatched those of the wounded not yet dead. One can imagine the tired, yet relieved, survivors shooting and bayoneting scores of bleeding and groaning warriors who hadn't had the strength to flee. What is astonishing is that after news of these events reached London, not a word of protest was lodged against the slaughter of these helpless Africans. The victory brought joy and pride, and its aftermath was considered normal and unremarkable. Nowadays such an incident would stir up a very different reaction. Howls of disapproval would arise from the press and Amnesty International, for it is now considered unacceptable to execute the wounded, even if they are enemies, and even if they are African. Because the standards of what constitutes murder have changed, a war crimes tribunal would likely be convened. Today even those on the wrong side of a conflict are believed to have a right to medical treatment.

Another example of shifting attitudes toward wartime killing was revealed during World War II. At the beginning of the struggle, bombardment by aircraft was new—it having only been experimented with in the First World War. Initially both sides expected this technique to be directed against military targets. Dropping bombs on unarmed civilians seemed barbaric and was castigated as murder, the equivalent of the recently banned use of poison gas. When subsequently German bombers inadvertently dropped ordinance on a suburban London neighborhood, Winston Churchill was so outraged that he ordered a retaliatory strike against Berlin. This, in turn, infuriated Hitler, who gave orders for what came to be known as the London Blitz. Ultimately, before the hostilities ceased, civilian area bombing had become the norm. The avowed goal was now to demoralize the opposing population so they would not prosecute the war as aggressively.

When finally Harry Truman[14] authorized use of the atomic bomb against Hiroshima, dissenting voices argued that this too was murder. Why, they wondered, had he not dropped a warning device off the Japanese coast? Absent from this debate, however, was a comparable indignation regarding what had come to be described as "conventional" bombing. Even though the firestorms occasioned by raids against Hamburg, Dresden, and Tokyo caused tens of thousands of deaths, these had come to seem ordinary. To call them murder, or even to contemplate bringing charges against those responsible, seemed absurd.

To continue this line of thought, war must not be imagined the only domain in which there are disputes regarding what constitutes killing. Arguments about what to prohibit also abound in legal systems, medicine, and personal relationships. Take the case of dueling. In the middle ages, jousting was considered the noble way to settle a quarrel. The individual who succeeded on the field of honor was thereby held to have earned God's judgment. Later, swords took the place of lances and offended gentleman demanded satisfaction from one another. The romanticism of this custom was rousingly captured in the swashbuckling novels of Alexander Dumas. Later still pistols replaced swords. Since these required less practice to master, members of the commercial classes might now challenge each other in emulation of their more aristocratic compatriots. When, however, matters reached this climax, the seeds of a counter-norm were sown. By the beginning of the nineteenth century people were not only prepared to condemn dueling as murder, but to hold the offenders accountable. One of these was Aaron Burr.[15] After serving as Vice President of the United States, he blamed Alexander Hamilton for his defeat in a bid for the Governorship of New York State. This spurred him to extend a challenge that was answered when the two met on the dueling grounds of Weehawken,

New Jersey. Burr emerged victorious, but the subsequent uproar ruined his political career. Ultimately he found it expedient to leave the United States and pursue revolutionary conspiracies in adjacent Spanish territories.

More familiar perhaps—because they are closer to us—are controversies about the nature of abortion, euthanasia, suicide, drunk driving, and animal rights. Abortion, lest one forget, is portrayed by some as murder and by others as a lifestyle choice. Likewise, as recently as the 1950s, drunk driving was reckoned to be a routine human imperfection. When fatal accidents occurred, they were chalked up as just that—accidents. Nowadays they are likely to be prosecuted as vehicular homicides and result in years of imprisonment. To go a step further, some vegetarians[16] and anti-vivisectionists insist that killing animals is murder. More than a few have even been heard to mutter that "animals are people too."

The depth of confusion engendered by these debates is manifest in the euthanasia controversy. For years prosecutors in Michigan have been bringing murder indictments against Dr. Jack Kevorkian[17] for his flagrant efforts to publicize physician-assisted suicide. They even went so far as to invoke an unwritten "common law" in their campaign to convict him. And yet jury upon jury has refused to find him guilty. Once they were exposed to videotapes of the deceased expressing a desire to die or to their relatives tearfully testifying to the last agonies of a loved one, they seem to have had a "there-but-for-the grace-of-God" experience. It is plain that both sides are passionate regarding their version of murder, but it is equally plain that they evaluate the situation differently.

One might imagine that there must somewhere exist absolutely clear instances of the murder rule. Some cases, to be sure, are definitely clearer than others. Strangely, however, the gray areas are not confined to narrow borderlands, but cover a major expanse of the landscape. For instance, it might seem that when a man attacks and brutally kills his ex-wife by slashing her neck from ear to ear, he has violated the sixth commandment. What could provide a more central example of murder? Nevertheless, the O.J. Simpson affair provides striking counter-evidence. In his first trial Simpson's lawyers dedicated much of their effort to discrediting Nicole. They wished the jury to perceive her as a loose woman who contributed to her own demise. In its extreme form, their argument (much of it unstated) was that a woman who shamefully engaged in fornication within earshot of her children deserved to die. Her ex-husband, though he denied complicity, had a right to be outraged, and consequently, if he lost control, he was within the bounds of normality. Had this line of reasoning been made explicit, it is probable that an American jury would have rejected it. Brazilian jurists, on the other hand, have found it convincing and exonerated husbands, and ex-husbands, who have brutally slain their wives and lovers.

Lastly, there is the Golden Rule—which many treat as the thirteenth commandment. In its simplicity and universality it seems indisputable. But here too ambiguities rob what appears to be a firm principle of its solidity. If this sounds implausible, ask yourself, what, in the end, does the rule mean? Certainly not, "If I like ice cream, I should give you some too." Intuitively, the Confucian[18] formulation, that is, "Do *not* do unto others what you would *not* have them do unto you," comes closer to what is intended. Nevertheless, many people have strange ideas about what they ought, or ought not, inflict on others. Thus, when a TV reporter asked a Brooklyn teenager if he thought it was appropriate to force the music blaring from his car stereo upon bystanders as much as two blocks away, he responded that if they did not like what he was playing, that was their problem. They "should" like it. In his view, he was merely educating them in the basics of sound musical taste.

THE CHARACTER ISSUE

This lack of exactness regarding the nature and content of moral rules has discouraged many moralists. They continue to crave precision, but the perplexities regarding where to draw the requisite lines impel them to seek an alternative. If objective moral facts—such as rules—cannot be agreed upon, then maybe the key to how morality operates is available in the structure of the human mind. Their strategy is thus to seek a mental faculty that can infallibly distinguish good from bad. One of the candidates for this task is "character" traits. According to this gambit, being an intrinsically virtuous person, as opposed to a fundamentally evil one, will unfailingly point an individual toward what is right or wrong. Sadly, however, here too things are not what they seem. Despite the best of intentions, once again confusions arise to prevent a recognition of how morality actually functions.

If the character theory sounds plausible, consider for a moment how one might try to define virtue. Virtuous people are presumably those with a predisposition to do the right thing. Given a choice between alternatives, they select the one most people would agree is correct. As with moral rules, however, it is not clear which dispositions constitute virtues or how these are to be adopted once identified. Despite this, character appears to some the gold standard of our moral universe. They believe it a guarantee that its possessors will reliably treat others decently. In their view, because character traits are stable and dependable, if someone possesses the right ones, he or she will exhibit desirable behaviors. Unfortunately, this optimism is undermined by disputes about what needs to be internalized and how this can be fixed in place. But whatever character is, if we are unable consistently to recognize and replicate it, then celebrating it is unlikely generate improvements.

Looking back upon history, as a monograph on virtue by the philosopher Alastair MacIntyre[19] has demonstrated, makes it evident that different societies, and eras, have reached different conclusions about what counts as rectitude.[20] Consider the Homeric virtues. Homer's warrior heroes had a highly developed sense of honor, but it was quite distinct from our own. While it is true that they too valued courage, it was the courage of the battlefield. Nowadays we read the Iliad with an admiration of Achilles and Hector, but do not subscribe to their belief that only in mortal combat can one prove one's mettle. Nor do we share the ancient Greek attitude toward hospitality. Odysseus, in his wanderings after the victory at Troy, was captured by the Cyclops Polyphemus. Instead of being treated as an honored guest—as a wandering stranger ought—he and his men were imprisoned to provide food for the giant. Rightly incensed by this breach of honor, the "crafty" (itself a virtue) Odysseus plotted a suitable revenge. When he ultimately escaped by blinding his tormentor with a stake thrust into his single eye, we are given to understand that justice was served. Although we too take pleasure in this triumph of virtue, should a contemporary traveler elect a similar revenge, we would be appalled. Living in a world overflowing with strangers, our attitude toward hospitality is less emphatic for the obvious reason that travelers today require fewer private protections in a world amply provisioned with constabularies and hotels.

Coming closer to home, other variations in what constitutes virtue are detectable. While the American Experiment was still in its infancy, Benjamin Franklin[21] became famous, in part, by offering his fellow citizens what was regarded as sage advise. In his *Poor Richard's Almanac*, he offered such timeless wisdom as, "Early to bed and early to rise, makes a man healthy, wealthy, and wise," "God helps those who help themselves," "The used key is always bright," "Little strokes, fell great oaks," and "Don't throw stones at your neighbors', if your own windows are glass." From these one can readily infer that among the virtues to which he subscribed were frugality, responsibility, and effort. But do we, in our contemporary prosperity, feel the same? Do we, for instance, in our consumer society, honor people who voluntarily spend less money on the basic model of an automobile when a more opulent one is within reach?

To bring our review of virtue up to date, it is also necessary to consider what William Bennett,[22] our contemporary chronicler of virtue, has seen fit to include in his *Book of Virtues*. Among the character traits that made his cut are: self-discipline, compassion, responsibility, courage, honesty, and loyalty. These certainly demonstrate a continuity with Franklin, but need to be compared with an alternate compendium of virtues prepared by Colin

Greer and Herbert Kohl.[23]   The latter felt compelled to write *A Call to Character* as an anodyne to what they considered Bennett's conservative agenda.   Thus in their book they decline to include four virtues endorsed by him, namely, friendship, work, perseverance, and faith, but add ten others: integrity, creativity, playfulness, generosity, empathy, adaptability, idealism, balance, fairness, and love.   Which constitute the "real" virtues I leave the reader to decide.   But remember, there are also potential entries not considered by either of these experts.

Should we, however, overcome this hurdle, another quickly rises to block the way.   Suppose we all agree that courage is a virtue; how is it to be inculcated?   Merely urging others to acquire a backbone does not of itself instill this propensity.   Consider the poem "If" by Rudyard Kipling.[24]   It is one of my favorites.   Every time I peruse it, I am inspired to face life's battles with renewed vigor.   The poem reads as follows:

> If you can keep you head when all about you
>   Are losing theirs and blaming it on you;
> If you can trust yourself when all men doubt you,
>   But make allowance for their doubting too;
> If you can wait and not be tired by waiting,
>   Or, being lied about, don't deal in lies,
> Or, being hated, don't give way to hating,
>   And yet don't look too good, nor talk too wise;
>
> If you can dream—and not make dreams your master;
> If you can think—and not make thoughts your aim;
> If you can meet with triumph and disaster
>   And treat those two impostors just the same;
> If you can bear to hear the truth you've spoken
>   Twisted by knaves to make a trap for fools,
> Or watch the things you gave your life to broken,
>   And stoop and build'em up with worn-out tools;
>
> If you can make a heap of all your winnings
>   And risk it on one turn of pitch-and-toss,
> And lose, and start again at your beginnings
>   And never breathe a word about your loss;
> If you can force your heart and nerve and sinew
>   To serve your turn long after they are gone,
> And so hold on when there is nothing in you
>   Except the Will which says to them: "Hold on!"
>
> If you can talk with crowds and keep your virtue,
>   Or walk with kings—nor lose the common touch;

If neither foes nor loving friends can hurt you;
   If all men count with you, but none too much;
If you can fill the unforgiving minute
   With sixty seconds' worth of distance run—
Yours is the Earth and everything that's in it,
   And—which is more—you'll be a man my son!

Bennett includes this ode to personal fortitude in his section on courage, and it is easy to see why. Trust yourself when all others doubt you; treat triumph and disaster alike; be prepared to lose all and begin again; these are certainly guideposts for the brave. They are also a recipe for winning in a world full of terrors. Nevertheless, they are a recipe without precise directions. This becomes glaringly apparent to me when I reminisce about the past. Thus the older I get, the greater my tendency to reflect on the trials I have experienced. I too have been lied about, and hated, and had my "truths" twisted by knaves. And I too have learned to persevere in the face of negative pressures. Yet when I was younger, I did not know how to do any of these things, nor could I have learned merely by being enjoined to. Though Kipling's poem is ostensibly directed at a young man, what young man understands how to keep his dreams from becoming his master? Or how to lose without lamenting his bad luck aloud? These attributes are acquired only through painful trial and error. It is experience, not exhortation, that hones them to a fine edge.

Worse still is the fact that apparently unambiguous appeals to virtue expose us to pitfalls and quandaries not contemplated until too late. Calls to character have a curious way of praising inclinations to action that end up being self-defeating. Virtues such as courage and honesty seem self-evident, but are actually composed of many strands, each of which has many wrinkles. A child's eye view of courage might, for instance, include a willingness to throw oneself on a hand grenade to save a comrade's life; it is far less likely to meditate on the implications of changing one's job because of an arrogant boss. Just how misleading calls to virtue can be is demonstrated by a well-loved parable. Hans Christian Anderson's[25] *The Emperor's New Clothes* is a delightful peon to honesty. It begins, as do many fables, with the phrase "Many years ago" (and evidently far away), and continues, "there was an Emperor who was so fond of new clothes that he spent all his money on them." One day there appeared in town two rascals who were intent upon taking advantage of the sovereign's weakness. They promised him that, for an appropriate fee, they could weave a fabric that was uncommonly beautiful, but, more than this, would have the unusual property of being invisible to anyone who was either unfit for office or exceptionally stupid. Since no one from the emperor on down wanted to admit to such flaws, all claimed to see, and admire, the garment made from this material, even though, in reality, it did not exist. When the day came for the monarch to show off this attire, he organized a procession through the center of his capital. Not wanting to appear foolish, his subjects too initially fawned over their ruler and cheered his remarkable costume. That is, until a small child piped up, "But he has nothing on!" When the child's father then urged the others to "Just listen to the innocent," it was not long before all were crying, "But he has nothing on!"

Bennett, commenting on the moral of this tale, notes that "trusting ourselves is the best road to the truth" and that "honesty, unlike new clothes, never goes out of fashion." Evidently he must be unaware of what Paul Harvey would call "the rest of the story." In Bennett's version the Emperor continues with the procession as if nothing had happened, but the real conclusion to the tale is less sanguine. Shortly after the sovereign had passed by, elements of the royal guard barged into the crowd where they picked up, and hustled away, both the child and his father. They were then taken to the palace dungeon where they were questioned, the boy fairly gently, but the father rather brutally. Later that same day the secret police picked up the mother and she too was subjected to torture. Eventually all of the close relatives were rounded up. During their cross-examinations, each, including the child, was asked the intent of his subversive behavior. Were they part of a larger conspiracy to overthrow the government? Perhaps they were in league with a foreign power? If so, who were their fellow conspirators? Unless they were willing to comply with these demands by furnishing answers compatible with the expectations of their inquisitors, they were beaten, deprived of sleep, or sent to solitary confinement. None was killed, but they were shipped to faraway prison camps. Sadly, within the year the father got into an altercation with a guard and lost his life. Luckier, the mother was a decade later released into the community, where she remarried, albeit unhappily. Other friends and relatives caught in the web of suspicion fared unevenly. Some got off with a stern warning; others were imprisoned. As for the child and his sister, they were sent to separate foster homes. For the most part, their crime was no longer mentioned by their keepers, but neither were they allowed contact with family members. When the boy grew to manhood, he became an ardent supporter of the emperor. All his life he attributed his youthful indiscretion to brainwashing by his parents and loudly reviled them as traitors. As for history, it records the emperor as one of the most successful of his line. The special suit of clothes is regularly cited as evidence of his splendor and commentators still stand in awe that no one has been able to duplicate its brilliance.

The real moral of the story is, of course, that honesty is not the uncomplicated quality of mind sometimes portrayed. On the contrary, a naive and unexamined honesty can be deadly. If, for instance, Anderson's tale persuades a person to become a whistleblower,[26] he may on this account lose his job, family, and tranquillity. In giving the impression that honesty is usually rewarded, the parable misleadingly encourages the guileless to take enormous risks they may not even recognize as hazardous, a circumstance that is hardly ideal.

The same sort of indeterminacy, of course, plagues the liberal virtues. Greer and Kohl, in praising the value of "playfulness," tell us that it is "a basic survival skill," that "without the ability to look at the world and oneself as slightly silly and out of joint, it would be impossible to live through the horrors and absurdities we encounter every day." At first blush, this has the ring of truth. Life does indeed need to be leavened with fun. But one must also look a little deeper. Take the selection that Greer and Kohl cite to back up their thesis. I refer to an excerpt from James M. Barrie's[27] *Peter Pan.* Peter Pan is, as we know, the much beloved flying, pirate-fighting, resident of Neverland who vowed never to grow up. In the story, he charms the Darling children with visions of frolic, magic, and—dare one say it—irresponsibility, if they will only follow him to his home, there to reside forever. They are sorely tempted, but when ultimately they choose otherwise, we readers are disappointed at their selling out. Yet which is best, to grow up and become an adult or to refuse and remain an eternally fun-loving child? In the real world, the choice should be obvious.

Play, psychologists tell us, is essential for coming to terms with life, especially among children. Yet in this era of MTV, it has, for many, become *the* goal of life. I, an aging member of the Pepsi Generation, remember when the good life was portrayed as an endless party on the beach. According to the media at least, the current X-Generation has gone beyond this by moving the gala into every aspect of their existence. If so, the lesson embedded in the Peter Pan legend contains disturbing overtones. Just as the *Emperor's New Clothes* presents a mistaken portrait of honesty, it fatally distorts the consequences of spurning adulthood. Those who manage to remain forever young do not on this account preserve their happiness. Quite the contrary, in failing to perform the essential tasks of life, they habitually let themselves and their loved ones down.

One finds a comparable predicament when contemplating vices rather than virtues. They too are not what we imagine and therefore can be misleading in what they recommend. Consider the seven deadly sins. Virtually everyone is aware that this inventory exists, but most could not itemize it. Derived primarily from the Christian tradition, it includes: sloth, lust, anger, pride, envy, gluttony, and greed. As should be evident from even a perfunctory perusal, we don't all agree on the offensiveness of these, never mind on their being automatic tickets to hell. Many economists, for example, believe that greed is the driving force behind successful economies. Likewise, many therapists argue that without being able to implement vigorous, albeit controlled, anger, people become so passive they cannot achieve even modest satisfactions.[28] Similarly, many civil libertarians passionately defend the right of people to be overweight. They contend that just because some individuals are compulsive eaters—perhaps for genetic reasons—they do not deserve to be stigmatized.

In addition, Stanford Lyman[29], in his review of the seven deadly sins, makes a strong case for pride. In his words: "Pride comes or goes—after or before a fall. Ever potential in the hearts of men, it nevertheless finds varied opportunity for expression and form. Its sinfulness is by no means sure. Sublimated as honor, dignity, or self-confidence, it serves as a sign of morality, a surety of character, or an incentive to succeed. Honored as patriotism, national prestige, or ethnic-hyperconsciousness, it establishes a nonrational basis for state security, restores damaged dignity, and gives additional ground for psychic self-sufficiency." What is more, humility is spectacularly overrated. Indeed, it is often a cover story for secret pride. If Lyman is correct in this, most of us do not understand sin any better than we comprehend virtues or moral rules.

SCIENCE TO THE RESCUE

With such an abundance of quandaries, it is evident why people sometimes seek expert advice in determining what is moral. There has to be, they reason, an objective source of guidance to cut through these thickets. Given its marvelous track record in physics, chemistry, and more recently in biology, science is an obvious candidate. Its practitioners are well-educated professionals who possess the knowledge, temperament, and investigative tools to solve difficult puzzles. Why not let them arbitrate moral dilemmas? Unfortunately, scientists are human beings.[30] They are not merely observers of the morality game, but also players in it. Like everyone else, they have private agendas they bring to the table and shamelessly promote. As a result, they tend not to be neutral, even when they claim to be. What they put forward as an unbiased description of reality is often really a disguised form of prescription, and what they insist to be discovered truths may actually be rationalizations for prior commitments. Far from habitually offering disinterested investigations, a closer inspection reveals a pattern of evaluative judgments that are not open to disconfirmation.[31]

One of my favorite prototypes of this tendency comes from Stalinist Russia.[32] It is the Lysenko case. In the 1930s, Joseph Stalin claimed that he was building socialism as a prelude to communism. As his grip on the Soviet government tightened, he justified his more repressive measures as essential to laying the industrial and agricultural foundations for a society in which the state would eventually wither away. If this meant forcing peasants onto state-controlled communes, or directing millions of slave-laborers into building a grand canal in the Arctic or into extracting mineral wealth from Siberian waste lands, it had to be done. Only firmness could prevent the ever-present reactionary forces from undermining the will of the Soviet people.

One of communism's articles of faith was that all men (and women) are created equal. Inequality was merely an historical artifact that arose from class warfare. Once the capitalist class was finally overthrown by the proletarians, and after the economic might of industrialization had created sufficient wealth, all people would live in harmony and prosperity. An important condition of this, however, was that the remnants of the bourgeois mind-set be eradicated. People needed to be reeducated so that the new socialist-man could come into existence. Fair-minded, and giving, these paragons of virtue would recognize the validity of the maxim, "From each according to his ability; to each according to his need," and act correspondingly. This was possible because people were infinitely plastic. Believers in the supremacy of nurture over nature, true communists knew that any person could rise to the top if properly indoctrinated. The key was education, whether in the schools, through media-based propaganda, or at the behest of omnipresent political commissars.

Into this cauldron arrived Trofim Denisovich Lysenko. An agronomist by training, he claimed to have developed a process for imparting the characteristics of winter wheat into spring wheat. By a technique called vernalization in which seeds were moistened and then refrigerated, they could be made more productive. In other words, by manipulating their environment these biological entities could be altered in accord with human desires. Here, indeed, was nurture grandly triumphant over nature. Moreover, if specific acquired characteristics could also be passed along from one generation to the next, as Lysenko asserted they could, the circle would be complete. It might then also be possible for properly treated human beings to be converted into self-perpetuating idealists who possessed the motivation required for true communism.

Having furnished precisely the sort of moral rationale Stalin was seeking, Lysenko was made president of the All-Union Academy of Agricultural Sciences, a member of the Supreme Soviet, and head of the Institute of Genetics of the Soviet Academy of Sciences. From this lofty perch, he became virtual czar of Soviet biological research. Consequently when he decreed that Mendelian theories of genetics were heretical, their pursuit came to a standstill. To violate this mandate was to risk a trip to the Gulag. Only gradually was Lysenko's moralistic stamp removed from what was supposed to be science. With Stalin's death, he lost his position as president of the All-Union Academy of Agricultural Sciences, but it was not until 1965 that he was removed as director of the Institute of Genetics of the Soviet Academy. Apparently orthodoxies expire slowly, especially when they are officially labeled scientific.

Should it be smugly imagined that only a totalitarian state could spawn moralized versions of science, it is essential to be aware of the case of Margaret Mead. A student of Columbia University's Franz Boas,[33] himself a seminal figure in American anthropology, she produced a series of popular monographs that, to this day, are cited in the textbooks as classical studies of human relationships. Although Boas is less widely recognized by the general public, he was the source of her inspiration, and of what today has become an integral part of our conventional wisdom, namely the concepts of "cultural determinism" and "cultural relativism." At the turn of the century, Boas confronted a social science beguiled by Darwinism. Biology was riding high and seemed perched to explain virtually everything that human beings did, including their cultural evolution. Darwin's cousin Francis Galton went so far as to proclaim that society must be renewed by controlling who reproduced, a program he dubbed "eugenics." Progressive in his politics, and anti-racist in his convictions, Boas could not abide this potentially repressive philosophy. Feisty by nature, he was prepared to fight, and fight he did. His riposte was that "culture" differed from biology and that it was culture that most determined human action. In other words, like Lysenko later on, he asserted the primacy of nurture over nature. In his view too, human conduct was plastic, and hence, should individuals be instructed dissimilarly, they will grow up differently.

Before Boas, small non-Western societies were routinely described as "primitive" or "savage." As a result of his influence, they became "pre-literate." Due to his incessant promotion, they were accorded the respect he believed they deserved. Probably Boas' most significant contribution was the insight that a specific society could not be fully understood, except in its own context. Because all societies are extremely complex, an element that may not seem to make sense takes on a different shading when perceived in relation to other elements. As an example, the Indian taboo[34] against eating beef appears extreme unless it is recognized as preserving draft animals in an agricultural community subject to periodic droughts that might tempt farmers to sacrifice them for food. His conclusion was that all societies possess a dignity worthy of admiration, and that social scientists, in particular, must acknowledge this if they are to understand their subject matter. It was, however, a small step to "ethical relativism,"[35] that is, to a belief that the moral worth of a society can be judged only in its own terms. In this view, all societies are created equal and possess the same ethical validity. To malign them is merely a sign of ignorance that can be remedied by accumulating the necessary knowledge. Doing so reveals that, if anything, in their simplicity, and honesty, smaller societies possess a greater claim to respect than do the more corrupt Western ones.

Mead's role in Boas' universe was to gather data to establish the correctness of this perspective.[36] As one of his acolytes, she was packed off to do research in the South Seas. Specifically, she was to engage in an ethnographic study among adolescents in the Samoan Islands. After a period of living among them, she would return to the United States where she would write a report detailing the nature of their culture. In this she was spectacularly successful. The volume that grew out of her efforts, *Coming of Age in Samoa*,[37] became the best selling anthropology book of all time and permanently altered the intellectual landscape, not only of America, but of the entire world. It seemed to prove, once and for all, that there was no single biologically derived "human nature." Here was a group of people who did not conform to Western expectations. They clearly did not go through the same sort of adolescent turmoil that until then had been deemed universal. In scientific terms, this was a negative case that confirmed the potency of culture vis-a-vis genetics. Mead argued that teenage Samoan girls regularly, and guiltlessly, indulged in premarital sex without any negative consequences. Satisfied and mentally secure, these members of a peaceful and contented community offered an example that a deeply conflicted and anxiety-ridden industrial society would do well to emulate.

This interpretation was widely accepted as true. Anthropologists and lay persons alike fell over themselves in their acclamation of it. John B. Watson,[38] the behavioral psychologist, Bertrand Russell,[39] the analytic philosopher, and H.L. Mencken, the iconoclastic journalist, were unanimous in their approval. Boas himself joined the chorus in lauding "her painstaking investigation." By providing vivid testimony to an exotic way of life, she had breathed life into it and awakened people to possibilities not previously contemplated. Maybe humans could reshape themselves into loving, cooperative, and community-spirited beings, if, that is, they had the will to do so.

For more than half a century this vision went virtually unchallenged, but in 1983 the romantic daydream was shattered by Derek Freeman.[40] After decades of on and off investigation, he concluded that Mead was wrong in most of her particulars. Samoa was not an exception to the rule, but an instance of inadequate research grossly misinterpreted to fit a predetermined agenda. According to Freeman, Mead, the true believer, unconsciously extended a gift to "Papa Franz" in the form of confirmation of his convictions. Mead's portrait of Samoa was almost lyrical. She described a South Sea paradise come to life in scientific apparel. For her, it was a "casual" society—a place of "ease"—in which there was little conflict and a great deal of nonpossessive love. Because children were raised gently and non-punitively, almost exactly as Jean-Jacques Rousseau had prescribed, they grew into happy and well-adjusted adults. With parenting chores spread over many relatives, they knew no guilt, and hence could be cooperative rather than competitive. As importantly, they became nonaggressive adults who spurned war, sin, and jealousy in favor of freely chosen lovemaking. The way Mead told it, for them "sex is play and permissible in all hetero- and homosexual expression[s], with any sort of variation as an artistic addition." Not only did they regard spontaneous sex with acceptance, but because they considered it a "light and pleasant dance," they expected teenagers to be promiscuous and their parents to take adultery in stride. In such a society, rape was virtually unknown, as were delinquency and frigidity. Boas supported this assessment by declaring that "with the freedom of sexual life, the absence of a large number of conflicting ideals, and the emphasis on forms that to us are irrelevant, the adolescent crisis disappears."

Yet as Freeman has demonstrated, almost all of this was a fairy tale. Samoans, by their own account, and that of most other observers, were never the lighthearted, pleasure seekers Mead imagined them to be. Far from being untroubled sensualists, they lived in a world obsessed with rank and etiquette. Not only were they aggressive and competitive, but they disciplined their children harshly and placed a high valuation on virginity. Moreover, rape, murder, and guilt were all present, as were war, jealousy, and deceit. Indeed, when shown her book, the Samoans could not recognize themselves in Mead's exposition. Her confidants, they suggested, "must have been telling lies to tease her."

It is easy to see how this could have happened when one reviews the circumstances of Mead's research. Most of us, when we pick up a book, assume its validity. It seems to have been produced by a disembodied authority. Yet Margaret Mead was a real person, who, when she went to Samoa, was just twenty-three years old. Although she had recently finished her doctorate, she had completed only two years of graduate study in anthropology and had virtually no previous field experience. To be sure, she had done library research on the Polynesians, but it did not concern the Eastern Polynesians or the adolescent period. To add to this, when she arrived in Samoa, she did not speak the language, and because she had difficulty in picking it up, never became fluent. One might have supposed that Mead would have tried to compensate for these handicaps by living among the Samoans. For all but ten days, however, including the mere six months she stayed on the island of Manu'a, she resided with Westerners, because, as she explained to Boas, she could not abide the starchy local cuisine.

When it came to the research itself, Mead relied on informants. But not just any informants; twenty-five adolescent and preadolescent girls. Because she was a small person, she fit in among them. It was primarily from what they said, not what she directly observed, that she drew her conclusions. As a consequence, it is easy to comprehend how she could have been misled. How, indeed, could these young girls have understood much about their own society? And how in the space of six months could they have conveyed its complexities to a stranger? Why also would they have come to trust a young [41]foreigner, who, as it happened, lived with a Navy family at a time when there was friction between the Navy and the indigenous peoples? Accuracy under these conditions defies credulity, except, of course, for those primed to believe. Even scientists, it seems, can be led astray by their moral certitudes.[42]

Chapter 3

Messianic Stickball

THE STICKBALL MENTALITY

If morality is not what we believe it to be, then what is it, and how is this related to idealism? The answers to these questions are surprisingly complex. Perhaps the best way to approach them is through a metaphor. In some ways, how adults play the morality game is paralleled by how children engage in team sports, particularly when they do so without adult supervision. Back in the Brooklyn of my youth, one of our favorite pastimes was stickball. From early spring to late fall, groups of neighborhood boys could be found playing this game in the streets, against brick walls, and in school yards. A variation of baseball, stickball is specific to urban settings. Without grass-covered fields on which to lay out regulation diamonds or the financial resources to acquire store-bought balls, gloves, or bats, it was as close as many of us city kids could come to the real thing.

As the name implies, a "stick," or more correctly, a broom or mop handle, was substituted for the bat, while a pink rubber ball—much like a tennis ball minus the fuzz—took the place of a rawhide one. In Brooklyn, the latter was called a "spaldeen." Made by the Spaulding Company, with its logo plainly emblazoned on its surface, this was beyond the pronunciation of most of the Jewish and Italian kids with whom I hung around. I am not even sure that any of us associated the black ink trademark with the name of the ball. Nor did we have gloves when we played. These were unnecessary with something as soft as a spaldeen. As to the bases, they were catch-as-catch-can and varied with the location of the game. If it were being played in the street, as was most common, home plate might be a manhole cover, a

45

piece of linoleum cut to size, or a chalk square scrawled on the pavement. The other bases might also be chalked in, but could coincide with a sewer or take advantage of a parked car. If the game were being played against a wall, the plate would be marked out against it so as to provide the pitcher with an unmistakable target. If played in a school yard, where painted bases were available, our practice was to divide the diamond in half so that what would have been second base was redesignated third.

The ground rules were a bit trickier, especially in the street. Foul lines might be established by utilizing prominent points of reference, for example, the edge of a building, but this left the problem of determining exactly where the line fell in the area between the plate and the designated feature. A similar problem arose with placing the outfield limit, that is, the spot beyond which an uncaught fly was an automatic home run. When we were younger, it was the second "sewer," but as we grew older and stronger, it became the third. The difficulty with this was that it lay across Avenue S, where traffic might interfere with tracking down a batted ball. Other local hazards, for which ground rules were needed, included the trees and cars. Depending upon the season, the maple trees on 8th Street or the cottonwoods on Avenue S might deflect a spaldeen. The question, in this case, was how to score such accidents. Similarly, the number of cars parked by the curb could fluctuate with the time of day or the day of the week, and might conceivably interfere with a base runner or a thrown ball.

Also problematic were the parameters regarding pitching and batting. Unlike a baseball, a spaldeen could bounce quite decisively. This made it possible, especially among the younger kids, to permit on-a-hop pitching. Whether this was to be on one or two bounces was, however, an open question. Another peculiarity of the spaldeen was that it could produce a wicked curve. If given a spin, when thrown on a bounce, it might dart sharply off to a side after it landed. The issue then became, was this fair? Even if pitched on a fly, a spaldeen could break two or three feet. How then was one to determine if it had crossed the plate? This was obviously troublesome without the presence of a neutral umpire. When the game was played against a wall, the chalked in target would leave a mark on the ball, but on the street opinions were often divided. There might also be controversies about how many strikes constituted an out. Younger players favored an unlimited strike rule with an out being determined by what happened to the batted ball or by reaching a fixed number of foul balls, but older teens, in deference to their greater skills, preferred a two-strike or two-swing rule.

Even the equipment could be a source of contention. Because nothing was standardized, specific bats and balls made a difference. Mop and broom handles did not, after all, come in a single gauge. Some were longer and some shorter, some thinner and some thicker, which influenced how easy it was to hit a ball or how far it would go once struck. Likewise, some spaldeens were bouncier than others. Those retrieved from a sewer were notorious for being dead. In such a case, what constituted a home run might have to be altered. Often the resolution of these matters depended upon who owned the equipment, for the possessor might threaten to go home if he weren't satisfied. Yet another complicating factor was who the players were. Besides age, there were the issues of how many players would be on the field and how good they were. Usually this depended upon who turned up. Because the games were spontaneous, as few as four or as many as twelve might take part. How the sides were chosen thus became another point of discord. This was especially serious if there were too many players and some had to be excluded. Because such decisions were usually made by the team captains, who was selected for these positions, and how they were to determine their picks, became critical. Favoritism was not out of the question, nor was cheating, so one had to be careful. Sometimes the sides were decided by who arrived first, or who was friends with whom, or who was the best hitter. It was even possible for a bully to barge in and demand that things be done his way.

Under such circumstances, it was inevitable that bickering was a routine part of the process. In fact, it was normal to spend more time on deciding which rules to follow, and how to apply them, than on the game itself. Before any contest started the players stood around in loose circles discussing, gesticulating, and arguing about what to do. Some kids would make quiet suggestions about what was most appropriate, but others angrily demanded that things be settled their way. Many would try to maneuver the conclusions in their favor. Thus, someone who could not hit a curve might try to get these excluded, while another would seek broader foul lines to accommodate his errant swing. Each, of course, expressed his desire as neutrally as he could, thereby trying to make it seem as if it were the fairest option. After the game began, however, the fights persisted. Without a trusted umpire to make the close calls, not only could balls and strikes become points of debate, but so too would safe and out calls.

Extensive fights were especially likely if the players were of different ages. The older boys tended to become impatient with the younger, whereas the latter felt threatened when their seniors tried to impose a solution. The decibel level really escalated when the boys from 9th Street came over to play our 8th Street crowd. A culture clash ensued with each side determined that its standards prevail. Jean Piaget,[1] the Swiss psychologist who studied marble players in his native country, described rule negotiations among his subjects as relatively civilized, yet in Brooklyn civility had nothing to do with the matter. We all wanted to win, especially against the 9th Streeters, and weren't too fussy about how we accomplished our goal.

The primatologist Frans de Waal,[2] in a discussion of how morality evolved from animal behaviors, describes something akin to my experience when reflecting upon his own youth. He writes, "Like every European boy, I could barely walk when I learned to play the world's most popular sport. [Which in his world was soccer.] Before I knew it, along with the fun...I was receiving important moral lessons. Team sports, with their rules and expectations, [I found] are a microcosm of society...." de Waal believes this was so in soccer because it was "not the almighty adult who kept an eye on you..., it was your peers and equals!" In the beginning, these others enforced "simple rules....[but] gradually [these became] more complex and precise, until one day an older boy shout[ed] 'offside'...and the most frustrating regulation of all [was] introduced." As importantly, "this knowledge [was] acquired via endless debates about what one did versus what one should have done...." Indeed, we "boys seem[ed] to enjoy these legal battles every bit as much as the game itself."

For me, these "endless debates" were instantly recognizable. The points of contention may have differed, but the spirit was the same. Nevertheless, unlike de Waal, I loathed them. My desire to win was as keen as anyone's, but if an older boy suddenly enforced a regulation with which I was unfamiliar, I felt imposed upon—almost as if he were cheating. Though he may merely have been trying to be fair, it felt as if I was being bullied into submission by somebody too strong to oppose. Still and all, it was the interminable nature of these disputes that most rankled. Nothing ever seemed to get settled. Just when an agreement appeared to be reached, someone else barged in with another suggestion. This happened continuously. Sometimes I would stand back, as if I were an uninvolved observer, and wonder if rationality had a chance to prevail. Why, I asked myself, couldn't we just play fair? My only solace came from a conviction that one day I would be an adult and part of a fraternity from which this sort of pettiness would be banished.

What I failed to grasp, but as de Waal has pointed out, is that team sports are indeed a microcosm of society, and, as it turns out, specifically of morality. Unregulated fighting is indigenous to each. Surprisingly, adults also engage in petty, interminable skirmishes. Although I expected adult rule-setting to be a determinate affair—entailing inviolable regulations judiciously enforced by a cadre of mature arbiters—when I arrived in the promised land, I discovered a set of standards more in flux than those of stickball. For obvious reasons, our street game was not codified, and mutated from neighborhood to neighborhood and instance to instance, but so, it appears, does morality. Its dimensions are no more fixed, or clear, than were our foul lines. This, for me, was a shocker. So was the fact that adult moralists are no more fair than were my childhood friends. They too are determined to win, often at any cost, and will distort their principles when necessary. Not to put too fine a point on things, the morality game apparently is governed by the same mentality as stickball. Both are free-floating performances that may appear stable, but that are, in reality, played by contestants who constantly make adjustments while adrift in a sea of uncertainty and unrest. As a result, the measures upon which they temporarily agree, to cover what they must, have to be elastic. But to be elastic, they need to be vague and turbulent. Paradoxically, confrontation and confusion are the norm; it is stability and reason that are not.

A WELL-KEPT SECRET

Yet most people do not recognize the plasticity of morality. Like my former self, they expect it to have firm boundaries established quite apart from the machinations of the players. Nobody has let them in on the secret that moral rules are created, and maintained, by human beings; that is, by people just like themselves. As with stickball, its regulations have no existence separate from what they themselves decide. Contrary to what most hope, neither nature, nor a merciful Divinity, intervenes to certify what is right or wrong. Indeed, were a supreme authority to descend from heaven and try to intercede, in all probability, no one would listen. The truth is that morality is up to us—with our limitations, imperfect knowledge, tribal hatreds, trivial jealousies, insatiable desires to triumph, nagging puzzlements, and ever-present insecurities. As Emile Durkheim wrote a century ago, society gives birth to moral rules and it is society that enforces them. For better or worse, whenever social standards are in place, so are people—people with the same boundless foibles, potential for mischief, and exalted aspirations as you and me.

Although many of us imagine morality to be something ethereal, it is merely a species of social activity.[3] As something we do, not something discoverable sitting under a bush or hiding out behind a comet, to understand it, we must recognize how it operates. What kinds of rules does it impose and how are these learned, expressed, created, enforced, or changed? Such basic questions must be resolved before we can determine what is right or ideal. Only then is it possible to comprehend how standards of perfection go wrong, why they are ignored, and why they sometimes insist on objectives that are far from perfect.

Informal Rules Moral rules are no more precise than are those of stickball. Obviously stickball has no official rulebook, but neither does morality. Codes such as the Ten Commandments may seem to belie this, but despite their apparent specificity, are not the standards we live by. The paradox of morality is that what we say we do is not what we actually do. The situation may be compared with highway speed limits. Everyone knows that precise maximums are enacted by state legislatures and posted on metal signs along the roadway. We also understand that these are not the limits enforced by the state patrol. No one tells us what will get us pulled over—it varies with the time and place, but during the course of driving we develop a sense of what to expect. This is what is meant by describing such rules as "informal." Another set of informal norms involves Christmas gift giving. Theodore Caplow[4] writes of how these gifts are decorated, selected to demonstrate familiarity with the recipient, and scaled to match the value of the relative status of the parties. To not wrap a gift, or to over or under give, would be faux pas of the first magnitude. No one explicitly instructs us on these points, but they are nevertheless in the atmosphere.

Informal standards are unofficial, inexact, and often ambiguous. As opposed to more formal rules, they are not overtly acknowledged or honored. Usually they remain unwritten, and when stated, fluctuate in their formulation, which often is totally plastic. They can nonetheless be quite potent. Typically we learn informal rules from examples, not precepts or authoritative pronouncements. Just as we ascertain the true speed limits by observing who is pulled over, so we discover moral standards by noticing who is punished or rewarded. People do, to be sure, say things such as "lying is wrong" as if these were indisputable commands, yet it is usually impossible to recognize exactly that to which a specific prescription refers without extensive experience. In the course of living we encounter, and internalize, numerous unstated—and often unstatable—qualifications to ostensibly unimpeachable prohibitions. And herein lies the essence of moral rules. It is in these qualifications—these exceptions—wherein the real standards reside. It is they that provide their remarkably malleable substance.

Consider a few of the qualifications to the lying rule. Although at first blush it seems simple and straightforward, what would be right in the following circumstances:

- A woman asks her husband to tell the truth about the dress she is wearing—whether it makes her look fat—and it does.
- A man asks his wife how his lovemaking stacks up against that of her previous lovers—and it doesn't.
- The Nazis knock at your door in the middle of the night to ask if you are hiding Jews—and there is a family cowering in the basement as you speak.

- A job interviewer asks you what is your worst fault—and you have a tendency to be lazy.
- You are assigned to write advertising copy for a new automobile—and have just read that Consumer's Union rated it last in its classification.
- Your boss is upset about losing an account and heatedly inquires who was responsible for failing to send out some promised materials—and it was you, but you need the job.

From the preceding it should be clear that not only is lying sometimes acceptable; often it is mandatory. But let us go a step further. Though these qualifications are common knowledge, from whence do they derive? Surely no one ever sat down and provided a list. The real rule against lying, the one we honor, is modified by a myriad of exceptions learned slowly and unconsciously. For the most part, they are never verbalized, not even in our own minds. It is certainly not as if a single, consistent principle were propagated once and for all. On the contrary, the ones we respect are continuously under repair and continuously open to reinterpretation. What moral rules prohibit is so complex, and so open to change, that simple, immutable proscriptions are impossible. Their absoluteness would inevitably distort what was intended.

Philip Howard[5] has made a similar point about laws in his book *The Death of Common Sense*. As he asserts, "Universal requirements that leave no room for judgment are almost never fair, even when the sole point is to assure fairness." He quotes former Supreme Court Justice Benjamin Cardoza to the effect that an "over-emphasis on certainty may lead us to...intolerable rigidity." The clincher, however, is found in manifold examples he presents. Howard begins with a story about the Missionaries of Charity. In 1988, this order of nuns headed by Mother Teresa was intent upon expanding their good works into New York City. It planned a project for the South Bronx, which at the time looked like a bombed out area with derelict buildings and brick-strewn lots covering many square miles of formerly residential neighborhoods. After consulting Mayor Ed Koch, they agreed to take over two fire-gutted buildings for $1 apiece and to invest $500,000 for their reconstruction. The goal was to create a temporary care shelter for sixty-four homeless men. All went smoothly until it came time to obtain approval for these renovations. Because the nuns were pledged to poverty, they did not want to install modern conveniences such as elevators. The city's building code, however, contained a provision that <u>all</u> renovated multistory buildings must possess an elevator. After extensive hearings, the sisters were told that a waiver would not be forthcoming, even though the requirement would add more than $100,000 to their costs, money they did not have. Rules, after all, were rules; never mind that this would result in the project falling through—which it did.

A second illustration from Howard involves a brick factory in Pennsylvania. As do most industrial facilities, it came under the purview of the Occupational Safety and Health Administration (OSHA). Mandated by federal legislation to protect the well-being of the American worker, this agency has instituted a plethora of workplace regulations. One of these requires that interior railings be exactly 42 inches high. Because the brick factory had some older partitions 39 and 40 inches high, its owners were ordered to take corrective action. In one area alone they were forced to spend several thousand dollars for a cut-off switch on a conveyor belt already surrounded by guard rails. Though no one was thereby protected, the regulation was satisfied. Insistence on this sort of mindless conformity is similar to something that occurred when I worked for the state rehabilitation agency. During a period of expansion, it contracted with a builder to install a series of individual interview rooms. As the undertaking neared completion, however, a state inspector noticed that the walls extended clear to the ceiling, while the contract, in accord with state regulations, specified partitions precisely six feet in height. When the contractor offered to complete the ceiling-high partitions at no extra cost to the government, this delighted the counselors, for it promised them privacy with their clients. The inspector nevertheless was adamant. He insisted that the completed walls be torn out and replaced with smaller ones. And despite the extra time and money, this was done.

When the same sort of formalism is applied to ethical considerations things can get grim. Although official moral statements tend to be short, the situations to which they are applied are usually enormously convoluted. As a result, when flexible interpretations are disallowed, what is demanded is often out of phase with what is needed. The consequences of this can be alarming. Consider murder. We have already noted how the character of prohibited killing has shifted over the centuries. What, indeed, would the modern world be like if private dueling were still condoned? Consider too what would happen if future adjustments were reflexively forbidden. Among the refinements currently under discussion is a redesignation of anti-personnel mines as unlawful. Should this shift be precluded despite a Nobel prize being awarded to its advocates? Similarly, judging from a spate of recent court cases, many people wish to stigmatize cigarette manufacturers as purveyors of death who ought to pay compensation for the medical expenses of their victims. Should they be required to desist from these efforts? And ought AIDS carriers who deliberately engage in unprotected sex be treated as killers? Advocates of this modification argue that knowingly, but surreptitiously, passing on a deadly disease is more than irresponsible; it is tantamount to murder. Are they wrong to try to change our minds?

Even in stickball, when the players are unable to reinterpret the rules, the game suffers. With moral questions, of course, the need for flexibility is more pressing. The complexity of the behaviors to be controlled is such that it virtually cries out for qualification. This is why moral regulations are not only expressed informally, but transmitted informally as well. As has already been suggested, the primary device for passing along ethical mandates are examples—which are inherently informal. In compiling his *Book of Virtues*, William Bennett[6] reconfirmed this a vital truth. By choosing to convey his selections through parables, poems, and fairy tales, he, in essence, endorsed these as the appropriate modality for instructing young and old alike. He knew that stories capture the attention and influence behavior far better than do abstract principles.

Indeed, morality is the domain of the object lesson. These, far more than verbal precepts, provide its heavy lifting. As even a casual inspection reveals, when indicating what is required, people typically point out their desires, even if this "pointing" is accomplished through words. Myths, legends, works of fiction, plays, biographies, history books, Bible stories, fairy tales, newspaper articles, television programs, and movies all present models for emulation. Though ostensibly entertainments, these routinely provide unofficial precedents that invite behavioral imitation. More common still is the background chatter through which people praise some performances and spurn others. Conversations wherein we bemoan Mary's treatment of John or inquire into the details of Harry's recent divorce tend to be disparaged as gossip, but they are the life blood of our moral universe. They teach us what others really believe, not merely what they feel compelled to utter on official occasions. Likewise, who is sent to jail, invited to a party, or publicly honored are more revelatory of people's attitudes than are a year's worth of self-conscious pronouncements.

Yet examples are intrinsically imprecise. People may nod in joint approval as an admired person walks by, or cackle in disgust as they dissect the details of a juicy scandal, but still come to different conclusions. Examples are like paintings. Their particulars seem distinct, but what is noticed, and how it is evaluated, varies. As we listen to the story of Chicken Little, or King Canute ordering the tide to recede, the morals we draw are not always consonant. Or when we read about Noah and the Ark, the Good Samaritan, or Lot and his daughters, our judgments differ with our stage of life. Finally, when we discuss the Viet Nam War, Watergate, or the Paula Jones affair, our prior political allegiances are evidently more influential than what is either important or true.

Polarized negotiations If moral prescriptions are indeterminate, and open to both interpretation and revision, how can people ever agree on a shared meaning? Perhaps they cannot. Perhaps the regulations they endorse are really solipsistic and a matter of individual decision. Yet were this the case in stickball, the game could not be played. If every player reinterpreted its rules however he wanted, chaos would ensue. Teammates could not coordinate a throw to first base, opponents would never know when a pitch was on its way, and score keeping would deteriorate into nonsense. A similar lack of predictability in dealing with morality would be utterly subversive. If its rules shifted with every player, and every moment, there could be no such thing as rule enforcement. Since what was required would be unknowable, it could not be insisted upon. People would simply act, and react, without any consistent pattern or hope of benefit.

In stickball this dilemma is overcome via chronic debates during the game. The constant wrangling I found so distasteful is, in fact, a mechanism that enables the participants to coordinate their behaviors. If thought of as a species of contentious social negotiation, it becomes recognizable as a tool for aligning divergent interests. The players may start out at odds, but after engaging in a prolonged period of pushing and pulling—not all of it pleasant—arrive at a mutually acceptable compromise. Temporarily, at least, they commit to a shared interpretation that allows particular plays to stand unchallenged. Once this is achieved, until an unexpectedly ambiguous situation arises, or their interests again clash, they possess a modus vivendi. Tomorrow, of course, will be another day and what seemed settled today may have to be renegotiated then.

An important footnote to this process, and a stabilizing influence, is that the parties do not begin from scratch every time they gather together. Each new contest has a known history and predictable repercussions. First-time players do not invent its rules; they learn them from those who have played the game before. Specifically, older kids informally administer standards they believe to be legitimate, while younger ones discover not only the general shape of the game, but also how to challenge its particulars. Though informal, stickball has traditions that are honored even as they are reformulated. Similarly, when insisting on an individual modification, the players maintain an eye an the future. Unless they are aware that what is decided today can serve as a precedent for next week's game, they may be seduced into institutionalizing a practice that ultimately proves more favorable to their opponents.

As paradoxical as it may seem, morality is also negotiated. Although its standards are thought immutable, even sacred, they are continuously modified as people judge what they, and others, ought to do. There are even identifiable teams to which individuals adhere as they battle over specific meanings. This might appear absurd, given the fact that few, if any, of us sign on to a distinguishable company of moralists, but it is so. In stickball, of course, the two contingents are immediately perceptible, there being a limited number of players engaged and the contest occurring at a definite time and place. With morality, however, the alliances tend to be more diffuse. Because the negotiation is informal, these lurk under a cloud of diversionary tactics and denials. Occurring here and there, now and then, and without definitive recognition, the struggle, and its participants, tend to fade from view. They can, nevertheless, be discerned once we know where to look. One of the areas in which this sort of altercation is today visible is the abortion[7] controversy. The rules about when and how a pregnancy should be terminated are obviously under intense debate, with questions regarding the acceptability of late-term procedures or the need for parental consent by teenagers being hotly disputed. Although there are some noncommittal players who occupy a middle ground, a seemingly unbridgeable chasm separates the pro and con factions. They are obviously pitted against each other—despite the fact that both want to be perceived as positive, the one for life and the other for choice. Each likewise portrays itself as on the side of the angels, as fighting the good fight against adversaries who are neither decent nor fair. In other words, as in stickball, both sides want to win and to do so through default if possible.

Abortion negotiations are, therefore, rather hard edged. Like most moral affrays they are manachean affairs that are so polarized it is difficult to perceive them as negotiations. Clearly, the parties do not sit quietly at opposite ends of a conference table trying to hammer out a compromise. Far from seeking areas of accord, they are intent on defeating each other. Thus, charges of bad faith and claims of unrivaled compassion are hurled with reckless abandon. The pro-choice side, for instance, stresses the agonies of mothers who bear unwanted babies, the tragic hardships of the children so conceived, and the butchery of desperate women forced to utilize back-alley abortion mills. The pro-life faction, in its turn, counters with pictures of bloody fetuses tossed on stomach-turning scrap heaps, pious quotations from the Bible that confirm the sanctity of life, and tales of persons whose parents almost aborted them but who, at the last moment, were spared to grow into happy, productive adults. Moreover, neither of these alliances is very particular about the language it employs. Those who favor abortion are habitually castigated as "murderers," while those opposing it are portrayed as wanting to deprive "innocent" women of their "freedom." Similarly, one faction insists that only God should make the decision about which babies survive, while the other, with equal fervor, asserts that this must be the sole prerogative of the mother.

When these two warring camps do get down to discussing details, there is an oddly surreal quality to the conversation. It may, for instance, sound as if they are seeking a scientific understanding of when life begins, whereas in reality there is little disagreement regarding the facts. Although one side claims that life is initiated at conception and the other points to the quickening, these are moral definitions, not biological ones. Likewise, if the question concerns which exceptions to a ban on abortion are appropriate, the weight assigned to specific reasons, for example, the health of the mother, rape, a fetal defect, family poverty, or single motherhood, depends on the antecedent commitments of the antagonists; with their religious affiliations, attitudes toward sexual liberation, and social class origins being more efficacious than any particular arguments they may make.

The parties are also less than gentle with each other. More often than their piety might lead one to suspect, they distort their respective positions and adopt coercive tactics. Because the other side is typically regarded as depraved, rules about fair play are suspended. In stickball, the players may try to get away with what they can, yet ironically because morality is considered more serious, what is regarded as permissible often goes to greater extremes. Not surprisingly, adversaries evaluated as "evil" are thought to merit what they get. Sometimes even "termination with extreme prejudice" is acceptable. Thoroughly representative of this attitude are attempts to impugn the motives of the opposition, with their resistance often attributed to moral turpitude rather than honest disagreement. In the abortion dispute, for instance, the pro-choice faction regularly depicts its competitors as misogynists. The sole reason they object to abortion is obviously that they hate women. By the same token, the pro-life group is convinced that those who condone abortion ignore the sanctity of life, and in their callousness overlook the slippery slope down which they, and others, must inevitably slide on their way to murdering their own grandmothers.

Nor is what the other side of a moral debate says carefully evaluated. The conviction of those who oppose them is that they are so vile that they would not refrain from deceit were this of the slightest advantage. Giving undue weight to their arguments might, therefore, risk one's being corrupted. There could, moreover, be nothing in their words that is worthy of consideration. As might be expected, this sort of cynicism contributes to making moral negotiations very intense. Despite the fact that the players belong to shifting sets of alliances in which today's friends can become tomorrow's adversaries, their interactions are generally both rigid and polarized. Unlike stickball, in which the coziness of the stage makes it apparent that inflicting an injury on a current rival might handicap tomorrow's teammate, the vastness of moral deliberations facilitates myopia. When one's opponents are typically anonymous, it is tempting to caricature them as "bad guys" who have to be vanquished if the equilibrium of the world is to be maintained. One's objective must obviously be to defeat them, once and for always, so that they no longer pose a threat. Elsewhere, in *Hardball Without an Umpire*,[8] I have labeled this disposition the "good guy-bad guy" syndrome and characterized it as entailing a division of the moral universe into two competing groups, one of which is to be cherished and the other stomped upon. The tendency is to regard these as mutually exclusive and locked in inevitable, and mortal, combat. Recent attitudes toward rape provide an illustration of how far this proclivity can go.

Katie Roiphe[9] in her book *The Morning After* describes what happened when an alleged increase in sexual attacks became a compelling issue on college campuses. The first gambit of the anti-rape forces was to redefine the transgression so that it would cover the full range of behaviors they wished to condemn. To achieve this, they turned to feminist theorists. As early as 1975, Susan Brownmiller[10] asserted that rape "is nothing more or less than a conscious process of intimidation in which *all men* keep *all women* in a state of fear...." According to Brownmiller, "the typical American rapist might be the boy next door." To make this allegation plausible, however, virtually every form of sex had to be reinterpreted as rape. As Roiphe observes, the revised "definition of date or acquaintance rape [now] stretches beyond acts of violence and physical force....even [to include] verbal coercion or manipulation." She then quotes the anti-pornography crusader Catherine MacKinnon,[11] who has written, "Politically, I call it rape whenever a woman has sex and feels violated." But this would mean, as Roiphe astutely notes, that rape "becomes a catchall expression...used to define everything unpleasant and disturbing about the relations between the sexes." As if to underline this assessment, MacKinnon goes on to argue that "the major distinction between intercourse (normal) and rape (abnormal) is that the normal happens so often that one cannot get anyone to see anything wrong with it." Given this attitude, any man who demonstrates unsolicited sexual interest becomes fair game. The domain of rape is so broadened that the activists can censure every male who expresses a heterosexual fondness of which they disapprove.

Roiphe relates how the rape reformers next organized demonstrations to "take back the night," inflated the statistics on campus rape, and compiled voluminous case histories of women whose lives had been ruined by male violence. In such a climate, outright fabrications were not beyond the pale. One of the incidents Roiphe describes involves someone identified as "Mindy." For four years, Mindy regaled *Take Back the Night* rallies with an account of how after leaving a Princeton eating club a boy she knew "started hitting on me in way that made me feel particularly uncomfortable." He was then said to have followed her across the quad and dragged her back to his room. "Although I screamed the entire time, no one called for help, no one even looked out the window to see if the person screaming was in danger." Her litany of degradation continued with a vivid narration of how he shouted obscenities at her, raped her, banged her head against a metal bedpost, and ultimately drove her to drop out of school for a year in order to regain her self-respect. This event was so traumatic that as she poignantly concluded, "My rape remains a constant daily reality for me."

Unfortunately for Mindy, and her supporters, her accusations did not stop there. Having also claimed to report the alleged rape to campus police, when, in fact, she had not, and then attributed a callous indifference to a university administrator to whom she had never spoken, unlike many moral accusers she was found out. In truth, the alleged incident, though heart-wrenchingly delineated, never occurred. Still, although Mindy was forced to print an apology in the university newspaper, and to defend the honor of the male student she had slandered, she remained unrepentant. As she later explained, "I made my statements...in order to raise awareness for the plight of the campus rape victims." Apparently, because this had worked, morally she felt on firm ground. In other words, the righteousness of her agenda justified the creation, and propagation, of a vicious fiction.

This brings us to a very peculiar fact about morality and moral negotiations. People often get away with lies, and villainies, in the name of doing good. How morality works, including how nasty its negotiations can get, is a well-kept secret precisely because we who play the game hide what we are doing from ourselves. In stickball, the participants may seek to conceal their personal interests, but if they get caught, little is lost. The rule they wanted may not be adopted, but no one is ostracized or diminished in stature. In morality, however, life itself can hang in the balance. The rules being contested are so pregnant with meaning that efforts to conceal abuses and/or to perpetrate manipulations often escalate beyond reason. People literally refuse to see what is happening right before their eyes lest they recognize something they do not wish to see. They may even punish those with the temerity to force them to do so. As a result, concealments often work very well.

But why people are so determined to avoid reality is itself an interesting question. As Sigmund Freud might have observed, our reactions to morality are over determined. We are uncomfortable with the game's realities for a variety of reasons. One of these is akin to my reaction to stickball, namely that we find conflict per se offensive. If moral hostilities continue for too long a period, or are too vigorous, many of us are moved to withdraw. Instead of openly engaging in the battle, we pretend that all is well and invoke euphemisms to conceal our disagreements. After all, aren't we all in favor of sexual freedom and therefore opposed to rape? And don't we all want to protect life and therefore oppose murder? Any person outside this alleged consensus is surely beyond contempt and unworthy of notice. A second source of discomfort is our aversion to uncertainty. Life is so strewn with pitfalls that most of us crave definite answers. Were we to recognize moral altercations for what they are, we might have to acknowledge that the rules we live by are fluid. Going on a date, for instance, might arouse anxieties about what to do. Is it permissible to touch private areas or must one ask permission? To perceive that there is no single correct answer unequivocally preventing error would itself be threatening. Lastly, during the morality game we often disguise what we are doing because we are determined to win. Consciously or not, we know that the rules we support stand a better prospect of acceptance if their pedigree is obscured. For example, overtly advocating punishment for normal, consensual sex, as MacKinnon does, would fail to persuade. Redefined as rape, the same facts elicit the desired agreement because this verbal realignment disarms potential opponents and prevents them from recognizing what is being attempted.

A curious emblem of our discomfort with morality is the boredom we experience when discussing it. When I was in my twenties, and a participant in group therapy, one of the members of our circle would periodically yawn. Just as the rest of us were getting into a rowdy altercation, she would throw back her head, cover her mouth, and make an unmistakable sucking sound. If asked what she was doing, she would ignore the question, but immediately urge us to change the topic to something more stimulating. The therapist would soon intervene to explore the origins of her reaction. Almost invariably we discovered that the subject of our discussion held painful associations for her. When, for example, we explored the modes of affection prevalent within our respective families, she disclosed the loathing she experienced at her family's custom of forcing the children to kiss their parents goodnight, regardless of their desires. The recollection of this counterfeit love distressed her so much that she would literally break into tears if we wouldn't change the topic.

The listlessness that arises during moral deliberations has similar foundations. Our impulse to change the subject also originates in a desire to feel less threatened. Consider the fact that the mechanisms through which morality operates are not particularly difficult to comprehend. How then have they come to feel so mind-numbing? Consider too that for millennia, rather than examine the actual nature of moral activities, people have preferred to embrace comforting myths. Even as I write, I am aware that when I become too technical, I risk alienating my readers. It is as if in becoming aware of what is really going on, we might overturn the moral order of our personal universes.

Intense emotions   One of the constants of stickball controversies is their volatility. The game proceeds smoothly for a time and then suddenly, often unexpectedly, someone lashes out at someone else. A ball is dropped, or a bat swung half way, and a thunderous confrontation erupts, with everyone milling about not quite sure of how to terminate the clash. Whatever else may be true, the encounter's intense emotionality cannot be denied. Anger, ridicule, and contempt permeate the atmosphere and capture the attention of all. Whether or not they were initially involved, the players cannot escape having their feelings stirred by the enveloping currents. Surprisingly, the same is true of morality. Its rules, and the mechanisms through which these are created and enforced, are likewise saturated with strong emotion.[12] As strange as it may be to admit, anger, guilt, shame, and disgust are the hallmarks of moral interactions. Edwin Lemert,[13] one of the grand old men of deviance theory, in writing about evil asserts that "to perceive evil is not only to see with meaning but also to see with strong feelings." He notes that in describing evil, we routinely resort to such emotionally saturated words as "crooked," "twisted," "unclean," "dirty," and "rotten" and argues that because our goal is an "emotionally charged consensus," we invoke provocative symbols to influence others.

Unequivocally at the center of our moral debates is anger. It is used to advocate specific rules and then to enforce them. Yet this may seem counterintuitive, for anger is clearly nasty, hardly the stuff of something as sublime as morality. Mean, harsh, and vindictive, it seems to specialize in inflicting pain, not in supporting goodness. Nonetheless, anger is what gives moral rules, and moral arguments, their substance. It stiffens their spines and gives them clout. Indeed, without it, the morality game would be a wishy-washy exercise in begging others to supply amorphous benefits. Simply listening to what people say confirms this primacy. Although when morally aroused, people hardly ever utter the word "anger," its essence habitually flavors their discourse. As we have seen, when an ethical question is raised, there is an "edge" to the discussion. One can hear it in the tones of voice; one can discern it in the hardness around the eyes and the tautness of the mouths. Although people may insist they are not angry, their displeasure forces its way to the surface.

If morally active people do acknowledge their anger, it is generally by way of euphemism. They may not admit to being "angry," but will admit to being "indignant," or "outraged," or "shocked." Oddly, even as their fury spews forth, they remain uncomfortable about labeling it as such. Apparently to do so would highlight the conflict and risk its escalation. It might also suggest that the moralist is a person whose displeasure is capable of being challenged. Unlike moral indignation, which appears to be both impersonal and elevated, garden-variety anger is visibly human and, therefore, fallible.

Nonetheless, moral diatribes are ubiquitous. Our propensity toward anger is strikingly on display in the work of Susan Faludi.[14] A Pulitzer Prize winning journalist, *Backlash*—her book-length defense of feminism—bears the subtitle *The Undeclared War Against American Women.* This pugnacious metaphor was at the time popular among militant feminists, serving also as the title for Marilyn French's[15] 1992 best seller *The War Against Women* and a widely reprinted article by Lori Heise,[16] *The Global War Against Women.* The image summoned up is, of course, of unprovoked slaughter and therefore of a need for vigorous defense. Were this representation the case, it would certainly justify anger. Those who have been attacked have not only a right but also a duty to be offended. Their hostility is an indispensable shield against assaults that must be repelled.

Yet the imagery in which Faludi indulges makes the extent of her moral fury plain. Her thesis that feminism is in danger of subversion by malicious enemies—that a virtual conspiracy exists to deprive women of their happiness and freedom—fuels an evident desire for a payback in kind. According to her, "A backlash against women's rights is nothing new in American history. Indeed, it's a recurring phenomenon; it returns every time women begin to make some headway toward equality...." As she reports the matter, all across the American landscape forces have gathered to turn back the clock. In the press, cinema, television dramas, and fashion industry, in advertising agencies and at political gatherings, conservatives have demonstrated an intent on transforming women into silent Barbie dolls. Instead of treating them as competent human beings, they habitually glory in savaging, defaming, and dismissing them.

Yet Faludi, in her wrath, is at least as guilty of caricature as are those she castigates. Because she so clearly perceives them as "bad guys," she is convinced that they deserve to be assailed. The depth of this rage, and her inclination to defend it, is apparent in how she concludes her work. "The backlash decade," she writes, "produced one long, painful, and unremitting campaign to thwart women's progress. And yet for all the forces the backlash mustered—the blistering denunciations from the New Right, the legal setbacks of the Reagan years, the powerful resistance of corporate America, the self-perpetuating myth machines of the media and Hollywood, the 'neo-traditional' marketing drive of Madison Avenue—women never really surrendered." The bad guys may have been malevolent, seeking to "cripple" equal employment enforcement, to undermine a twenty-five-year-old anti-discrimination law, to flood newsstands with slanderous misinformation, to permeate television sets and movie screens with visions of nesting housewives, and to cram retail store racks with demeaning garter belts and teddies; nevertheless women courageously resisted by going to work in record numbers, postponing their wedding dates, and buying all-cotton Jockeys as opposed to the flimsy silk items foisted on them.

If this indictment seems overdrawn, it is a reflection of what rage can do. In the heat of battle, intense anger literally distorts what those in its grip see. Rather than trying to understand the other side, they endeavor to bludgeon them into submission, accusing them of every imaginable transgression. Who, concurring in Faludi's passion, would want to give these vicious anti-feminists a chance? Who would not be tempted the pile-on and pound their weasel-like torsos into the turf? But this too is the product of intense anger, which mobilizes support by eliciting complementary anger in similarly inclined others.

Guilt, as opposed to anger, is a more transparently moral emotion, but also more internal. It enforces ethical standards by means of a mental voice that demands compliance. Guilty people are often besieged by a personalized anger that gives them no rest or leeway. "How could you do that!" it shouts. "What kind of person are you?" The result is that when a person is committed to a specific rule, it is held in place by his or her own tendency toward self-punishment. Western societies are especially prone to utilizing this device to maintain social order. If the conventional wisdom is to be believed, Catholics and Jews, in particular, are often consumed by private demons that terrorize them into dutiful submission. A sense of sin, or filial piety, impels them to honor imperatives taught by their families or faith.

East Asians, in contrast, prefer shame as their primary internal enforcement agency. To lose face in China or Japan has the same potency as sin in Christian lands. Yet shame is more difficult to explain than guilt. We all know what it feels like to have dismissive fingers pointed our way, but most of us would be hard pressed to explain why this is uncomfortable. Ridiculing eyes may make us want to sink through the floor, but we usually fail to connect this with the preservation of social standards. Nevertheless, this is the principal function of shame. Because embarrassed people want to shrink from sight, the proscribed behaviors become less visible. They cease being models for emulation and therefore for immoral conduct. If this seems improbable, consider how likely it is that you would want to duplicate the actions of someone red-faced with shame. Consider too how difficult many people found it to condemn President Clinton when he shamelessly asked to be allowed to get on with the business of the nation despite the Lewinsky affair. His lack of visible embarrassment sent the message that he had nothing to be ashamed of.

Lastly, but surprisingly effective as a moral enforcement agent, is disgust. Though difficult to place, this is the feeling people experience when confronted with rotting meat or fresh excrement. In such cases, it prompts them to avoid the contaminated substance. The emotion is utilized within morality because when undesirable human conduct is treated as if it were contaminated, it too becomes something to be shunned. The result is thus comparable to shame. Because its object is avoided, it becomes less visible and hence less likely to be copied. Edwin Lemert[17] provides a wonderful illustration of how this operates in Melanesia. A man whose behavior is found unacceptable may, in this culture, be told to "'go copulate with your wife', or conversely, a wife at odds with her husband may tell him to 'go eat excrement' or 'eat your mother's excrement.'" Obviously, one would not want to do such things, certainly not in public. Being seen in this light would be mortifying and hence unthinkable. In contemporary America, of course, these injunctions will not work. Our disgust is more apt to be expressed as contempt. We say things such as "You make me sick" or "The very sight of you makes me want to puke." Either way, the disdain can be jarring.

SELF-APPOINTED MESSIAHS

Stickball and morality have a lot in common, but in one respect they part company. They may both be riven with informal rules whose specific meanings are adjudicated in polarized negotiations, which are themselves permeated by strong emotions, but stickball is taken less seriously. Few of its devotees expect it to save the world—it being "just a game." With morality the "just" disappears, as does the "game" part. From the perspective of the players, the quality of human life, and not merely of an afternoon's enjoyment, is at stake. As a consequence, they are intent on getting things right. They not only want moral questions to work out; they want them to work as well as possible.

The upshot is that many moralists become proselytizing idealists in a way that stickball players do not. I can vouch for the fact that no Brooklyn kid ever appeared on 8th Street claiming that if only we erased the Spaulding logo, the game would soar to heights so ethereal it would reconfigure our lives. Nor did any of my friends insist that an insight into how to swing a bat endowed him with an authority that must be respected if we were to be happy thence forward. In morality, however, such avowals are commonplace. There is always someone claiming to know the *best* way to do things and, therefore, to deserve deference. An illustration of this process was evident in the prophesies of the Paiute Indian medicine man Wovoka.[18] A little more than a century ago, he convinced thousands of native Americans that their problems were due to a moral defect that could be corrected if they dedicated themselves to the Ghost Dance ceremony. They were assured that if this ritual were performed correctly, it would reverse their tragic history of military losses to whites. The world would literally be reborn, with all Europeans disappearing, and all Indians, living or dead, reunited in a life free of death, disease, and misery. In the version adopted by the Sioux, even the white man's bullets would lose their power to penetrate Indian flesh and the buffalo would return to repopulate the plains.

Messiahs,[19] big and small, with their large-scale and seductive promises, are essential players in the morality game. Whether they swear that they can save the world, or merely a small part of it, they are a driving force in determining what people will believe and how they will apply it. The ideals they introduce, or simply champion, are rallying flags around which others gather. They are, as it were, visionaries, whose vividly portrayed pictures of a glorious future induce others to dedicate themselves to their fulfillment. Whether these ideals encapsulate an entire way of life, or a specific standard of conduct, they become guideposts that help their acolytes decide which rules to adopt. As such they are crucial to formulating moral commitments and to enabling individuals with disparate inclinations to align themselves in an apparently coherent philosophy. In so doing, they convert private reactions into all-consuming public institutions.

Ideals are, in fact, a species of shared dream. In essence, they are fantasy goals that possess an ability to inspire and to coordinate actions. Some of these may be utopian, and others prosaic, but all are uplifting. In their very simplicity, they motivate us by pledging marvelous outcomes for conformity with specified criteria. In a sense, ideals are "if only" statements. If only people will do such and such, specific benefits must inevitably accrue. Only then will we be happy, safe, and secure. Among the shining hypotheticals that have in recent years been propagated are:

- If only adequate welfare supports were made available to all eligible persons,...
- If only competent therapy were universally accessible to the emotionally distraught,...
- If only everyone faithfully complied with the letter of God's dictates,...
- If only adults retained the open innocence, and honesty, of youth,...
- If only sexuality were natural and liberated from an artificial sense of guilt and shame,...
- If only the male libido were civilized and made more respectful of women,...

All of these contingencies assume that their aspirations are not only feasible, but that once attained will deliver the goods. Exactly how this is to happen, and what it will look like when it does, are left vague. Indeed, the expected advantages are typically treated as we do the concept of heaven. Thus, if asked what paradise looks like, most of us allude to clouds, choirs, and streets paved with gold. Sometimes we also insist that it contains no pain, disputation, or illness. Yet were we pressed, we would have to admit that we have no idea what the place is actually like. In fact, most of us expect that we will find out only after we are dead. Our idealized visions of the future are similar in that people are convinced of their desirability without being able to corroborate their particulars.

Ideals take the form they do because of the nature of morality. All three of the game's major aspects are exploited to inspire and, intentionally or not, to mislead. Thus, because moral rules are informal, the ideals they sponsor also tend to be informal. They are never exact descriptions of what is, but generalizations of what might be. Cobbled together from bits and pieces of our biographies and fantasies, they delineate a mode of life presumed to be so fulfilling that it clamors for realization. In a sense, they are examples, not of what has been, but what should be. As such, they are as imprecise as any example. No matter how well thought through, they cannot include all the relevant details and are, therefore, prone to overlooking crucial elements. Although they may convincingly depict what they recommend, they are closer to fairy tales than verbatim accounts of impending developments.

Ideals are also laden with emotions. The images they invoke habitually incite strong feelings. So emotionally attractive are the states of affairs they recommend that people eagerly dedicate themselves to their actualization. In a real sense, they induce an emotional craving. Meanwhile, that from which they offer deliverance is portrayed as worthy of revulsion and hence in dire need of rejection. Because it is "bad," it must be angrily renounced. This affective element is what makes idealism so potent. Were its dreams incapable of arousing passion, they would be like other reveries—merely passing fancies that tickled the imagination but were easily relinquished. Once their feelings have been engaged, however, people find themselves committed. What was merely an idle musing becomes a goal for which one may lay down one's life, pledging never to rest until it is complete in all its tenuous particulars.

Finally, commitments to ideals are forged in the same sort of polarized negotiations as are moral rules. They come into existence as part of the process of creating shared meaning systems. Players with a particular moral point of view to purvey—in sociology they are called moral entrepreneurs—typically find these visions invaluable in furthering their causes. The emotional vivacity of these public dreams suits their purposes by acting as rallying points. Easy to see, and follow, they can be waved before the faithful to invigorate them as they gird for combat. The goals that these activists favor thus become shared symbols, that is, issues, to which all swear allegiance. They then serve as "guide-ons" toward which people gravitate even as the smog of battle swirls around them.

Nevertheless, as icons in a polarized contest, ideals are manipulated to achieve an effect. When all is said and done, those who attach them to their standards are in search of followers. They truly are messiahs in the sense that they promise salvation to those who will join them. As such, their visions are not conceived of as hypothetical accounts of what is possible, but as ineluctable realities that cannot be denied. From the point of view of these partisans, that which they predict is so enticing that in a struggle with opposing visions, they will invariably triumph. Yet this desire for success is often taken too far. Its very intensity, coupled with the nature of ideals, makes excess virtually inescapable. Because an ideal's ability to persuade depends on its being alluring, the promises it makes tend to be inflated. Designed, as it is, to carry people away, it conveys an exaggerated impression of its potential consequences. In its ambiguity, and emotional fervor, it tempts people to ally themselves with imperfectly understood goals, which sometimes, like Hitler's agenda for Europe, are remarkably dangerous. It may also induce people to remain faithful to disastrous objectives long after their limitations have been revealed. Without pausing to investigate their provenance, or progeny, dedicated idealists persist in pursuing their central ambitions until they are themselves defunct.

Ideals are theoretically pure. They are usually thought to inhabit a plane several notches above our more mundane concerns. Yet this is deceptive. Ideals are human artifacts. They are ideas about what is possible, not transcendental guarantees of happiness. Moreover, in their simplicity and motivational energy, they tend to distort the options available to us. While some of what is promised may meet our needs, some may not. Just because something is beguiling does not mean it merits pursuit. One must be chary of embracing an elegant dream lest it turn out to be a nightmare that sports multicolor plumage and makes sweet noises.

Chapter 4

Dreams or Nightmares

UTOPIANS

"Wretch! Wretch! Utter wretch! Keep thy hands from beans!"

It became a mantra among us. Both of my college roommates and I had been philosophy majors. As a result, when we moved in together, it was like joining a free-floating seminar on just about everything. Night after night we would discuss the fate of the world until six o'clock in the morning. If some idea struck us as particularly inane we would ridicule it, in our superannuated adolescent fashion, by invoking the above injunction against eating beans. One of us had encountered it while reading ancient Greek philosophy and it seemed to epitomize the sort of foolishness that thousands of people take seriously. As we were later to discover, ideals, though they make admirable rallying points, when closely inspected, frequently fail the intelligibility test. Oftentimes downright squirrelly, they are not so much visions of a transcendent epoch to come as cartoon illusions dressed up to look substantial. Purporting to be solid and luminous, they tend instead to be dramatically incomplete and dangerously misleading.

Yet in our levity, my friends and I demonstrated the effortlessness with which it is possible to reject ideals associated with other people. Should these be sufficiently different from our own, they are easy to dismiss without being given a fair chance. On the other hand, once adopted, these shared dreams take on a life of their own. When looked at from the outside they may appear bizarre, but after they become our own they are treated as sacrosanct. Indeed, they may feel so true that they appear to need no defense whatsoever.

Whatever their quirks, ideals in their many aspects, including private ambitions, utopian projections, and romantic schemes, have long influenced our laws, therapeutic contracts, and personal relationships. However much they may be praised or disparaged, there is reason to believe they will remain part of our social scenery for millennia to come. So too will the confusions and abuses to which they are prone. To dream of something better than what exists, is part of what it is to be human. It is to manipulate the future inside one's own head in preparation for transforming it on the outside. As such, idealism is a mixed bag. Many of its visions are heralds of improvements to come, but others are siren calls into oblivion. The problem lies in distinguishing between these—and even more in disentangling those that are a combination of both. Because the potentially real and the fantastic look very much alike, separating them is often next to impossible.

But as difficult as it is to ascertain what would improve our personal situations, we usually muddle the task further by the manner in which we treat our ideals. Because they seem so certain, they do not invite inspection. Instead, we cling to those in which we already reside our faith merely because we have come to believe in them. Furthermore, the complexity of the connections between what is and what we would like to see happen makes it nearly impossible to verify their suitability to our purposes. However wise we are, we make guesses, then await events to determine if we were correct. For as long as there have been written records, we have accounts of visionary expeditions into the future; some of which panned out, but others of which terminated in tragedy. Sages, holy men, and politicians alike have all proposed versions of a better universe to come, and while some of these are still with us, others have vanished into an unmourned past as their defects have been exposed.

Utopianism[1] has a distinguished yet excruciatingly painful history. The quote that so fascinated my roommates and me was culled from followers of the Greek philosopher Pythagoras.[2] Still studied, he is one of the first idealists of whom we have written documentation. Best known for his theorem about right triangles (the sum of the squares of the sides equals the square of the hypotenuse), Pythagoras organized a secret religious society in the south Italian Greek colony of Crotona. Among the imperfectly understood doctrines of this sect, the best known are their beliefs in the transmigration of souls and that numbers constitute the true nature of things. By combining these two ideas, they came to the conclusion that the goal of mankind must be to elevate the soul so that it can be reborn into a higher station, ultimately to be liberated from the wheel of birth. What is more, to achieve this, it was necessary to promote justice, which itself needed to be expressed numerically. On a more practical level, the Pythagorean society was dedicated to sexual equality, the dignity of slaves, and respect for animals. By engaging in a variety of purification rites, which included ascetic and dietary rules (including the prohibition against beans), they hoped to encourage a moral renaissance. For awhile this appeared to be successful, but ultimately the rigidity of their demands alienated their neighbors, who, in a sanguinary coup, ejected them from the community. As was to recur many times in the succeeding centuries, what some regarded as an ideal, even spiritual, formula for living struck those upon whom it was imposed as dictatorial and impious.

If he lived today, Pythagoras would probably be considered a cult leader. Along with Jim Jones of Jonestown, David Koresh of the Branch Davidians, and "Bo" Applewhite of Heavensgate, he would be described as the charismatic founder of a doomed utopian order. Because his doctrines are not currently fashionable, his methods of promoting them exacting, and the fate of his community disastrous, he would be dismissed as an aberration. As such, his views are usually judged an oddity, a peculiar footnote to history that makes for interesting reading, but need not be seriously entertained.

A more mainstream idealist, whose projections are still respected, is Plato.[3] Also Greek, but Athenian and almost two centuries Pythagoras' junior, his works, which continue to be regarded as classical, are required reading for all modern students of philosophy. Indeed, they are so admired that many contemporaries view themselves as Platonists. Plato's image as sober, level-headed, and wise is such as to ensure that his views are not rudely dismissed. To understand him, however, one must begin with Socrates. Plato's honored teacher, and the hero of his dialogues, survives in the popular imagination as a kindly old gentleman scuffling along the streets of Athens, persistently but inconveniently pursuing the truth. Presented as constantly asking questions, he is alleged to have taught the young to challenge their elders and to cling to their integrity in the face of rampant hypocrisy. Known for his simplicity and modesty, he is especially remembered for his response when told that the Delphic Oracle considered him the wisest man alive. After first rejecting this designation, Socrates regained his composure to suggest that this could only mean that he, unlike most others, was aware of how great his own ignorance was. With this unquenchable disposition toward exposing human shortcomings, if necessary by revealing his own, Socrates became, in Plato's account, anathema to the untutored mob. In the end, their envy was to consume him. Brought to trial for his devotion to virtue, he was convicted and sentenced to death. But even here Socrates' larger-than-life spirit survived. To the end, he retained his dignity. After drinking the prescribed hemlock, he resumed his imperturbable philosophizing, his last words being: "Crito, I owe a cock to Asclepius; will you remember to pay the debt?"

As moving as this account is, it is nonetheless misleading, as it fails to place Socrates in historical context or to indicate why these events transpired. Instead of depicting him as a man of his time, it offers up a timeless incarnation of intellectual rectitude. In contrast, Socrates' opponents, rather than having their views delineated with sensitivity or accuracy, are presented as boorish ruffians, absolutely unworthy of our sympathy. Yet who were these so-called thugs? They were none other than the people of Athens. It was a jury of five hundred of its citizens that decreed him guilty of corrupting their youth and of not believing in the state gods. This was a serious step, and perhaps even an unjust one, but why did they feel compelled to take it? Was it merely because they wished to silence a voice of rationality and decency?

I.F. Stone,[4] a long-time political reporter noted for his fierce integrity, did not think so. In his *The Trial of Socrates* he reminds us that Socrates' Athens had recently been at war with Sparta. Familiar to us as the Peloponessian War, this contest did not go well for the Athenians. After a series of disasters, their home territory of Attica was invaded and their cherished olive trees cut down. This turmoil, not too remarkably, produced a home-grown aristocratic conspiracy dedicated to overthrowing the city's democratic institutions. When it succeeded, its leaders installed a hated oligarchy that later came to known as the Thirty Tyrants. This regime did not last long, but when it was toppled, it left a shadow of fear and hostility that took decades to efface. It was in this atmosphere that the trial took place.

Socrates, as Stone reminds us, was sympathetic toward the Spartans. A military community based on strict discipline, Sparta was the antithesis of democratic Athens. It was not a place of commerce or intellectual ferment, but of hard-working, helot agriculturalists presided over by a company of austere soldier-landlords. The Athenian gods that Socrates is alleged to have disparaged represented the very different occupations of his fellow countrymen. Understandably, these craftsmen and merchants could not appreciate their values, as epitomized by Pallas Athena or Hephaestus, being ridiculed. Neither did they welcome their cherished freedoms being exploited to make them look foolish in the eyes of their children. Not too strangely, such activities struck them as subversive. Stone speculates that had Socrates, who was convicted by a mere sixty votes, appealed to his judges' commitment to free speech, he might well have escaped censure. Stone suspects that Socrates deliberately provoked his peers in order to achieve a martyrdom that would further his opinions. With the assistance of Plato's celebratory writings, this was more than accomplished. After more than two millennia, he is still perceived as a champion of free speech and justice, while his democratic accusers are repudiated as ignorant oppressors.

Plato, however, did not limit his assault on democracy to recounting the death of Socrates. Although, over the centuries, like his mentor, he has ceased being a real person, he was, in fact, a flesh and blood human being who in his time was locked in desperate conflicts with other real people. We remember him as the founder of the Academy and for promulgating an Idealist philosophy, but he was also an Athenian aristocrat, originally named Aristocles ("Plato" being derived from *playts,* which means "flat" and presumably described the shape of his forehead), who was sympathetic to the institutions of Sparta. With personal connections to the Thirty Tyrants, he was far from the disinterested scholar we today assume. Understood in this context, his most influential work, the *Republic,*[5] takes on new dimensions. Instead of being a dispassionate examination of the requirements of a just society, it is transmuted into a political tract. The social arrangements it recommends were not merely the disembodied product of an intellectual inquiry, but propaganda intended to persuade his fellow Greeks of the merits of a preferred social order.

Although Plato's utopia has been misleadingly translated as a "republic," it was not one in the modern sense. (In the original Greek the work was entitled *Politeia.*) It was, in fact, a monarchy whose ruler may have been selected for merit, but who was still its indisputable ruler. As almost everyone knows, Plato's predilection was for a "philosopher king." In his view, the sovereign must be someone dedicated to truth and justice, and therefore only someone devoted to the pursuit of wisdom for its own sake would qualify. Although the potential leader might prefer to engage in private studies, for the good of all he must descend into the hurly-burly of the marketplace and assume his rightful station. Since others with less leisure were not in touch with the realm of pure essences, they could not possibly determine what the community ought to do; hence it was his duty to provide them with enlightened guidance. Their own happiness and safety depended upon it.

To put it bluntly, these are not democratic sentiments. That they have not been more widely repudiated is eloquent testimony to the attraction that many contemporary intellectuals find in elitism.[6] Apparently they too privately believe that members of the intelligentsia, like themselves, are the best suited for governance; that only such people are smart enough, and learned enough, to have valid insights into the nature, and solution, of human problems. Plato, in contrast, was quite candid in his forthright advocacy of social stratification. He wished to see his community divided into three estates, with a ruling class on top, a military elite of guardians in the middle, and ordinary people at the bottom. These were to remain distinct so that only those with the proper qualities would serve in the appropriate positions. Some social mobility was possible, but it was discouraged. Thus, Plato has Socrates say, "We shall tell our people...that all of you in this land are brothers; but the god who fashioned you mixed gold in the composition of those among you who are fit to rule, so that they are of the most precious quality; and he put silver in the Auxiliaries, and iron and brass in the farmers and craftsmen." Despite the fact that everyone's soul possessed a reasoning, a spirited, and an appetitive element, these were distributed unequally, a truth that needed to be factored into a determination of individual vocations. Furthermore, because children were generally like their parents, most could be expected to follow in their paths.

No doubt much of this elitism will fall flat with modern readers. Many of Plato's other objectives will, however, strike us as entirely reasonable. When, for instance, he advocates placing more value on reality than appearances, or in promoting the equality of women, most of us will applaud. Nonetheless, other notes remain as discordant as his snobbishness. Thus, when it comes to reforming the family, his brand of social engineering seems extravagant. In particular, in discussing the marital arrangements that should prevail among the guardians, he declares that there must be a law specifying that "no one man or one woman are to set up house together privately: wives are to be held in common by all; so too are children, and no parent is to know his own child, nor any child his parent." When Glaucon, Socrates' interlocutor, responds that "it will be much harder to convince people that [this] is either a feasible plan or a good one," Plato has his champion continue by contending that "no one would deny the immense advantage of wives and children being held in common, provided it can be done." Families, in his view, were a superstition that needed to be outgrown, for, as Socrates next argues, love should not interfere with breeding the best human stock and social rewards should be distributed according to merit, not from any family favoritism.

The details of Plato's defense of this scheme are disconcerting. As to why breeding should be controlled by the rulers, he has Socrates assert that "there should be as many unions of the best of both sexes, and as few of the inferior, as possible, and that only the offspring of the better unions should be kept"—in other words, that eugenics is best. To guarantee that the children of these liaisons are raised properly, they are to be taken from their parents and placed under the care of men and women appointed specifically for this purpose. These will start by superintending the nursing of the children. "They will bring the mothers to the crèche when their breasts are full, while taking every precaution that no mother shall know her own child." All relationships are thus to be completely equalized because "disunion comes about when the words 'mine' and 'not mine,' 'another's' and 'not another's' are not applied to the same thing throughout the community."[7] Were children to begin life by clinging to someone they called "my mother," invidious distinctions would surely follow. Only if all children are treated in exactly the same fashion can they grow into "citizens bound together by sharing together in the same pleasures and pains, all feeling glad or grieved on the same occasions of gain or loss."

For some reason, many utopians appear to be hostile to the family;[8] they seem to find its particularism a threat to the socially imposed blueprints they prefer. Modern descendants of Plato have turned up in as ostensibly diverse locales as Soviet Russia, Mao's China, and the Israeli Kibbutzim. Thus, children were initially raised on the latter by nurses in communal facilities so that they might grow into a band of selfless siblings.[9] Ultimately, however, these arrangements collapsed as reality intruded. Contrary to the hopes of their architects, the mothers found that they could not bear the sacrifice demanded of them. To not be allowed to love and care for one's own infant was simply too painful. Nevertheless, to hear Margaret Mead[10] tell it, Samoan children raised in common by a group of relatives escaped strong personal attachments, which in turn inoculated them against intense emotions and repressive relationships. Even John B. Watson,[11] the American pioneer of behavioral psychology, favored impersonal childrearing. In his books on the subject, he urged that babies not be indulged. Research, he claimed, proved that parents who responded with alacrity to crying infants prevented them from mastering their feelings. Scientifically speaking, predetermined feeding schedules, and a determination to avoid spoiling, were more appropriate.

Those who have had children will surely find these recommendations unpersuasive. Their theoretical character is inevitably revealed by the vicissitudes of daily living. Nevertheless, idealistic speculations, no matter how exorbitant, have had their attractions. Even though Plato's dreams never came to fruition, they did inspire a myriad of alternative earthly paradises. One of the more prominent of these gave its name to an entire genre.[12] In the year 1516, in the city of Louvain, the English jurist, Thomas More,[13] later Saint Thomas More, published a slim Latin volume entitled *Utopia*.[14] Purportedly the account of a journey to a newly discovered island, it was actually a scheme for reforming Tudor society. Probably not intended as a model for discrete legislative initiatives, it did attempt to highlight flaws in the contemporary social fabric and to advance other possibilities.

"Utopia," which literally means "no place," or "good place," was described as a functioning nation, but one very different from those of early modern Europe. Its relatively peaceful and rational citizens lived in a state of contentment, presumably because their polity was organized along lines sharply at odds with those with which More's audience was familiar. A lawyer by training, More was a humanist scholar by aspiration. He and his circle were deeply impressed with the achievements of ancient Greek authors such as Plato and sought to emulate them. *Utopia* was thus an exercise in creative conjecture, intended to stimulate thought first and action second.

The community that More envisioned was primarily urban and communistic in design. Anti-feudal in spirit, most of its members, after serving a period as agriculturalists, earned their living as craftsmen and merchants. Work was required of all who were able, but because the trappings of nobility were absent, most of this was productive and, therefore, no one needed to labor more than six hours a day. Those who governed the community were not hereditary rulers, but *syphogrants* who were ordinary citizens temporarily elevated to perform this task. Because More perceived a lust for possessions as the root of social injustice, the Utopians were described as living a virtually money-free existence. They did have gold, which they used to pay their mercenaries, but it was held in such contempt that they used it to make chamber pots and the chains for their prisoners. Abiding in a tolerant, albeit pre-Christian association, they also permitted a diversity of religious thought. Though advocates of a belief in a deity, they did not force others to concur in this. They likewise encouraged equal treatment, and therefore dignity, for women.

The emphasis More placed on comradeship can be seen in his description of Utopian eating arrangements. "Each street," he tells us, "had spacious halls....[to which were] assigned thirty families...to take their meals in common." "Summoned by the blast of a brazen trumpet....[they sat] down at three or more tables according to the number of the company. The men sit with their backs to the wall, the women on the outside, so that if they have any sudden pain or sickness, such as sometimes happens to women with child, they may rise without disturbing the arrangements and go to the nurses," which, incidentally, were provided gratis by the government. Ordinarily, "the duty of cooking and preparing the food...[was] carried out by the women alone, taking turns for each family." Although people were allowed to dine at home "yet no one does it willingly since the practice is considered not decent and since it is foolish to take the trouble of preparing an inferior dinner and an excellent and sumptuous one is ready at hand in the hall nearby."

More had a reputation for being an affable man and this disposition was palpable in his invention. Pleasure was consciously valued by the Utopians, as were peace and prosperity. Yet More was also a man of contradictions. The same tables at which his citizens convivially, and solicitously, dined were served by slaves who performed the heavy and dirty labor. Though acclaimed as a "man for all seasons," the real Sir Thomas More was capable of barbarities when these served his convictions. Remembered today for his dignity in going fearlessly to the scaffold rather than betray his beliefs, he was also capable of beheading others. It should be recalled that within five short years of the publication of *Utopia*, Martin Luther upset the equilibrium of Renaissance Europe. His challenge to the Pope, which initiated the Protestant Reformation, was received by More as a threat to Christianity. Commissioned by the bishop of London to write vernacular works to challenge the Lutheran heresies, he did so with a vengeance. Afterwards, as Lord Chancellor of England, he was an active prosecutor of these infidels, sending many of them to their deaths. This latter More was evidently not the same one who disciplined his daughter by beating her with a peacock feather, but rather the religious fanatic who periodically wore a hair shirt so abrasive it caused his flesh to bleed. This Thomas More regretted his authorship of *Utopia*, for he feared the tolerance it espoused had given aid and comfort to heretics. What had once seemed to the scholar in him an ideal became a symbol of unconscionable laxity that the politician sought to expunge.

DYSTOPIANS

Most of the ideal communities constructed by intellectuals have remained within the realm of fantasy. While Thomas More straddled the divide between the worlds of letters and politics, most literary speculations have continued only as speculations, and therefore have had limited effects—either for good or ill.[15] In the hands of politicians, however, ideals can be lethal. Henry VIII's daughter Mary I, after she became queen, was known as Bloody Mary[16] precisely because she put her idealism into practice. A dedicated Catholic, she was determined to return her nation to the one true faith, even if this meant hanging hundreds of resisters. That these Puritans were equally passionate in their convictions did not endear them to her; rather it hastened their demise.

Certainly many politicians are opportunists, more intent on advancing their careers than on creating a utopian polity. Some, however, have co-opted the idealism of their times for their own purposes. Though not true believers, they have sought to influence those who were. Among these was Napoleon Bonaparte.[17] Still revered by the French, he tied his fortunes to the principles of the French Revolution. Throughout his climb to power, he claimed to be the agent of "liberty, equality, and fraternity." Verbally the patron of democracy, as a practical matter he sought to erect an empire for himself and his descendants. Hundreds of thousands of his countrymen were to die in this attempt, yet until the end he was perceived in heroic terms.

Our own century, however, has provided far better evidence of the destructive capacity of political idealism, especially in the hands of committed utopians. It may sound unsophisticated to label Adolf Hitler[18] an idealist, but he, most assuredly, was one. His vision of a perfect world strikes us as monstrous rather than admirable, yet for him, and many of his "brown shirts," Nazism was the highest ambition to which anyone could aspire. Intended as a model for a flawless society, it was conceived as a vehicle for restoring honor, progress, and purity to the entire world.

As he explained in his preface to *Mein Kampf*,[19] on April 1, 1924 Hitler entered jail in the fortress of Landsberg am Lech. Arrested for having led an abortive coup against the Weimar Republic, he took advantage of his imprisonment to write about his life and cause. Rather than allow himself to proceed at the mercy of what he called "the foul legends about my person served up by the Jewish press," he decided to elucidate what he really stood for, primarily for the edification of his adherents. This work, which many thought of as fiction, was a blunt avowal of his actual goals. Often crass, it better than any single indicator demonstrates the substance of his idealism. Although Hitler was later condemned for slavishly following its plans, the book communicates visions to which he was indeed committed. Whether or not perverse, he thought them exalted and worthy of dedication.

Central to Hitler's hopes was the restoration of the German people to their deserved place in the sun. A devotee of the Social Darwinist ideas of the late nineteenth century, he believed that evolution had uniquely fitted them for leadership. The heirs to an immaculate Aryan genetic endowment, they were smarter, purer, and more active than other racial strains. It would even be fair to say that they were the only true human beings; hence upon their success hinged the success of the entire species. In his words, "Anyone who speaks of the mission of the German people on earth must know that it can exist only in the formation of a state which sees its highest task in the preservation and promotion of the most noble elements of our nationality, indeed of all mankind, which remains intact." This would require that "the German Reich as a state must embrace all Germans and has the task, not only of assembling and preserving the most valuable stocks of basic racial elements of this people, but slowly and surely raising them to a dominant position."

If it is imagined that such blatant partiality cannot possibly be idealistic, that in its obvious unfairness, it fails the equity test, one must understand that ideals are not always fair. Pythagoras may have sought fairness, but Plato did not. As he would cheerfully have pointed out, his central concern was justice. Nor was Sir Thomas More always fair. Both in his writings and political career, he allowed some people to be treated better than others. How unfair idealists can be is evident in the doctrines of John Calvin.[20] This

Protestant divine taught that only God's mercy permitted some souls to be saved from perdition. Since, in their sinfulness, everyone deserved to descend into hell, it was only through His infinite grace that Jehovah spared a small assemblage, the so-called elect. They, therefore, deserved superior treatment even here on earth, which, in Calvin's theological enclave at Geneva, they received.

Hitler was no less convinced of the entitlements due the German people and of their consequent need to suppress lesser tribes. Again to quote him, "The stronger must dominate and not blend with the weaker, thus sacrificing their own greatness. Only the born weakling can view this as cruel...." He then pointed to natural law as confirming the need to keep groups distinct. "The consequence of...racial purity, universally valid in Nature, is not only the sharp outward delimitation of the various races, but their uniform character in themselves. The fox is always a fox, the goose a goose, the tiger a tiger...." It therefore followed that a German could only be a German, a Jew a Jew, a Slav a Slav, or a Gypsy a Gypsy. Ultimately this justified the expulsion and elimination of inferior stocks, who because of their biology were incapable of salvation. To fail to do so risked "lowering the level of the higher race" and producing a "physical and intellectual regression." The Jews, in particular, were a parasitic people who, like syphilitics, epileptics, and the retarded, had to be isolated and/or liquidated lest they contaminate the whole.

Also prominent among Hitler's ideals were his beliefs in community and leadership. The blue-eyed, blond German people were notable as individuals, but were even greater as a collectivity. They possessed a "folk" spirit that needed to be nurtured in group activities and celebrated in cultural achievements. In music, art, and mass rituals, the state must reaffirm Germanic solidarity and its devotion to greatness. In this, the nation required the ministrations of a unifying leader. If Aryan talents and dynamism were to be brought to fruition, they could not rely on the flaccid authority of a degenerate democracy. What was needed was the discipline of a social movement such as the Nazi Party and the strength of character of an outstanding chieftain, that is, the party's Fuhrer, Adolf Hitler. "Leadership requires not only will but also ability...and most valuable of all is a combination of ability, determination, and perseverance." Even more than this, "the future of a movement [and hence of a people] is conditioned by fanaticism, yes,... intolerance." In sum, only an unyielding commitment could succeed and only Hitler could provide it.

The idealistic character of Hitler's vision is verified further in the intransigence of his rhetoric and the mechanisms he used to promote his words. One of the first politicians to harness the full panoply of modern mass media, he regularly utilized stirring images and soaring cadences to inspire the man on the street. From the Nuremberg rallies with their thousands of waving flags and hobnailed paraders, to his impassioned radio speeches and cinematic extravaganzas, he appealed to the sentiments and longings of ordinary men and women. If they were tired of disorder in the streets, he would give them discipline; if they felt betrayed by the Versailles Treaty, he would tear it up. As was to be confirmed in countless newsreels, the emblems of his new Germany would be its clean-cut young people. With their heads tilted forward scanning the horizon in search of the magnificent victories to come and striding out in muscular unison to invigorating teutonic military rhythms, they were to epitomize its confidence and promise.

Hitler was also fortunate in the person he chose to translate his philosophy into public theater, that is, Joseph Goebbels,[21] the Nazi minister for propaganda. After the party came to power, Goebbels was made virtual czar over the mass media. Among his responsibilities was oversight of the film industry. A subtle communicator, if a heavy-handed ideologue, he knew how to stimulate sympathy for ideas that might otherwise seem brutal. By appealing to the prejudices, and apprehensions, of his audiences, he manipulated them into concurring with Nazi objectives. Where Hitler preferred heavy-handed documentaries, such as Leni Riefenstal's *Triumph of the Will*, which blatantly extolled German excellence, or Fritz Hippler's *The Eternal Jew*, which decried Jewish perfidies, he championed entertainments that enlisted the viewer on the side of "virtue." One of the more effective of these was the film *Jew Suss*. The story of an ambitious Hebrew, it chronicled his rise to power at the expense of more honorable Germans. Worst of all, however, was his lascivious harassment of a beautiful, innocent, flaxen-haired German maiden. Included too in the film were depictions of Jewish religious festivals portrayed as sadistic animal tortures. These, it was made plain, were conducted in lieu of direct vengeance aimed against gentiles. The effect was electric. The movie aroused a moralistic frenzy to defend imperiled Aryanism. Audiences hated Suss, and therefore all Jews, and wished a violent end to their threat to the underdog Germans.

Another twentieth century political idealist was Mao Tse-tung.[22] Although Hitler is now almost universally reviled, Mao has retained his standing among many radicals. Also fanatical in his attachment to profound civic change, he represented this as beneficial to·all peoples, not just the Chinese. The leader of a peasant-oriented revolution, he was honestly committed to a Communist millennium that would theoretically provide equality and prosperity for everyone. As importantly, in his righteous ardor to promote this ideal, throughout his career, he took enormous risks on untried strategies. From the Long March through the Great Leap Forward and the Cultural Revolution, he continuously demonstrated a willingness to put his philosophy to the test.

The mark of an idealist is often not merely a desire for power but also loyalty to a vision. Mao exhibited this time and again. Not only did he fight intrepidly for his beliefs, but he consulted them in determining what should be done. Where opportunists grasp at whatever works, and autocrats impose whatever has been historically successful, he took chances on hypothetical possibilities. Communism for most of us is a bundle of conjectures, but for him its forecast millennium was as solid as if it already existed. As a result, he did not hesitate to manipulate events in a manner that seemed likely to actualize it. In this sometimes he won, as with the Long March, but at other times lost, as with the Great Leap and the Cultural Revolution.

In particular, The Great Leap, which was launched in the 1950s, was intended to speed China's transition to superpower status. Through sheer hard work and will power hundreds of millions of Chinese proletarians would be mobilized to create the sinews of an advanced manufacturing nation. An infrastructure that others had taken hundreds of years to accumulate would rise, almost instantly, through their collective efforts. Symbolic of these exertions was to be the formation of a decentralized steel industry. In backyards across half a continent, under the dedicated direction of Communist Party cadre, ordinary farmers would build thousands of iron-producing furnaces. Without the need for expensive centralized equipment, these would so increase the volume of ferrous metal that a flowering of industrial production would ensue Needless to say, this did not transpire. The quality of the steel generated was so low that it was unusable. Even worse, to reach the state set-quotas, the peasants melted down preexisting implements, rendering these unavailable for the tasks they had previously performed.

Another of Mao's idealistic aspirations that failed to live up to its billing was his War Against Sparrows. Mao himself had conceived this plan for destroying the "four pests" that made rural life miserable. Sparrows were targeted, along with rats, flies, and mosquitoes, because they ate grain, thereby stealing it from the mouths of the poor. The object was to muster gangs of peasants equipped with nets and clubs to surround these little birds and slaughter them by the millions. On one level, the peasants were victorious. In thousands of villages, sparrows were trapped in trees, shooed off of rooftops, or smashed in gardens. The trouble was that the next spring these dead birds were not on hand to eat the insect pests that also thrived on grain. It soon became evident that the avian depredations had been insignificant compared with that of these others. The result was a devastating famine in which millions of Chinese starved to death. What seemed like a good idea on paper was clearly not one in the field. Like so many purely mental constructions, it had not taken into account the myriad of complexities found in nature.

Mercifully, the Cultural Revolution that came along a decade later did not repeat the errors of its predecessor. It managed to invent a whole new set, however. Also the brainchild of Mao, it sought to upset the bureaucratic strongholds erected subsequent to the overthrow of Chiang Kai-Shek's Nationalists. These had become competing sources of power that he found intolerable. To his mind, they were betraying his revolution. Wasn't communism supposed to empower the masses? Weren't the peasants supposed to be in charge of their own destinies? Those who now presumed to direct their efforts must, therefore, be capitalist-roaders who needed to be torn down and humiliated. They obviously had to be reeducated to the virtues of work, and, if need be, sent to collective farms to renew their communist dedication in manual labor.

As his minions in this bottom-to-top reform, Mao found eager adherents among the young. Taught from infancy that he was their savior, teenagers, in particular, were ripe for exploitation by his seductive calls to action. Adolescents, moreover, are natural idealists. Not yet privy to the complexities of the adult world, they are nevertheless impatient to make their mark. Moreover, because they do not understand where the actual problems lie, they depend on their imaginations and the promises of their elders for guidance. From their perspective, this makes things look simple. Obviously what is right is appropriate for everyone and must command universal obedience. Furthermore, since the young are certain that age tends to bring corruption, their unsullied innocence is needed to enforce rectitude. As a result, bands of schoolage children, liberated from their classrooms, wandered throughout the countryside tearing administrators from their offices, compelling them to wear dunce caps, and hanging them from jury-rigged scaffolds. These disruptions were catastrophic. The business of the nation almost ground to a halt. In some areas there was even evidence of cannibalism. Apparently some disgruntled persons took advantage of the disorders to obtain the ultimate revenge on their superiors. Idealism, it seems, when too literal can be quite hazardous.

If there is any doubt of this, one need only look to Mao's disciple Pol Pot.[23] After a visit to China during the Cultural Revolution, he was inspired to return home and implement a rural utopia. Invigorated by the glories of Ankor Wat, he intended to restore Kampuchea to its former regional dominance. A soft-spoken visionary, none of his comrades could have imagined the lengths to which he was prepared to go. Once in power, however, when city-living "intellectuals" hinted that they might resist his mandates, he ordered that they be indiscriminately killed. Millions of living, breathing Cambodians were shortly converted into bleached out skeletons in his infamous killing fields. Nothing wa⌐oing to stop him from turning his ideal into reality.

SEXUAL LIBERATION

One of the more unexp⌐ns aspects of many ideals is our inability to pin them down. The simpl⌐trically upon which they are based can in practice be confusing and eve⌐, opposed to each other. What is right, and needs implem⌐, is therefore often subject to intense debate. People not only⌐ they are sometimes 180 degrees at odds. Sadly, both sides of⌐ .itretemps may tend toward extremism and thus be significantl⌐ouch with reality. One of the areas in which this predicam⌐merged with alarming regularity is that of sexual standa⌐t everyone is in favor of sexual liberation, but just what this ⌐een hotly disputed. Some have fought for tighter strictures, w⌐ve demanded a loosening of these regulations. How far apart ⌐oe is dramatically discernible in the contradictory aspirations of ⌐ristian Fathers and postmodern hippies.

earliest days the Christian Church contemplated sexuality with a ⌐d eye.[24] Contemporary interpretations of what the Doctors of the Church intended are divided, but there exists a consensus that most were wary of carnal pursuits. For example, when St. Paul advised his flock that it was better to marry than to burn, he made it abundantly plain that it was holier to be celibate than sexually active. Even within marriage, sex was to be indulged solely for procreation, not recreation. Other churchmen were more adamant. One was Origen. Especially influential within the Greek Church, in his quest for perfection, he physically castrated himself at the age of eighteen. Taking literally Christ's New Testament exhortation to be celibate, he was determined to avoid any sexual provocation whatsoever. Less intemperate was St. Augustine,[25] who, after leading a dissolute younger life, encouraged his communicants to emulate Christ. For him, this meant dismissing with carnal passions if possible. Perceiving women as temptresses, he was resolute in the opinion that the only legitimate excuse for copulation was the preservation of the species. Almost a millennium later, St. Thomas Aquinas continued to hold that "a marriage without carnal relations is holier" and insisted that priests, monks, and nuns be abstinent—a position the Catholic Church maintains to this day.

The tradition that sex is debased, and consequently that sexual liberation lies in being free of its tyranny has had many adherents. One of its more extreme expressions was found among the Shakers.[26] An offshoot of the Quakers, this religious sect reached it zenith in nineteenth century America.

Of all the period's communistic societies, it was the most successful. In
terms of sheer numbers, Shaker com... unities overwhelmed the others. At
one point, they were home to 6000 a... members and over the course of
more than a century almost 20,000 pe... identified themselves with its
principles. This compares with the Fo... societies with an aggregate
membership of 4500 and the Amana comm... ith 1800. Even today the
Shakers are celebrated for their accomplishme... most everyone is aware
of the simple yet elegant furniture they prod... But they were also
excellent agriculturalists, inventing numerous ... to make animal
husbandry more efficient. They were even respo... creating new
breeds of animals such as the Poland China pig.

But where are the Shakers today? They are no long... creating new
failure was not, however, attributable to a lack of commit...
Nor did they succumb to internecine battles. On the cont... us. Their
way of life worked very well for those who embraced it. ...enuity.
what hurt them was their own idealism. Pivotal to their belie...aker
with the early Christian Fathers, was a dedication to celibacy. But ...
this, to be a Shaker, one had to be personally celibate. It was not en...
advocate chastity or to study it in the abstract; one had to dwell in a S...
residence among other celibate Shakers. As a result, new mem...
continually needed to be recruited from the outside. Since there were ...
children to indoctrinate in the faith, others had to accept it voluntarily.
Predictably, when this process dried up, so, unfortunately, did they.

The pivotal role of the sect's chastity ideal can be traced back to its
founder, Mother Ann Lee. Born in Manchester, England in 1736, she is said
"in early youth...[to have] had a great abhorrence to the fleshy cohabitation
of the sexes, and so great was her sense of impurity, that she often
admonished her mother against it...." As an adult she was prevailed upon to
marry, but when none of her four children survived, she plunged herself into
religious devotions. By all accounts, she possessed a charismatic personality
that soon brought her a significant following. Yet shortly thereafter
persecution emanating from the more established churches convinced her
that only by migrating across the ocean could she observe her evolving
beliefs in tranquillity.

Once in America, Ann Lee's communicants surged in number and
eventually were organized into the communal houses for which they became
famous. These were strictly segregated, with men and women leading
parallel but separate lives. Their buildings featured a bilateral symmetry
with doors, bedrooms, and dining areas set apart for each gender. One of the
primary ways in which the sexes did interact—their work assignments
otherwise being gender specific—was in the common room where their
prayer services were conducted. Although men sat on one side and women

on the other, they sang and danced in plain view of each other. Contrary to the staid image entertained by many outsiders, they were enthusiastic worshipers who threw themselves into their rituals with a Dionysian fervor.

Also contrary to conventional opinion, their celibacy was not an expression of anti-woman sentiments. Mother Ann firmly believed that God had a dual personality that was half masculine and half feminine. The male spirit was embodied in Christ, while the female was manifested in Mother Ann herself. It was sexuality that she perceived as evil. She asserted that it was "the root and foundation of human depravity...the very act of transgression committed by the first man and the first woman in the Garden of Eden....wherein all mankind were lost from God...." According to David Mosely, one of her followers, she held that men and women were equally responsible for the fall. As he reported, she "exposed the subtle craftiness of that filthy nature in the males, by which they seek to seduce and debauch females; and all the enticing arts of the females to ensnare and bewitch the males, and draw them into their wanton embraces." These convictions were so firmly maintained that they lasted for as long as the sect did. Indeed, so faithfully did its adherents suppress the demands of carnality that they undermined the body of believers that might have sustained their commitments. In essence, theirs was an idealism that self-destructed.

Less overt in their contradictions, but perhaps no less headed for destruction, have been those moralists who have advocated "free love." Neither free, in the sense that it has numerous adverse consequences, nor loving in that it actually weakens personal commitments, this defense of sexual promiscuity has placed its brand on the twentieth century. Since at least the 1920s, but with stirrings going back much earlier, intellectuals have asserted that sex is natural and beautiful. Margaret Mead was not alone in portraying physical intimacy as an inherent good that must not be abridged by social constraints. Herself a product of the roaring twenties, she attained maturity in a world animated by flappers, drenched in illegal alcohol, and awash with popularized Freudianism. Ever since the end of the First World War, the old European order, replete with its doddering Emperors, immobilizing bustles, and Victorian rigidities, had been swept away by a rising tide of advancing hemlines, uninhibited jazz, and intellectual adventurism. A world in which millions had just died from poison gas and machine gun fire hardly seemed the place for an allegiance to home, hearth, and sexual fidelity. It was instead a time to party. The poet Edna St. Vincent Millay,[27] herself embroiled in a life of promiscuity, captured the prevailing sentiment in her 1920 verse *A Few Figs from the Thistles*:

My candle burns at both ends;
It will not last the night;
But, ah, my foes, and, oh, my friends—

It gives a lovely light.

Sigmund Freud[28] was, in stark contrast, no libertine. Though the self-proclaimed ambassador of childhood sexuality, he never intended this to justify unrestrained sexuality.[29] He was, after all, a psychiatrist, and when he spoke of the libido, he had in mind a form of biological energy that during different periods in one's life activated different parts of the body, ultimately settling in the genitals. If a child were traumatized, and therefore fixated at a particular moment of development, it was therapeutically necessary to return him to the scene of his injury. It was not, however, useful to teach him or her that mental health depended on sexual spontaneity. Freud never imagined that a lack of inhibition was psychologically beneficial. A prig in his personal life, he certainly did not countenance a life without restraint. But this was not how he was perceived. Millions of people who had not read his books were sure that his research corroborated the value of unrestricted passion and exulted in the prospect of setting their own ids free.

A particularly celebrated partisan of free love was Lord Bertrand Russell.[30] One of the preeminent philosophers of the first half of this century, he was an avowed enemy of Victorian repression. In a slim volume originally published in 1929, he propounded a logical case for lifting sexual controls. A virtual manifesto for sexual liberation, his *Marriage and Morals*[31] argued that unless outdated standards were modified, people would be condemned to lives of gratuitous misery. Modernity, in essence, demanded that adults of both sexes understand their situation and renounce time-worn superstitions.

A controversial figure, Russell was barred from institutions of higher learning on both sides of the Atlantic. His pacifism during World War I caused him to be dismissed from Cambridge University, while a legal battle over his sexual views caused the revocation of an appointment at the City College of New York. Nevertheless, Russell was extremely influential. The author of the *Principia Mathematica*, he helped lay the foundations for advanced mathematics and hence for the sort of programs without which modern computers could not operate. Also prominent in logical positivism and analytic philosophy, he set forth arguments that are still debated in academic circles. Yet it was his political activism that attracted the broadest attention. His public atheism, libertarianism, and antiwar views made him an outcast among many, whereas ironically, as the century wore on, his eloquently written self justifications won him not only converts, but also a Nobel prize in literature.

Born into the British aristocracy, Russell's grandfather, Lord John Russell, had twice been Prime Minister. Both of his parents, however, died before he was five and he was raised by his grandparents. Since the elder Russell himself died when Bertrand was six, it was his religiously exacting grandmother who dominated his childhood. Though his parents had been notorious freethinkers who intended to instruct their younger son in their own atheistic utilitarianism, this so horrified her that, when she found out, she determined to undo whatever damage had already been inflicted. Nonetheless, when Russell became an adult, he looked back with a romanticized pride upon the convictions of his parents. An uncommonly good student, he buried himself in his studies, ultimately authoring dozens of books. He was also socially active, marrying several times and having numerous sexual affairs, many of which were scandalously public. In his autobiography, he candidly admits that upon entering his first marriage, "Neither she nor I had any previous sexual intercourse.... [hence] we found, as such couples apparently usually do, a certain amount of difficulty at the start."

Against this muddled background, Russell's social idealism may productively be interpreted as a search for both love and family. Overly intellectualized and anticonventional in its details, it is consistent with what he believed to be his family heritage and with the defense mechanisms that enabled him to cope with an emotionally barren childhood. Restless, and never completely successful in his quest, Russell both infuriated and enthralled his contemporaries. It was as if he had to validate his personal life solutions by inducing others to agree with them too. Yet brilliant as he was in this enterprise, the ideals for which he fought were not as comprehensive as he believed. Although he sought to be systematic, like most idealists, he failed to consider the full implications of his positions. As with Thomas More, who had not realized where religious toleration could lead, or Chairman Mao, who did not foresee the repercussions of slaughtering sparrows, or the Shakers, who discounted the consequences of celibacy, he did not completely recognize what was entailed by radical sexual liberation.

According to Russell, "Historically,...sexual morality, as it exists in civilized societies, has been derived from two quite different sources, on the one hand [from a] desire for certainty as to fatherhood, on the other [from] an ascetic belief that sex was wicked, except in so far as it is necessary for propagation." In other words, the necessity of determining paternity so as to be able to transmit heritable lands within the family, coupled with millennia of religious superstition, had combined to keep unnatural traditions in place. In his view, fathers who wanted to dominate their ancestors, and religious zealots who believed it marginally better to marry than burn, created a custom that now cried out for reconsideration. Women and children, in particular, had to bear the brunt of the old regime. The old-fashioned institution of marriage literally deprived females of their freedom of choice and consigned a large number of them to prostitution. Likewise, the need to internalize artificial taboos had encouraged patterns of socialization that compelled children to remain ignorant of sexuality and/or to experience guilt over their natural impulses. Menstruation, masturbation, and sexual exploration, instead of being milestones on the road to healthy intimacy—the way they were in Mead's Samoa—had come to produce unnecessary feelings of wickedness and inadequacy. The old-fashioned family was, in sum, an outdated hotbed of repressed emotions and unresolved jealousies that had to go.

Fortunately, argued Russell, modernity, as engendered by the industrial revolution, had made such change possible. With its increasing wealth, society had become more democratic and more stable. Newly constituted welfare states had even begun to emerge that could both mandate, and provide for, the well-being of families. Instead of being compelled to assign fathers the role of ultimate provider, government agencies might now assume this task. Additional freedom was also permitted by the invention of reliable contraceptives. Because the negative consequences of indiscriminate female copulation could be controlled, the need to deny women the same pleasures as men was obviated. It would even be possible for people to engage in trial marriages to determine if their love could survive cohabitation. Said Russell, "For my part, while I am quite convinced that companionate marriage would be a step in the right direction, and would do a great deal of good, I do not think that it goes far enough. I think that all sex relations which do not involve children should be regarded as a purely private affair...."

Russell did, however, caution that the evolution of this new ethic would put a strain on the family, a situation about which he felt ambivalent. At one point he wrote, "The break-up of the family, if it comes about, will not be, to my mind, a matter of rejoicing." Yet he believed this could be endured. Love, he assured his readers, was essential for growing children, but he was also convinced that a single parent, with government assistance, could provide it. He likewise believed that with complete liberty adult love would flourish and that couples would be able to establish sounder family units. Thus he asserted: "The doctrine that I wish to preach is not one of license: it involves exactly as much self-control as is involved in the conventional doctrine. But self-control will be applied more to abstaining from interference with the freedom of others...." In other words, his new sexual ethic was about doing one's own thing and allowing others to do theirs.

Among the factors that Russell seems not to have contemplated is that a reduced emphasis on sexual commitment might interfere with love, not facilitate it. Contrary to what he imagined, decades of experience with trial marriages have demonstrated that these reduce the chances of marital stability.[32] Nor have one-parent families proven an outstanding success. Even with substantial government support, these have produced a lost generation of college drop-outs, prison drop-ins, and marital incompetents. An "if-it-feels-good-do-it" philosophy, unhampered by internal constraints, is apparently not the best grounding for love or happiness. There is something about intimate relationships that seems to require internalized restraints. Perhaps the old rules about sexuality were not merely about male selfishness, or religious prudity, but about establishing the groundwork for trust and cooperation. If so, social demands that people remain faithful may be a precondition for interpersonal love and devoted childrearing.

In retrospect, Russell was perhaps less inflammatory than many of his contemporaries imagined. Appearances to the contrary, he was aware of the pitfalls of unrestricted sexuality, but he nonetheless concluded that, with care and rationality, the outcome would be superior to the traditional alternatives. Other advocates of sexual freedom have been less circumspect. Starting in the 1950s, and coincident with the arrival of more reliable contraceptives, Hugh Hefner[33] promulgated the Playboy Philosophy. This belief system extolled recreational sex as a sophisticated and harmless option for the up-to-date hedonist. As long as there were two consensual partners, what they did between themselves was their business. What counted was that it be fun for both. Even more flagrant in her idealization of sex has been the pop diva Madonna. Her recent picture book of public nudity entitled *Sex* purports to be an exercise in carnal emancipation. Its expressed goal is to teach people to shed their sexual inhibitions and take pride in their unadorned bodies. She assures us that if only others emulate her, they too can be fulfilled. Since then, of course, she has had a child out of wedlock, an experience that she has similarly described as life-affirming.

WELFARE MOTHERS

Ideals that seek to reinvent a significant portion of human experience can go seriously awry. The proportion of our lives they typically try to amend is so extensive that they are bound to leave out important factors. Although the images they broadcast may be compelling in their simplicity, they cannot begin to replicate the intricacies of reality. Unhappily, even moderate ideals can be gravely mistaken. Their errors may be on a smaller scale, but can be equally dangerous. The problem is that even humble problems are inordinately complex. They may seem to be accessible in their entirety, yet in most cases vital elements remain unconsidered. The upshot is that even modest idealism can be immoderate in its outcome.

This became evident to me while I was working for the New York City Welfare Department. After serving a stint as a caseworker, I was transferred to an employment counselor position at the Tremont Welfare Center in the

South Bronx. This work was not particularly strenuous, with no home visits to make, but it was frustrating. Physically able clients had to be called in on a regular basis to be referred to a small pool of not very exciting jobs that they were not especially eager to fill. For the most part, we, professionals and clients alike, went through the motions, somehow hoping that a modicum of good would emerge from the enterprise. Most of us agreed that there had to be a better way that some day someone would discover, but in the meantime none of us knew what it might be.

And then it happened. The Department developed a plan to help AFDC mothers achieve independence. These single parents, many of whom had been on assistance for years, were to be offered an opportunity to help themselves. Those who were high school dropouts would be encouraged to enroll in an equivalency program and, to facilitate their participation, would be provided with a basketful of benefits. In addition to their monthly allotments, they would be given funding for clothes, transportation, and books, and supplied with day care for their children and tutoring sessions for themselves. If they succeeded, they would then be offered further opportunities. Most significant among these was the prospect of enrolling in college. Here too, for a period of from four to six years, they would be supported in their studies. At the end of the line, those who graduated were to be offered a job with the department, coming in as paraprofessionals whose responsibilities would include intakes, routine counseling, and elementary paperwork.

We employment counselors were ecstatic. Finally, our clients were being given a real opportunity with a real payoff. Hard work was to be rewarded and in the end those whose lives had been going nowhere would assume control over their destinies. It therefore came as a surprise when, in the middle of an animated discussion about how the program would operate, we were interrupted by our clerks. One of them, a short woman with very intense eyes and closely cropped hair, looked at us imploringly, yet incredulously, and asked, "How can you talk like that? How can you even think of doing that to us?" Instantly the room grew quiet. We counselors had no idea of what she meant. Do what to whom? We were simply talking about how to make a self-help program work. What could possibly be her objection? And then the answers came tumbling forth. All three of the clerks were distressed almost beyond coherence. Taking turns, though in their agitation sometimes trampling on each other's words, they managed to make themselves understood. First, they reminded us that all three were single mothers. Two had even briefly been on welfare. Then they noted that they had worked at their jobs for years, and that, as we counselors could testify, they had done an intelligent and energetic job. We had to agree.

Did we also realize, one of them inquired, that the dropouts we proposed to help were their peers?[34] They lived in the same neighborhoods, shopped at the same stores, and had friends and family in common. Many had even been their classmates. The difference was that they—the clerks—had stuck it out and obtained their high school diplomas. Nor had they become unwed mothers. Though they too had had to endure poverty and discrimination, they had married, had children, and only subsequently had been deserted by their spouses. Yet even in this predicament, they behaved responsibly. Welfare was for them a temporary expedient. Believers in hard work, they had gotten jobs as soon as they could. Nor did they quit these, despite the pressures of raising families on their own. They were determined to do the right thing, and so far as they could tell, they were doing it. But what was to be their reward? The dropouts, the ones who had been irresponsible, would get the special breaks. They would be the ones to receive an opportunity to go to college and to get their Bachelors degrees. And then they would be the ones given paraprofessional jobs that paid better than clerical ones. Ironically, after years of following the rules and exerting untold efforts, our clerks would get to be bossed around by women who had not worked as strenuously, not demonstrated comparable abilities, and not, incidentally, been as moral. Was this fair? Was this the appropriate compensation for their efforts?

We idealistic counselors did not have an answer.

Chapter 5

Extreme I: Radical Feminism
(The Last Bastion of Marxism)

OF TOILET SEATS AND CYCLING FISH

Several years ago, a female friend, a college professor, came to visit me at my home. I was living by myself fairly comfortably in a large contemporary house replete with multiple bathrooms. After chatting for awhile, she excused herself so that she could use one of these. When she returned, she indicated that she had something important to tell me. As a slight blush traversed her face, she hesitantly asked if I realized that the toilet seat in my guest lavatory had been in the raised position. Wasn't I aware that female visitors might, from time to time, want to use the facility and that it was only polite to keep the seat down in deference to them? She was positive that I did not want to acquire a reputation for being a male chauvinist pig.

This friend was not a radical feminist. A professional woman, though not yet a married one, she fully expected to be some day. Not to put too fine a point on the matter, she liked men and intended to enter a companionate relationship in which she and her husband would be mutually respectful. She was not, in short, a male basher. Why then, I wondered, did she caution me about the toilet seat? Surely she understood that this was my house and therefore arranged for my convenience. Nonetheless she also considered herself to be stating a self-evident truth. Keeping toilet seats down was an elementary courtesy. To do less was to betray an insensitivity that did not become a friend.

Two years later, a member of my introductory sociology class expressed a similar conviction. The course assignment was to produce a "description and analysis" paper. Each student was to go out into the world to observe and report on a specific social interaction. She chose the socialization patterns within her own family. As she later explained, she had two children, a boy and a girl, but the boy was resisting efforts to get him to put the toilet seat down. Though she and her daughter repeatedly reminded him, he would "intentionally forget." He was especially aggrieved when his sister told tales on him. The mother, in her turn, was frustrated by these events. Although she loved her son dearly, she did not understand why he refused to comply with a social norm. Indeed, in her paper, she interpreted the situation as a case of "norm enforcement."

In reading her narration, I was struck by how confidently she characterized the toilet seat standard as a norm. This did not, however, coincide with my personal experience. When I was a child, it had certainly not been so depicted. Neither of my parents ever intimated that putting the toilet seat down was required behavior. And yet, my female colleague had also considered it mandatory. What was going on here? Was there a social compact of which I was unaware? I knew that some feminists were pushing the toilet seat initiative, but had they achieved its universal adoption while I wasn't looking?

This led me to think about why the toilet seat rule should be presumed important enough to be a moral one. Implicit in the prescription was a conviction that each night thousands of innocent women, their eyes groggy with sleep, lurch into their bathrooms, fail to turn on the light or check the position of the seat cover, and tumble into the commode. When I mentioned this possibility to my classes, there were always several women who affirmed that it had indeed befallen them. Usually they conceded that they had not exactly tumbled in—that they had merely been shocked by the coldness of the porcelain as their bottoms grazed against it. I then wondered about what happened to men. How come, in the blackness of night, with sleep also robbing them of their senses, they never seemed to make the same mistake? After all, they too sometimes used the facility in the down position. Did they somehow remember the way it had previously been? Or were they, contrary to conventional wisdom, the family members with the sixth sense?

My female students rushed to disabuse me of this latter surmise. The difference, they explained, was that at night men rarely availed themselves of the seated position. They were thus not in as much jeopardy. Well then, I wondered, what about when they used the facility while standing? What would happen if drowsy men stumbled into the bathroom and failed to raise a lowered seat before taking care of their business? Wouldn't this lead to a terrible mess if their aim were off? It would be particularly untidy if the seat were protected by a fuzzy covering. And if this was so, then when men left the seat up, maybe it was because they were safeguarding women from having to perform the cleanup.   Notoriously lax about sanitary activities—but some of whom undoubtedly were in love with their wives—maybe they were expressing a perverse form of interpersonal consideration?

The more I mused about such permutations, the more I felt trapped inside a comedy routine.   There appeared to be a myriad of absurd points and counterpoints to which the genders might resort.   For instance, was it more difficult for one sex or the other to raise or lower the seat?   Or did men need relief because of their difficulties in hitting the target and women because they were coping with greater social pressures?   Or was this a matter of personal respect and of family hygiene?   What was glaringly obvious was that I had not heard any of these pros and cons expressed in a public forum. I was not even aware of there having been such a debate.   The only discussions to which I had been privy were one-sided affairs in which men were berated for their obtuseness.   Why, I asked myself, was this so?   Why had women become so strident and men so taciturn?   A significant change in social standards was apparently afoot without serious deliberation, with it simply assumed that one side was correct and the other depraved.

It also occurred to me that when other feminist ideals were at issue, there was a similar lack of scrutiny.   At this point, I was reminded of an aphorism for which Gloria Steinem[1] is celebrated.   In advocating that women can, and should, be more independent, she assured the ladies that "a woman needs a man as much as a fish needs a bicycle."   Where once wives were mere appendages of their husbands, she vigorously maintained that today's woman must realize that she can survive on her own.   Generally, an analysis of what she means ended here, the pithiness of the observation merely bringing knowing smiles to the faces of the faithful.   Yet the statement contains implications worthy of note.   It was not only about women learning to be their own persons—it also implied something disturbing about the nature of heterosexual relationships.

The image of a fish riding a bicycle, it must be admitted, is a memorable one.   Yet it suggests a situation that one never encounters in life.   Fish just don't ride bicycles.   They don't have the equipment for it; their fins cannot conform to the pedals or their tails to the handle bars.   Neither are their muscles properly located to power a mechanical device.   Does Steinem's metaphor, therefore, imply that women, when they interact with men, do so without suitable equipment?   Are they, as it were, incapable of using men? Or perhaps the implication is that women do not need men because they have nothing to gain from associating with them?   If so, the suggested area of exclusion is very broad.

But Steinem's maxim has graver implications. Bicycles are intended for use on land. When employed underwater, they are inefficient and ultimately futile. On the other hand, a fish on dry land is in deep trouble. Should one attempt to ride a bicycle, it would not be able to breathe and would quickly become desiccated and die. In other words, bicycle-riding is fatal for fish. It is not an exercise in which they might choose to engage should they have the urge. But is this happenstance supposed to indicate that relationships with men are equally lethal for women? If a woman made the mistake of desiring one, would she inevitably regret it? The claim seems to be that women don't need men at all; that such an association is habitually unprofitable and unfailingly catastrophic.

Like the toilet seat rule, the fish aphorism imputes dreadful qualities to men and to male-female relationships. It not only recommends that women be strong, and that men be considerate, but is profoundly pessimistic about the prospect of a fruitful collaboration between the two. This brings us the radical feminist ideal. Not all feminists are radicals, but those who are have been particularly active in determining the gender aspirations of contemporary society. They have set the tone for our discussions about sex, have constructed the agenda for legal reforms, and have been the most conspicuous as gender enforcement agents—regularly demanding conformity with their wishes and punishing their foes with an unquenchable zeal. As such, they are the principle authors of what has become a full-blown social disaster. This latter term is not chosen lightly. Radical feminism has rapidly become a blight on the latter half of this century.[2] Its excesses compare favorably with any in history; the ideal it espouses is as corrupt and as prone to inflicting pain as many of the worst that preceded it. In its extreme form, feminism has drifted dangerously far from its moorings to reality. Though unquestionably sincere in their faith, the radicals provide a textbook case of idealism gone awry. Like the Shakers and Nazis before them, they have neglected to measure their vision against what is possible and instead concentrated their attention on a narrowly conceived, and in the end, fantastic goal that has visited incalculable suffering on untold millions.

What then is it about radical feminist aspirations that makes them so destructive? Many people would surely aver that branding them harmful is to make a strong and, on the face of it, dubious claim. They conclude that most feminist objectives are no more than modest extensions of our shared democratic longings. This is certainly how the radicals would characterize their own proposals. They tell us that their intent is complete equality for everyone and liberation for downtrodden women in particular. In their view, because society has historically been unfair to the so-called weaker sex, it must be reorganized to allow them the same opportunities that have always been accorded men. At home, on the job, in politics, and in religion, they must be permitted to make their own choices and to demonstrate that they are as capable of competent performances as any man. They must especially be freed from the burden of oppression that has always been their lot. No longer can it be acceptable for biology to dictate that half of mankind be shackled to home and children, prevented from controlling their own resources, and intimidated by threats of rape and male predation.

Once upon a time, the radicals go on to assert, men had undeniable advantages in a world where strength and aggressiveness made a difference, but as society has become more civilized, the benefits of modernity have become, and must become, open to all. Where historically only men could handle eighteen-wheel trucks, power steering today enables women to drive the big rigs too. It may once also have been true that national destinies were settled on battlefields where only those who could manipulate heavy swords stood a chance, but nowadays modern electronics and missile technology allow ninety-pound "weaklings" to bring down jet planes and to blow up well-defended cities. Likewise, the spread of the ballot box has enabled women to speak for themselves on public issues, whereas the growth of bureaucracies has permitted them to control huge organizations even when these are composed mostly of men. Evidently while earlier times fostered a masculine mentality in which being tough was prized, social progress now places a premium on cooperation rather than competition. As a consequence, the day of the woman has arrived and the ladies must be allowed to assume their rightful station in life.

The new ideal, according to the radicals, must therefore be *androgyny*.[3] They are emphatic that gender per se cannot be allowed to determine anyone's social role. Because everyone, both male and female, has both masculine and feminine qualities, no one must be artificially constrained. Each person must be encouraged to display, and develop, all that he or she is capable of being. This means that aggressive women should be permitted to pilot combat vehicles, while sensitive men should be encouraged to become nursery school teachers. Old-fashioned stereotypes have to be dismantled so that people can realize their authentic selves. Even within dyadic relationships, men and women must be allowed to switch roles. There is simply no reason why women should not be breadwinners or men childcare agents. Indeed, true democracy, and true freedom, cannot emerge until all social tasks, and benefits, are evenly distributed. Anything less is unjust.

The flip side of women's liberation is, in the feminist lexicon, the civilizing of mankind. As the beneficiaries of past iniquities, men acquired a sense of entitlement, and a disposition toward violence, that must be reversed. Because their privileges were acquired at the expense of women, these have to be stripped away. The reality is that the victimization of women has become so glaring, men need to be warned to desist even if this entails some "male bashing." As was made plain in the toilet seat example and the bicycling fish aphorism, men have become the problem. Despite the urgent need for universal equality, since they are the ones guilty of insensitivity, selfishness, and violence, they are the ones who must be singled out to do the changing.

And what of the male response to these accusations? Oddly, most men seem to have been paralyzed by the indictment. It came upon them so suddenly, and so vociferously, that they have not known how to react. In my sociology classes, which are overwhelmingly female, time and again the men sit in stony silence when gender issues arise. Typically they stare at their feet or out a window. Rather than volunteer an opinion, they pretend not to be in the room. This may seem cowardly, but experience has taught them that whatever they say will be wrong. In private they may grumble over the allegations hurled at them, but in public—like George Bush debating Geraldine Ferraro—they hold their fire. They know that several factors handicap them, that, for instance, as gentlemen they face automatic repudiation if they are perceived as abusive to women. But more than this, they are confused about how to respond to an ideal they ostensibly share. Most American men are democratic at heart, hence when confronted with egalitarian appeals, cannot cavalierly reject them. Instead they mumble something about their devotion to fairness and reserve their distress for when among their male colleagues.

This atmosphere of idealistic intimidation has become pervasive. Two recent experiences epitomize it for me. Not long ago, at a meeting of Kennesaw State University's Academic Forum, I was prevailed upon to be the discussant for a paper about the relationship between social class and economic development in West Africa. The author, Akenmu Adebayo, a Nigerian-born historian, made a persuasive case that the evolution of effective modes of monetary exchange had radically altered the distribution of political power in precolonial Africa. In the middle of this discussion, however, apropos of nothing central to his argument, he inserted a description of the power relations between men and women. Apparently in hopes of being comprehensive, he noted that there existed gender-based power distinctions as well as economic ones. When I pointed out that gender stratification had different foundations from the socio-political variety, a female colleague, and friend, began making faces. With her lips pursed in silent rebuke, she implored me, "Don't go there! Don't go there!" Later, on the way out, she asked me if I had missed her signal. Because I had blundered along and made my point anyway, she feared that I had not noticed her efforts to warn me. As she then explained, I did not seem to realize that talking about such issues could only cause me grief. Whether or not my point was valid, too much candor would provoke the feminists in the audience and incite them to put me on their enemies list.

This pressure to squelch nonfeminist ideas comes in many guises. Those applying it may not recognize their kinship to the McCarthyites of the 1950s, but they are as relentless. Even when being jocular, a threat lurks behind their fellowship. To cite my second case, several years ago, at a meeting of the Georgia Sociological Association, a local professor read a paper on feminist humor. Much of this recapitulated the quips and anecdotes then being told at the expense of men. Males, he observed, were regularly ridiculed for their alleged immaturity, obtuseness, and unwillingness to ask directions when lost. Many of his examples, he admitted, were crude and vengeful, but in conclusion he praised them as a useful corrective. Where once men told coarse stories about women, the very boorishness of the feminists was a measure of progress. Fortuitously, sitting beside him on the dais was a woman who had just presented a paper on equal opportunity programs. Among other things, she had explained the procedures for litigating sexual harassment on campus. When asked what would happen if a man told comparable jokes about women, she unhesitatingly replied that this would be grounds for legal action. When her questioner continued by inquiring if women would be held to the same standard, she acknowledged that they would not. No one in the audience thought this as a double standard. Nor did anyone seem to suspect that radical feminist doctrines were anti-family,[4] anti-sex,[5] anti-child,[6] and ultimately anti-woman.[7]

THE MARXIST CONNECTION

Rush Limbaugh,[8] not exactly a paragon of neutral probity, is wont to refer to radical feminists as femiNazis. In this, he evidently seeks to highlight the brutality of their tactics. But he is wrong. The gender radicals are not Nazis—they have much more in common with Marxists. Although they share totalitarian impulses with both groups, as Carolyn Graglia[9] has noted, their aspirations are closer to the latter. This allegation will unquestionably strike many as rhetorical overkill, as comparable to Joseph McCarthy's campaign to characterize his opponents as tools of a Russian conspiracy. Nonetheless, referring to radical feminists as Marxists is not an exercise in name-calling. Like most extreme idealists, the nature of their goals, because they are so rarely subjected to a critical examination, may be misunderstood, but they are indeed collectivist. Often, on the word of their advocates alone, they are taken at face value, and their lineage is obscured, yet Marxist is an accurate depiction of what these gender activists believe and where their beliefs originate. Despite their democratic verbiage, extreme feminists are egalitarian in a Stalinist, not a Jeffersonian, sense. It is not by accident that among their fore-mothers one finds such left-leaning[10] spirits as Jesse Bernard,[11] Simon de Beauvoir,[12] and Betty Friedan.[13]

Ironically, whereas all around the world Marxist ideals have been falling into disrepute, with communist regimes from China to Fidel's Cuba having either lapsed or been converted into something less socialist, radical feminists have not been tarred by this debacle. Apparently they have managed to remain aloof from the rigidities, brutalities, and ineptitudes of their compatriots because few have publicly acknowledged their loyalty to a common underlying philosophy. On the contrary, the radical feminists stress their nonpolitical aspirations. Instead of avowing a desire for a communist style millennium, they bewail specific acts of "oppression." Case by case, they indict men for abusing their wives, for refusing to permit qualified women to rise to positions of authority, or for engaging in persistent sexual harassment. The "system," that is, the "capitalist" system, is implicated, but not usually by name. When reform is advocated, it is generally in a piecemeal fashion, for example, by introducing affirmative action on the job, female soldiers in the trenches, and nontraditional values into families. All this, of course, is done on behalf of "equality," "decency," and "fairness," and not on that of a Marxist utopia.

In private, however, the radicals are more candid. The typical woman-on-the-street would be shocked by the extreme convictions they express. Not only are they given to blaming capitalism, but when considering alternatives, they find themselves debating between alternate versions of socialism and communism. Thus, Alison Jagger,[14] in her book on feminist politics, considers only four options: liberal feminism, traditional Marxism, radical feminism, and socialist feminism. Needless to say, none of these envisions a future based upon a market economy. It is taken for granted that this is a bankrupt form of social organization that is beyond redemption.

One of the premier fore-runners of Marxist-style feminism was none other than Friedrich Engels.[15] As Marx's long-time supporter and collaborator, his writings on gender have proven uniquely authoritative. More than a century ago, at his colleague's behest, Engels reviewed the writings of Lewis Henry Morgan,[16] an American anthropologist who had recently produced a book on family relationships among the Iroquois Indians. Transfixed by what he encountered, Engels subsequently wrote a work relating Morgan's ideas to Marxism. Morgan, it seems, had come to the conclusion that prehistoric hunter-gatherer societies were organized quite differently from contemporary ones. Mistaking the matrilineal families of his subjects for matriarchal ones, he reasoned that women were once in charge of tribal life. Carrying this interpretation forward, Engels claimed that men had overthrown women in conjunction with the agricultural revolution. Because the men wanted to ensure unequivocal lines of paternity, largely to clarify the inheritance of land rights, women were held back, deprived of their former status, and converted into a species of property. Later versions of the capitalist marketplace only intensified this tendency. Since they too were property-oriented, inheritance was vitally important here also and this solidified the attitude toward women as mere objects.

Buttressed by this sort of theorizing, radical feminism has maintained a politicized and ideologized view of gender. Its central tenets, to this day, reveal a startling correspondence with Marxist ones. If we systematically go down the list of their respective beliefs, their shared ancestry is readily apparent.

1. First, Marx[17] characterized his system as based on "material dialectics." At its core was the doctrine that society is inherently divided into two conflicting groups. For Marx, these collectivities were social classes. During the course of history, two principal contenders always vied for dominance, with one achieving ascendancy. In the modern era, these rivals were the capitalists and the proletarians. In the Marxist lexicon the former were the owners of the means of production, while the latter worked for them as paid laborers—sometimes referred to as "wage-slaves."

Radical feminists, in comparison, adopt a similarly dichotomous world view. For them, it is not social classes but rather the two genders which are rivals for ascendancy. As such, these are thought to be in perpetual conflict. It is not merely that men and women are identifiably different, but that each person, from birth, belongs, as it were, to a gender-based party upon which his or her life chances depend. Each of us is, first and foremost, the member of a team that has locked horns in a virtual death struggle with the other. Failing to be loyal to one's own sex is, therefore, equivalent to treason.

2. For Marxists, what is at stake in these dialectical struggles is power. In the public realm, the contestants are thought to seek a monopoly on political or economic influence. Each presumably wants to win so that it can determine how social benefits will be distributed. But let us pause a moment. Before proceeding, it is first necessary to define what is meant by "power." In the abstract, power entails an ability to dictate social decisions, whether or not others wish to comply. This may sound dry and uninspiring, yet we human beings crave the sort of supremacy that power makes possible. In ordinary terms, we all wish to be "strong" and to be perceived as strong. As importantly, we tend to revile the powerless as "losers." Our virtually universal attitude is that it is better to be dead than the impotent cipher of a master one cannot resist—hence Patrick Henry's stirring declaration to "give me liberty or give me death." The result is that in the Marxist universe, the dominant class always seeks hegemony. Although its subordinates would

throw off their oppressors if they could, being overmatched, they are forced to submit.

In the "gender wars,"[18] for that is how the radicals conceive of the conflict, the goal is also power. The contestants may value money, military strength, and control of the ballot box, but they yearn for something else as well—gender-based power. This is thought to be a personalized form of authority, with men in particular seeking to terrorize women into submission. Thus, the hard-core feminists allege that from time immemorial males have employed force to intimidate females. This is the point of their engaging in sexual harassment; it is the objective of rape. It is why when a man tears the clothing off a date, and holds her down so that he can have his way with her, the intent is not physiological gratification but domination. He desires to send her, and all women, the message that resistance is futile. This pattern is believed to be so ubiquitous, and so demeaning, that according to Catherine MacKinnon "just to get through another day, women must spend an incredible amount of time, life, and energy cowed, fearful, and colonized, trying to figure out how not to be next on the list."[19] In sum, men are dedicated to establishing a patriarchy in which only their voices are heard. As with the capitalist oligarchy, their aim is for the few to hold sway over the many.

3. But the oppressiveness of capitalists, and of men, does not end here. As greedy as both are for command, they also seek dominion over social goods. In their overweening selfishness, they clamber after bigger houses, faster cars, and more compliant sexual partners. If they could, they would hoard all forms of wealth unto themselves, permitting the losers only table scraps. Marx's view was that the capitalist strategy was to concentrate property in the hands of fewer and fewer business owners, allowing the workers barely enough for subsistence. As mere instruments in the manufacturing process, the latter are compelled to create affluence, but at the same time they are allocated only the means of support needed to keep them alive and productive.

The word used to describe this sort of oppression is "exploitation." The idea is that capitalists, by virtue of their greater power, will appropriate everything, whether or not they are legitimately entitled to it. As Pierre Proudhon put it: "Property is theft."[20] Both he, and Jean-Jacques Rousseau[21] before him, interpreted ownership as an excuse for depriving people of the fruits of their labor. Only because individuals were foolish enough to fall for this ruse did they lose control over what was rightly theirs. Radical feminists, of course, allege that the same pattern exists within the family. In the bourgeois household, men are said to virtually own women, extracting from them whatever value they can. Not only do they prevent those in their custody from controlling their destinies, but they force them to work at tasks they would not voluntarily choose. Besides being sex slaves, women are compelled to perform degrading jobs such as cleaning toilet bowls and caring for small children. Though they might prefer to be captains of industry, they are relegated to fetching the coffee and chauffeuring the softball team. Even when allowed to discharge the same jobs as men, they are paid less and afforded lower esteem.

4. Amazingly, those on the receiving end of this abuse tend to comply. Instead of objecting, they glorify their oppressors, tamely blessing them for the few articles of charity they are provided. In the Marxist world, workers are described as trapped by a "false consciousness." They are so intimidated that they literally fail to perceive themselves as being exploited. When their employers explain how well they are being treated, they docilely accept this as factual and reinforce it with cultural norms mandating deference. Even when they conclude that life is unfair, they continue to submit. Taught to render unto Caesar that which is Caesar's, they fool themselves into believing that some day the accounts will be settled and they will obtain their rightful reward in heaven.

In male-female relationships a false consciousness[22] is also thought to prevail. A myth of love, rather than of employer generosity, theoretically persuades women that what is being done to them is in their interest. Just as battered spouses blame themselves for having provoked their mates, so do ordinary women convince themselves that their own needs are secondary to those of their husbands. If they must uproot themselves in the wake of his job transfer, or give up a college education for financial reasons, it is their duty and they must not demur. Nor must they earn more money than their husbands, or be scandalized by his sexual indiscretions. It is, in short, the place of women to be understanding.

5. Faced with a world of unequal and unremitting toil, Marx urged the path of rebellion. In the *Communist Manifesto*,[23] he and Engels demanded that workers take the future into their own hands, for, as they put it, the oppressed had nothing to lose but their chains. The capitalists might own the factories, but as a tiny minority could not effectively resist a majority mobilized in its own defense. If the masses of ordinary workers would just organize, and self-validate their inalienable rights, they would be unstoppable. They could then reconstruct the world along more reasonable lines.

Today much of this rhetoric has a hoary ring that echoes the street corner orator shaking his fist at the bloated tycoon. But this tradition is still very much alive.[24] It can be found at the conferences of professional academics from coast to coast. Whether these meetings are dedicated to literature, sociology, or history, they abound in paper sessions and panel discussions that make it plain that thousands of erudite feminists have devoted their careers to documenting the evils of male domination. Their fondest hope is to state their case so persuasively that it cannot be denied. Once this has been achieved, everyone will presumably realize what needs to be done. Similar attacks on false consciousness are also operative in "consciousness-raising" sessions. Often under the auspices of helping professionals, thousands of lay feminists regularly gather together to rehearse their indictments against men. Much as in group therapy, they recite the indignities visited upon them so that they may thereby have their suffering authenticated by other women who have endured a similar fate. Ultimately, the radical view of gender relations is endorsed as an established fact—as self-evidently real to the participants as the imperialist quest for world domination was to communist fundamentalists during 1930s.

6. The ideal endpoint for traditional Marxists was a "dictatorship of the proletariat." When workers overthrew their masters, they would institute a new world order in which everyone was completely equal and totally free. Liberated from an obligation to cater to the insatiable appetites of their bosses, like the citizens of More's utopia, ordinary people could work less arduously while at the same time providing more amply for everybody's needs. This would enable them to make choices about when and how to labor, and, as importantly, to treat everyone else as a human being entitled to personal dignity and self-determination. The economic might of industrialization would, as a consequence, be harnessed for the benefit of all.

Woven very much from the same cloth is the radical feminist ideal. Its paramount good is "androgyny." Alison Jagger[25] approvingly suggests that there should "be no characteristic, behavior or roles ascribed to any human being on the basis of sex." Moreover, according to the manifesto of a New York feminist group, "Sex roles themselves must be destroyed. If any part of these role definitions is left, the disease of oppression remains and will reassert itself again in new, or the same old, variations throughout society." In an androgynous society, everyone is hypothetically free to have any job irrespective of gender. Women would be as likely to be machinists as men, and men as apt to be nursery school teachers as women. Judith Lorber[26] is quite explicit about this. In her ideal vision of the future, to ensure "scrupulous gender equality, equal numbers of girls and boys would be educated and trained for the liberal arts and for the sciences, for clerical and manual labor, and for all the professions. Among those with equal credentials, women and men would be hired in an alternate fashion for the same jobs...until half of every workplace was made up of half men and half women."

In a sense, androgyny is the ultimate form of equality. Premised on the belief that there are *no* essential differences between men and women, it treats the genders as completely fungible, that is, as interchangeable. Thus its devotees emphatically deny that men are better at spatial skills or that women are superior at verbal ones. If there appear to be such disparities, these are strictly the result of socialization and can be corrected by equalizing educational opportunities, for example, by tutoring girls in math and boys in nurturing skills. About the only gender-based difference that the radicals accept is the superior upper body strength of males, which they then discount as irrelevant in a world chock-a-block with labor saving machinery.

7. Marxists are so confident of the propriety of their ideal that they believe it inevitable. Marx himself made light of the musings of utopians, but regarded his own predictions as scientific certitudes. He was convinced that they followed from an analysis of how societies operate. In Marx's view, communism is a favored child that rides upon a wave of history. A dictatorship of the proletariat is not merely desirable, it is where all industrial nations are headed. Since capitalism must succumb to its internal contradictions, no matter how stoutly the reactionaries may resist, they are doomed to be swallowed up by an unforgiving fate.

Radical feminists are in like manner infatuated by the certainty of their objectives. For them, androgyny is not merely a good; it is the optimal state of male-female relations. They are satisfied that given the opportunity, everybody will embrace it, for only it can meet their underlying needs. In consequence, anyone inclined to turn back the clock must inevitably fail. Susan Faludi[27] captures this spirit quite nicely. In describing those opposed to radical feminism as comprising a "backlash," she invokes the image of a surging crest that cannot be denied. Male chauvinists may try to subvert feminist advances, but they only create delay. Because androgyny is an inherent "advance," and because history only moves forward, they cannot prevail.

8. Yet the radicals, whether Marxist or feminist, are not content to allow history to unfold unaided. They wish to employ the power of social institutions, including the government, to ensure their victory. Traditional communists believed that before a dictatorship of the proletariat can evolve, the ground must be prepared by the prior establishment of socialism. Socialist societies are those in which the government owns and organizes the means of production. This enables them to create the economic foundation for communism. It also permits them to educate the masses in the skills and attitudes required for a world in which each gives according to his abilities and receives according to his needs. In its time, Stalinist Russia reaffirmed this sequence by dedicating itself to fashioning the new "communist man."

Feminists too want to reeducate people. Androgyny may be our natural condition, but they do not intend to gamble on its spontaneous flowering. Their strategy is to mobilize schools, therapists, and governmental agencies to teach everyone respect for women while simultaneously equalizing everyone's competencies. Feminists may portray these endeavors as teach-ins or sensitivity training, but they are clearly indoctrination sessions. They are definitely not open-minded quests for knowledge. Those who attend them often do so no more voluntarily than did Russian counter-revolutionaries when shipped to the Gulag. Moreover, the participants know in advance what is expected of them, that they will not be released until they publicly acknowledge the requisite views. Ultimately, like its Marxist predecessor, feminist reeducation is long on propaganda and short on autonomous decision-making.

Similarly, if men and women do not spontaneously distribute themselves in the expected proportions at work, at home, or in the political vineyards, government engineered coercion and/or private sanctions are to be used to redirect their efforts. Today this often takes the form of affirmative action programs and/or an aggressive political correctness. People are literally given jobs, or deprived of them, in accord with their ideological purity. In Soviet Russia, ideological discipline was enforced through Communist Party membership, whereas in the United States lawsuits and adverse publicity play a similar role.[28] But as has been suggested, this is nothing less than a species of feminist McCarthyism. People now look over their shoulders worrying if some innocent remark will be misconstrued with dire consequences for their careers and well-being.

In summary, the parallels between Marxism and radical feminism include all of the following:
- two conflicting groups
- contesting for power
- with the weaker being exploited
- but deceived by false consciousness so that it does not recognize
- the need to effect revolutionary change
- which will institute a profoundly egalitarian utopia
- that is in accord with the march of history
- yet in need of public enforcement.

There can be no doubt that many radical feminists have the best of intentions. There can also be little doubt that their vision is as susceptible to oppressive implementation as was the communist ideal or as would have been the Platonic ideal had any community been naive enough to adopt it. Politicized visions tend to become procrustean beds. Their "one size fits all" mentality promises universal freedom, but chops off the feet of dissenters. What is offered may be appealing, yet in practice is enforced through a reign of terror.[29] The question then, especially as it pertains to radical feminism, is this: Why the attraction? Why have so many intelligent, conscientious, and caring persons dedicated themselves to its attainment? If its potential for destruction is as great as was that of Marxism, why have more of them not realized this, especially with the grim example of Russia before their eyes?

THE DIVISION OF LABOR

To hear the radicals tell it, we are living with the consequences of a male insurrection that occurred some ten thousand years ago. It was then that men allegedly used the excuse of agriculture to confine women within the home. What is more, it is asserted that for these usurpers to maintain their domination, they had to assume the role of an occupying militia. Much as the Red Army resorted to indiscriminate rape when it battered its way into Berlin, males are accused of relying upon sexualized violence to sustain their hegemony. Every day, in every way, they must keep women in submission lest they discover their actual strength and instigate a counter takeover. Domestic brutality and sexual harassment may not be universal, but their threat is, and must be; otherwise they would lose their effect.

This Marxist-inspired scenario is, in fact, a fable. It has no more substance than Plato's myth about gold alloyed in the souls of the ruling class. The problem is that many feminists perceive it to be true. Because they are moralists who view events through ideological glasses, they see only part of the picture. Contemporary women do have legitimate grievances, but their nature and origin are different than commonly supposed. Instead of deriving from hierarchical sources, they grow primarily out of role and intimacy[30] problems. Many women are indeed unhappy, and desirous of a remedy, but not because men have intentionally enslaved them. The world is more complicated than that.

In the early 1960s Betty Friedan[31] wrote a book that sent shock waves through society. Her *Feminine Mystique* impelled millions of women to reexamine their lives and to experience a revulsion with what they saw. According to Friedan, modern housewives were descending into a suburbanized desperation. Shut up in ticky-tack houses, far removed from the real action, they were assigned housecleaning and childcare tasks whatever their individual talents or inclinations. If they desired, they might indulge themselves in television soap operas and ritualized self-beautification, but they could not make decisions of any consequence. These were reserved for men who were the dominant figures on the job and at home. While husbands might place their wives on a pedestal, exalting them for their femininity, this was actually a ploy to infantilize them and deprive them of respect.[32]

Friedan's nightmarish plot might have been overdrawn, but it was grounded in history. The process of confining women to empty domesticity had indeed been going on for some time and women were growing restive. Originally upper middle class women, but by the mid-twentieth century, lower middle class women as well, had become dissatisfied with their lot. Thorstein Veblen,[33] writing before World War I, pointed out that females had by that time become the emblems of conspicuous consumption. As industrialism had enabled families to prosper, they sought to demonstrate their success to outsiders. By adorning their women in fancy clothes and elaborate hairdos, and requiring them to remain as homemakers, the economic achievements of the whole could be confirmed. The result was often what Henrik Ibsen[34] assailed in his play *A Doll's House*. Nora, his heroine, it will be recalled, was forced by her husband to maintain a life of barren idleness merely to satisfy this bourgeois ideal. Nor was this ploy unique. In China, the same effect had earlier been obtained by binding the feet of well-bred women.

The real difficulty in the modern world was thus not the rapacity of men, but that industrialization[35] had deprived women of the roles they had previously occupied. They were not so much forced into a subordinate position as denied their former claims to equal dignity. Before the factory system separated home from work, both genders had been vital to family prosperity. There was, to be sure, a strict division of labor, with men plowing the fields and women doing the cooking and sewing, but both knew they could not flourish without the other. Today we tend to forget just how much effort was expended to achieve domestic comfort. We fail to consider that in an era before gas stoves and ready-to-wear garments, bread had to be baked from scratch and cloth woven from raw wool. Indicative of how far we have come is the term the "distaff sex." Though women are sometimes still referred to this way, almost no one remembers why. In point of fact, the distaff was a small hand spinning wheel used for converting natural fiber into yarn. Whenever women had nothing else to do, they could be found twirling it, hence they became associated with the tool. This was necessary because had they not, there would not have been sufficient material to provide their families with the few pieces of apparel they possessed.

One of the first achievements of industrialization was, of course, the mechanization of the clothing industry.[36] Spinning jennies and steam-driven looms made the production of factory cloth cheap enough for ordinary people to afford. Similarly bread came to be baked in huge commercial establishments, while grammar schools proliferated to serve inadvertently as babysitters. Even the availability of refrigerators made daily trips to the market superfluous. In short, the kinds of tasks for which women had once been essential disappeared. This was exacerbated by advances in health, which in lengthening life reduced the proportion of their lives that women devoted to childrearing. The upshot was that where men previously had been dependent on their spouses' domestic contributions—thereby endowing them with considerable power—this leverage was now fading. No wonder women experienced a malaise.

The central problem was thus a dramatic, and unplanned, shift in the gender division of labor. With the kinds of work from which they once attained prestige gone, women felt themselves disrespected because, relatively speaking, they were. Still, everyone needs to be needed. Gaining respect is even more meaningful than is achieving interpersonal dominance. Though many women interpreted this situation as a male plot, it in fact flowed from an unexpected economic revolution. What made men seem like the oppressors was that their roles, and hence their prestige, had not been as adversely affected. That they were close by, in intimate relationships, only served to drive this iniquity home.

The question quite naturally arose as to what to do about this imbalance. Because we human beings are rarely content to suffer in silence, women sought a solution. In this case, the answer seemed obvious. If male roles continued to be satisfying, why shouldn't they be available to women too? If men enjoyed authority, why shouldn't the ladies? If husbands were sexually active, why not their wives? And if boys attended college, or drove trucks, or played basketball, or killed Iraqis, why not girls? On the face of it, there seemed no valid distinction permitting one gender to be free and the other to be tied down by a host of outdated restrictions. Sigmund Freud may have declared that anatomy was destiny, but to the dispossessed this was the ranting of a neurotic man determined to safeguard his ill-gotten perquisites. Judith Lorber's demand that all occupations must be equally divided seemed more reasonable. Only this was even-handed. Only it provided women with the opportunities they deserved.

Yet as manifest as this may sometimes seem in a society that glorifies equality, it may not be what is best. Whatever the radicals may assert, there are significant differences between the genders.[37] To assume, as they do, that an equality of opportunity will inevitably produce an equality of results depends on people being identical in every respect. If there are variations in abilities and desires, these may eventuate in task disparities. The fact that men and women are concentrated in different occupations would then be due to choice, not to class-based discrimination. As those who pay attention to psychology and biology know, many physical, emotional, and cognitive distinctions have recently been uncovered.[38] Male and female brains seem to be wired differently, with women having larger verbal areas and broader corpus callosums. They also seem to use both of their cerebral hemispheres when problem-solving, whereas males tend to be more localized thinkers. Furthermore, male children, even as babies, seem to be more aggressive, and less adept at picking up emotional cues, than are their little sisters. As importantly, men appear to be more instrumental and competitive, while women are more expressive and relationship bound. Placed on a basketball court, the former tear into each other with trash talk, while the latter—though they too want to win—are more apt to be solicitous of friend and foe alike.

This instrumental/expressive division has been commented upon for decades. The sociologist Talcott Parsons[39] was aware of it. So, more recently, has been the linguist Deborah Tannen.[40] Parsons (with Robert Bales) pedantically defined the two concepts thus: an "instrumental function concerns relations of [a] system to its situation outside a system, [i.e.] to meeting the adaptive conditions of its maintenance of equilibrium," whereas "the expressive area concerns the 'internal' affairs of the system, [i.e.] the maintenance of integrative relations between the members." Translated into less obscure language, and related specifically to the family (itself a kind of system), an instrumental orientation tries to put food on the table, whereas an expressive one tries to keep the kids from killing each other. Tannen underlines this division by discussing how boys and girls handle conflict. Citing Marjorie Harness Goodwin's[41] study of how children play, she describes boys as having an affinity for hierarchical organizations and girls for the bonds of friendship. Males are apparently obsessed with determining who is the boss and if possible with becoming the boss themselves. They "particularly liked to play openly competitive games, such as football and basketball. Even for activities that were not competitive by nature, [they] often broke into teams to facilitate competition. The girls [in contrast] were not much interested in organized sports and games. They preferred whole-group activities such as jump rope or hopscotch." Moreover, "The boys ranked themselves according to skill at different activities and often boasted and bragged about the their abilities and possessions....[frequently arguing] about status—about...who had the power to tell whom what to do. The girls [on the other hand] argued about their relative appearance, their relationships to others, and what others had said about them." The distinction was clear. Boys wanted to get things done by grasping for power, while girls tried to make sure their relationships were in good repair.

Consider what happens when one takes a personal problem to a man. If he were told that someone was having a conflict with his boss, he would probably give specific directions on how to handle the situation. Like most men he would be intent on getting the job done and would provide a plan for achieving this. A woman, however, would likely have a different reaction. She would probably ask her confidant to elaborate upon the ways she had been mistreated and then commiserate with each violation. Concerned to preserve the equilibrium of the relationship, she would try to calm the roiling waters and would search for a peaceful resolution.[42]

Though in her writings Tannen is concerned with facilitating gender communication, she provides numerous examples of how men convert social encounters into contests in which to prove their mettle. Whether on the highway, at public meetings, or in the bedroom, they seek to demonstrate who is best. Women, in stark contrast, find this absurd. They do not see the point of always trying to be the fastest, loudest, or most domineering. Nor do they understand why men avoid crying in public. To them, tears are a sign of sensitivity. That men consider them an indication of weakness seems crazy.

Returning to the gender division of labor, if persistent male-female differences do in fact exist, and are not a temporary matter of socialization, then recommending that women adopt male roles, or conversely that men become more like women, must ultimately prove counterproductive. Even when the suggested modifications might prove socially useful, if they do not address the predispositions of those who must adopt them, they will be rejected. For an improvement to succeed, it has to be more than a fantasy. At minimum, it must be capable of making the lives of actual people better. Surprisingly, but as often happens, the changes that work generally emerge from unplanned, unchronicled, and uncelebrated events. When something goes wrong, as has with the sexual division of labor, people are moved in a piecemeal, uncoordinated, and frequently imperfect manner to rectify the situation. Far from the glowing symmetry of the self-proclaimed ideal, they individually, and in concert, seek concretely satisfying solutions.

This is what has been happening with regard to gender roles. They have been changing. But what is more, they have been changing in an identifiable manner. Although unheralded, it has not been the radical equality of the ideologues, but a refurbished instrumental/expressive cleavage that has emerged. Time and again men seem to congregate in positions that feature competition and task attainment, while women prefer nurturance and peacekeeping. Both sexes now work primarily outside the home, yet few are doing precisely the same thing as the other. Census data reveal that nearly all elementary school teachers are women, whereas machinists are overwhelmingly men. Likewise nurses, social workers, and secretaries tend to be female, whereas long-haul truck drivers, construction workers, and fire fighters are male. Despite unremitting propaganda encouraging people to cross over to nontraditional roles, most do not. Apparently jobs working with children, utilizing fine motor dexterity, and providing emotional support are more comfortable for women, whereas conflict, gross motor dexterity, and independence appeal more to men.

This pattern is present even in unexpected venues. A hundred years ago it was rare for women to be medical doctors; now this barrier has been breached. Nonetheless, men and women do not select medical specialties in the same proportions. Females opt more for family medicine and pediatrics, while males tend to become surgeons. Similar trends are visible in real estate, where women sell the private residences and men the commercial properties. Even among college professors one sees a growing dominance of women in disciplines such as literature, yet men retain their hold over engineering. More revealing still has been how the genders have dealt with the authority issue. In fields such as elementary school teaching, where women have a large edge in numbers, men are more likely to gravitate to supervisory roles. The same is true in social work and nursing. In business, although women have been climbing the corporate ladder at a dizzying pace, they are underrepresented at the top. This is often attributed to a "glass ceiling,"[43] but individual choice may have something to do with the matter. Statistical evidence suggests that women who succeed are less apt to be married and less apt to have children. Certainly the demands placed on ambitious executives have something to do with one's ability to juggle work and family. It also seems reasonable that those for whom children are a priority would opt out of the rat race.

There is also, however, the matter of aggressiveness. Some women, Margaret Thatcher for instance, are unquestionably assertive. In a power struggle, they can hold their own with anyone. Yet research going back to Maccoby and Jacklin,[44] consistently shows that men are on average more aggressive. Although we are dealing with overlapping normal curves here, the observable differences skew perceptions and therefore individual decisions.[45] From experience, men and women both conclude that in a literal battle the man is the one more likely to win. Individual matchups might turn out otherwise, but normal cognitive processes tilt the advantage toward him. Actually, when in graduate school, I did a study at a community mental health center that confirmed this. In the children's services unit, which contained some twenty professionals, half men and half women, only one supervisor was female and six were male. This riveted my attention and I made inquiries. Many of the men, I was told, so craved command that they had created their own supervisory positions. Most interesting of all was the unit's directorship. It had been contested by a man and a woman. Many thought that she was more qualified, but eventually the position went to him. When asked why, she explained that she had voluntarily withdrawn her bid. When probed for her reasons, she responded that the job was not worth the grief. The conflict engendered had so displeased her that she elected to defer to a colleague who found it more acceptable. The moral of the tale seemed to me that men often become the bosses, not because they are more expert, but because they are more dedicated to fighting for authority.

Of course, evidence of this sort does not prevent the gender radicals from denying there are differences or from trying to impose their vision of equality. An integrated military being one of their priorities, they begin by asserting that women can do anything that men can do, then wind up imposing revised procedures designed to blur the disparities. To illustrate, the Army switched to using sneakers in many of its drills when, during co-ed training, women recruits suffered higher rates of boot injuries; the Marines placed a yellow line half way up their climbing ropes and allowed women to stop there; and the Navy, to accommodate more females in its Search and Rescue teams, doubled the number of individuals required to do the job. Gender-norming has become standard operating procedure in many physical occupations, with females often graded as equivalent to men because they have shown "comparable effort." That this is a blatant form of denial, which may have dangerous implications for national security, is repudiated in the rush to be "fair."

Even in the home, there have been disruptions attributable to modifications in the gender division of labor. My grandparents had no such difficulty. They had a clear understanding about who was in charge of what. He may have been the one deferred to in public, but if he entered into her kitchen and began poking around the pots, she would shoo him away with a wooden spoon. By the same token, if she entered his workshop, he would gruffly order her to leave, which she meekly did. Neither was a particularly humble human being, but they knew their respective places and honored them. Nowadays, with so many women working outside the home, household chores obviously cannot be divided as they once were. If meals are to be prepared at odd hours, or children transported to little league games, spouses cannot stand on the same ceremonies as my grandparents. The question thus arises as to how they can—if at all—apportion their responsibilities. But more of this shortly.

In the meantime, we must not forget that radical feminists extol complete equality above all else. As importantly, however, they do not tell us why. Their passion may be convincing for many, but it is no substitute for reasons. What then are their arguments, especially since alternative ideals are readily available? Among these latter is the belief that "free choice" is superior to a sweeping gender congruence. Advocates of this competing standard assert the actual decisions of men and women, based on their personal preferences, should carry more weight than a hypothetical balance. Those who favor androgyny claim that the elimination of gender roles is essential and the only practical guarantee of individual freedom, but the opposition counters that gender complementarity is preferable and as capable of maintaining individual dignity. What cannot be disputed by either side is that both instrumental and expressive roles are necessary for effective social functioning. The dilemma therefore becomes how to provide for the two—and for justice toward both genders as well.

THE INTIMACY DILEMMA

If reshuffling our gender roles is a more compelling need than is demolishing some mythical male hegemony, what are the consequences of making androgyny society's principal objective? Contrary to the hopes of many moderates, paying obeisance to complete equality will not, of itself, bring universal happiness. Never in history has any society survived, never mind flourished, without a gender-based division of labor. The lines of separation may have modified over time, but there have always been social tasks that are primarily male or primarily female. Gender Marxists, of course, promise to alter all of this. Without fully calculating what is involved, they convert male-female relationships into a politicized class struggle. Based on less evidence than was educed in favor of the toilet seat rule, they contend that gender conflicts are hierarchical clashes best terminated by extirpating all traces of rank. Moralists that they are, they do not examine unwelcome facts, but agitate instead for dramatic solutions that are a priori assumed to be advantageous. Indications that this might limit the available options, or divert energies in unproductive directions, do not deter them.

Ironically, to insist that hierarchy is the central culprit in unsettling gender relations not only interferes with achieving a voluntarily reorganized division of labor, but also subverts a unique and invaluable aspect of human association. Heterosexual intimacy[46] is one of the cornerstones of social life. Entirely different in nature from the connection between capitalist bosses and their paid underlings, it is the key to stable families. Some cynics discount the validity of intimacy and insist that it is a myth. They will not admit that, while emotional closeness is admittedly fragile, its absence would be immeasurably worse and would diminish us all. It is nevertheless no secret that most adults strive to form permanent pair bonds, two functions of which are procreation and companionship. When these unions work, they are the matchless source of the interpersonal support that Christopher Lasch[47] referred to as a "haven in a heartless world." A man and woman in love are not rivals for dominance, but allies who can revel in each other's accomplishments—not master and slave, but partners in a shared quest.

Intimacy is, however, problematic.[48] As we all know, it does not always work. Couples fight and they get divorced. Sometimes they act as enemies who are not content unless they can submerge each other.[49] There is a vulnerability associated with closeness that apparently cannot be eliminated. When two people live in physical proximity, they grow to know one another as in no other relationship. They learn their respective strengths and weaknesses, and they achieve a propinquity that enables them to take advantage of what they discover. To summarize the situation colloquially, they are able to push each other's buttons. This, of course, breeds danger. Not only does each partner know where to attack, but given the fact that intimacy is supposedly safe, they may be lulled into letting down their own guards, thereby exposing themselves to injury from the other.

As a result, mutual confidence is crucial to intimacy. Successful lovers seek to understand and to accommodate each other. They know that they must provide ongoing evidence of their trustworthiness to allay fears that have a legitimate basis. In newly established relationships, couples almost daily tease, test, and reassure one another, thereby confirming the sanctity of their bond. Politicizing such an attachment would undermine it. When ostensible lovers become competitors for domination, their motives shift to defeating each other. Control, not mutual support, becomes their touchstone and they are prepared to be unmerciful. Power is indeed a part of all intimate relations, hence the length to which the parties go to reassure each other that it will not be abused, yet it cannot be the paramount consideration. In loving relationships, control has to be equitable and gentle. Although both parties have desires and demands, these need to be worked through in ways that both find acceptable. Were the gender Marxists correct, love would indeed be the tragic illusion that many of its detractors have long maintained.

To put the matter bluntly, a class struggle mentality, when it comes to gender, makes losers of men, women, and especially children. Neither sex gets to be what it is comfortable with being, but worst of all, because intimacy is undermined, family solidarity suffers. And lest the point be lost, when families suffer, so do their offspring. No society has ever risked eliminating families,[50] yet America, under the auspices of an egalitarian pipe dream, often seems on the brink of doing so. In casting men as quintessential villains, women as inevitable victims, and children as invisible bystanders, the nation is subjecting itself to an experiment of colossal proportions.

First, let us consider the status of men. As the whipping boys of gender Marxism, they stand accused of stacking the deck in their own favor. Ostensibly having hoarded power for millennia, they are now being asked to share their bounty. On this level, however, men seem not to have lost very much. As the designated family breadwinners, most of them have always apportioned their spoils among those they love. Unlike capitalists, who rarely invite their workers to share their bed and board, husbands typically delegate the direction of household affairs to their wives. Radical feminists will object that the operative word here is "delegate," and will assert that only when women have independent control over their own fortunes can they benefit from them. Pampered slaves are, after all, still slaves. But this is a caricature. Love and slavery are not compatible. Successful intimacy depends upon partners who truly care about each other and are prepared to treat each other as moral equals. Unless the happiness, and dignity, of both are accorded the same weight, the disrespected party will feel aggrieved and honest sharing aborted. Whatever their fantasies, few men dictate how their wives will live. "Delegating," in this case, means dividing responsibilities in ways that are agreed upon by both parties. Typically the arrangement is based on joint decisions, not unilateral ones.

Nor have men lost much in the workplace. Despite affirmative action, most historically male occupations remain male-dominated. Even though women have attained positions of authority at a phenomenal rate, just as the radicals complain, men have been able to maintain their supremacy. Some macho specimens may feel under threat, and some no doubt have experienced downward mobility, but these are few in number. Moreover, within heterosexual relationships, the tendency remains for the male to be economically predominant, if for no other reason than couples choose each other so that he is. This means that on a personal level relatively few men must endure a sense of fiscal failure.

The real loss experienced by men has been in terms of their reputations and their peace of mind. They have become the black hats of the contemporary gender wars.[51] But let us back up for a moment. For as long a time as we have evidence, there have been sexual tensions between men and women. Besides the vulnerabilities of sexuality, intimacy breeds a need to adjust power relations and this is often expressed in a jockeying for position. In the 1950s the public discourse that accompanied this process was tilted in favor of men. Women were encouraged to be sweet, docile homemakers, who, if they were too assertive, would be accused of castrating their partners. If there was a question of who initiated an illicit sexual encounter, the woman was apt to be blamed for being inappropriately seductive. Today it is the man who is automatically guilty. His unrestrained lust is universally regarded as the causative element. All a woman needs to do is accuse a man of having instigated unwanted lovemaking and he has no defense.[52] Whether or not she initially objected to his advances, she can, after the fact, claim victim status. As the sole arbiter of whether she felt uncomfortable, she defines the situation. Thanks to years of negative propaganda, the kindest and best intentioned of men are accorded less credibility than the most manipulative of women. Even to question the motivation of a woman is prima facie evidence of abusiveness.

The primary causality in all this has been trust. Men must now be on guard lest an ill-considered joke be adjudged offensive or an unsolicited overture be interpreted as harassment. At work, when in conference with a female, they must think twice about closing the door, or, when in a discussion about the merits of a woman, must fear being overly candid.[53]

Emblematic of what has occurred is the Clarence Thomas[54] affair. Though years in the past, it continues to haunt our body politic. Millions of women still regard Thomas as the epitome of insensitive masculinity. He may sit on the Supreme Court, but to their minds he is forever tainted by Anita Hill's accusations. In retrospect, this spectacle, which served as a morality play for a generation, remains distressing. Aside from the fact that we will never know who said what to whom, the significance attached to what were, in essence, trivial allegations is astounding. In calling the things Thomas is averred to have said trivial, I am acutely aware that I invite censure. Nevertheless, telling a trusted colleague, who does not protest, about a pornographic movie is not a hanging offense. Nor is a comment about a pubic hair on a coke can. These may have been coarse, and poorly expressed, but did not constitute harassment, especially since no negative career implications flowed from them. But this did not matter. In the circus atmosphere generated by the radicals, it was possible for a former colleague to solemnly accuse Thomas of looking admiringly at her backside as she walked down a hallway. In other words, normal male behavior became an indictable offense once the goal was to construct an object lesson in masculine knavery. The tangible harm inflicted on Thomas became irrelevant compared with the symbolic value of besmirching his character. (Amazingly, when the political winds shifted, Gloria Steinem, of all people, was able to defend Bill Clinton's groping of Kathleen Willie on the basis of his being able to take No for an answer.)

On a more mundane level, but ultimately a more harmful one, is a case related to me by my brother Joel Fein. A lawyer in the Tampa area, he had a client—let us call him Mr. Jones—who was remanded to jail for having made several phone calls to an ex-girlfriend. The two had a child together, which, when they separated, was placed in her custody. After Jones expressed an interest in maintaining his relationship with the child, she went to court to seek a restraining order. Initially this was rejected, but when she amended her request to include charges of physical abuse, it was granted. Although there was no evidence that this occurred, or that Jones had ever been violent in any circumstance, her claim that she was "very much afraid for my life and the safety of my newborn son" was taken as adequate documentation. Later, not realizing the extent of what was being prohibited, Jones made five separate phone calls to determine the child's health after his former girlfriend had first called to tell him that the boy was sick. He also made the mistake of asking her whether a reconciliation was possible. When she subsequently complained of this to the court, he was sentenced to five years of incarceration, one each for each of the five calls he made.

Although copies of her answering machine tapes revealed that at no time did Jones threaten her, merely attempting to speak to her made him culpable.

When my brother tried to get this decision reversed, the judge would not allow exhibits indicating that the tendency toward violence was hers, not his. While this magistrate admitted that his sentence was unusually harsh, he declared that he had a "gut feeling" that there was something "strange" about Mr. Jones. My brother believes that because Jones is a big man with a high-pitched voice, this rubbed the judge the wrong way. It is also probable that in an environment where men are routinely distrusted, the judge preferred to err on the side of the woman. He knew that if he were called to account, it would almost surely be for having failed to protect her. Sadly, even after Jones was incarcerated, his tribulations continued, for his ex-girlfriend next obtained an injunction on behalf of the child, which meant that Jones could not so much as send him a Christmas card.

But besides the damage done to individual men such as Jones, there is also the question of the harm done by subverting traditional male roles. For decades now, these have been under assault. It has been assumed, much in the manner of Bertrand Russell, that government bureaucrats can replicate the services men have historically provided, and, that given the turbulence of male behavior, perhaps should. To their credit, members of the religious right have strenuously objected to this maneuver on the grounds that it is an affront to family values. In the media, however, theirs have largely been discounted as retrograde voices whose concerns are disingenuous. More recently some sociologists, most notably David Popenoe,[55] have begun to tout the importance of fathers. They point out that children who grow up unprotected by committed male parents have increased chances of failure. On measure after measure, the data reveal them to be gravely handicapped. Less likely to go to college, more likely to be involved in the criminal justice system, less likely to be intellectually productive, and more likely to be divorced themselves, they tend to be poorer and less happy than their more sheltered peers. Without the benefits of male discipline, and horseplay, both boys and girls grow up more parochial and insecure.[56]

Feminist critics, of course, dispute this. Popenoe himself has been smeared and his observations dismissed. Thus when *Contemporary Sociology*,[57] the journal of reviews of the American Sociological Association, published an essay on his book *Life Without Father*, it was teamed with Judith Stacy's[58] *In the Name of the Family: Rethinking Family Values in the Postmodern Age*. More importantly, the editors chose as the reviewer Scott Coltrane, himself the author of a feminist-friendly work entitled *Family Man, Fatherhood, Housework and Gender Equity*.[59] Predictably Coltrane castigated Popenoe for presenting a fricassee of half-truths. As he candidly complained, "I found Popenoe's scientific rhetoric strained and his logic flawed, perceptions I expect most sociologists to share." He further revealed that "I found Stacey's sarcasm entertaining," but fretted that "her postmodern phraseology sometimes detracted from her point." Reviewers are supposed to traffic in opinions, but the bias here was blatant. Popenoe, although he presented statistics, was criticized for their inadequacy and for trying to "sound scientific," whereas Stacy, though she admittedly "gets personal...names names, gives dates, recounts observations, and offers opinions" was commended, Coltrane acknowledging that he found himself "smiling at her sardonic comments." In other words, because she was on the right side, he liked her despite her lack of hard data, whereas Popenoe, on the wrong one, failed to measure up irrespective of his citation of numbers.

But women too have been harmed and their traditional roles have also been under assault. They are currently being urged not to embrace the old-fashioned marks of femininity, such as modesty and indirection, and not to behave in ways regarded as "passive." What is wanted is a more muscular femininity in which allegiance to family life is minimized and that to extrafamilial duties is maximized. The modern woman is told that she should not hesitate to engage in body-building or in asking the man for a date. She can, they say, have it all—children, sexual fulfillment, and chairmanship of the board. One of those who has objected to this advice has been the historian Elizabeth Fox-Genovese.[60] Her *Feminism Is Not the Story of My Life: How Today's Feminist Elite Has Lost Touch with the Real Concerns of Women* is a richly textured exploration of what ordinary women experience. She begins by declaring that "the overwhelming majority of American women perceive feminism as irrelevant," and she becomes especially vehement when discussing families and children. As she puts it, "feminists who condemn women who choose to stay home are arrogantly denying to other women the right of choice they claim for themselves. In the name of what values do they dismiss devotion to children as capitulation to sexism and patriarchy? By any reasonable standard, the rearing of children is the most important thing that individuals—or, for that matter, societies—do." "The feminist hostility to the 'mommy track,'" she continues, "seems puzzling at best, irresponsible at worst. It reflects the revolutionary fervor that insists that the world should be entirely transformed—right now—in accordance with the revolutionaries' theories and dreams, to say nothing of prejudices." Though saddened by what she perceives as a likely rejection by feminist colleagues, Fox-Genovese courageously reaffirms the need to defend the rights of the young and of those devoted to caring for them.

Christina Hoff Sommers,[61] an academic philosopher by trade, is even more vociferous in her rejection of radical feminism. In her influential work, *Who Stole Feminism: How Women Betrayed Women*, she declares that the activists are both out of touch and disingenuous. "A surprising number of clever and powerful feminists," she writes, "share the conviction that American women still live in a patriarchy where men collectively keep women down. It is customary for these feminists to assemble to exchange stories and to talk about the 'anger issues' that vex them," for they seriously believe that they are engaged in a "gender war." Worse still, to triumph in this conflict, they are prepared to distort reality. Whether in a chimerical study that purports to show that the battering of women is responsible for most birth defects or a newspaper article that authoritatively reports physical abuse to rise 40% on Super Bowl Sundays, the feminist hyperbole machine has veered out of control to a degree with which Sommers does not wish to be associated. As a female who intends to be both a woman and strong, she insists that her chances are damaged by a proliferation of fictions that gratuitously insult men while dramatically misrepresenting women.

Carolyn Graglia,[62] in her *Domestic Tranquility: A Brief Against Feminism*, goes even further in making ringing defense of traditional female roles. Citing her own life story for support, she unabashedly admits that "I never envied males, but always loved being female and basked in the sensual satisfactions it affords me. Delight in my distinctive femininity distinguishes a woman like me from those feminists who claim that sexual differences are as inconsequential as the color of one's eyes. At the same time, while I have always believed sexual differences to be important—and reveled in those differences—I never found being female incompatible with being a lawyer. I did decide, however, that practicing law was incompatible with being the kind of wife and mother I wanted to be."

It is clear that a significant proportion of both men women are not well served by the gender Marxists. Nevertheless the real problem, and the real disaster, is the impact of radical feminism on families. It is the interaction between men and women, and ultimately between them and their children, that is most damaged in unduly celebrating androgyny. The quality of family life and even the existence of the family have been under assault, with the most dramatic evidence being a huge increase in the divorce rate and an even more troubling rise in the proportion of children born, and raised, out of wedlock.[63] The questions involved here are larger than individual preferences or private needs. Valid gender ideals must serve social, as well as, personal requirements—including the requirements of succeeding generations. To be more precise, families must accomplish functions over and above those pursued by their individual members. But more than this, they must find workable solutions to the dilemmas thrust upon them by the dislocations inherent in industrialization. The welfare of children matters even in a world awash in material prosperity. And children suffer when their parents cannot cooperate in raising them,[64] especially when those parents are in raucous conflict with one another.

Some, of course, deny the primacy of families. This anti-family bias is evident in the work of Stephanie Coontz.[65] An academic historian, she has been the recipient of the Washington Governor's Writer's Award and the Dale Richmond Award of the American Academy of Pediatrics. The thesis for which she has been acclaimed is that the traditional family unit is an outmoded myth. In her view, not only is the presence of fathers—and one must also suppose of mothers—not vital to the well-being of children, but "not until the 1920's did a bare majority of children live in a male breadwinner-female homemaker family...." Before then illness and accidents tore most families apart. As a result, she cautions against "romanticizing 'traditional' families." In her estimation, the future really belongs to flexible multicultural arrangements. "America needs more than a revival of the narrow family obligations of the 1950's whose (greatly exaggerated) protection for white, middle-class children was achieved only at tremendous cost to the women of those families and to all those who could not or would not aspire to the Ozzie and Harriet ideal."

Popenoe would surely respond by observing that contemporary families are being undermined, not by death and economic hardship, but by divorce and illegitimacy. He would also note that children are acutely aware of the difference between voluntary desertion and the ravages of death, and that they can cope more easily with the latter. Mothers who deny the relevance of men, or fathers who make personal gratification their overriding concern, exhibit a selfishness that would be breathtaking were it not so tumultuously defended by the gender reformers. Many women, to be sure, have derived significant relief from gender Marxism. Campaigns against domestic violence and for a reduction in legal restrictions against property ownership have not been mere egotistical diversions, but civilized improvements. Nevertheless, ideals that encourage indifference to family obligations are ill advised. They may spell liberation for a few, but occasion an ordeal for many more.

Whatever one may think of Coontz' thesis, the nuclear family has, in recent decades, been altered in ways that make it more difficult to satisfy its basic functions. Not only its division of labor, but the very incentives to remain within its boundaries, have been transformed. Specifically, neither men nor women need to remain married in the way they once did. The very effectiveness of the modern market economy enables men to purchase household services outside of matrimony and women to get jobs that pay enough to support themselves and their children. Staying together therefore becomes a luxury that is voluntary and problematic. Whatever the benefits of a stable heterosexual pair bond, the continuation of specific unions has come to depend on the personal choices of those involved. When they have neither the desire, nor the skills, to sustain it, it is susceptible to dissolution.[66]

Whether privately arrived at, or as a result of a cultural legacy, when intimate partners divide their areas of specialization, they thereby reduce the stress upon them and make it easier to work out their differences.[67] My grandparents' arrangement, with her in the kitchen and him in the shop, may not be everyone's cup of tea, but it was not merely an aesthetic, or traditional, whim. Their compromise served vital purposes. When predictable tasks are separated so that they do not overlap, the potential for inadvertent strife is diminished. Even though men are on average more aggressive than women, women too will fight with a vengeance for what they want; hence when both seek supremacy on the same turf, the collision can be frightful.[68] For example, if both are set on becoming president, and only one can, the loser inevitably will be offended. If, however, one wants to be an engineer and the other an executive, they can coexist harmoniously—the victory of one representing a victory for the other. The same applies a fortiori to engaging in childcare, providing economic support, and getting to the bathroom first in the morning. One way or another, compatible marital partners must develop mutually acceptable agreements regarding who gets to do what.[69]

A potential for role conflict, coupled with increasing family isolation, has other consequences as well. Prominent among these is the premium placed on intimates being able to achieve mutual understandings. Though men and women differ in their instincts and experiences, to be mutually supportive, they must recognize what the other is doing, and thinking, and be able to put themselves in his or her shoes. Empathy and insight become ever more crucial in getting past their personal interests and finding common ground. Specifically, a man's tendency to use the toilet seat alternately in an up and down position needs to be understood and accepted by the woman in his life and her tendency to take more time with her personal appearance needs to be understood and accepted by him. Radical feminism, by painting men as congenital villains and women as perpetual innocents, offers so elementary a world view that it short-circuits this process. The fairy tales it espouses, rather than providing practical guidance, encourage rivalries so intense that the parties can grow to hate each other. Once this occurs, they may refuse even to be sympathetic, the goal of each then becoming to vanquish the other and the devil take the hindmost.

Remarkably, just as social developments have made it imperative for couples to be mutually perceptive, radical feminists provide a cheering section that entices women to eschew compromise. Thus David Horowitz[70] relates how, in the early 1970s, at the beginning of the "consciousness raising" phenomenon, he urged his wife to attend a local women's group so that she too might become "liberated." After the first session, however, she came home "in a state of agitation, vowing never to return. 'They hate me because I'm a mother,' was all she said. Year later I learned from other members of the group that they had berated her for allowing me to 'oppress' her by 'making' her assume the housewifely role. They also told me that within a year of the group's formation, every marriage in it had dissolved." This sort of unsympathetic interference can, to be blunt, be terminally toxic to relationships that are difficult to maintain in any event. That it presents itself as providing a bastion of liberty is ironic and inexcusable.

In the past, the inevitable injustices of family life were controlled primarily by informal sanctions. Relatives and friends chided the parties—and sometimes shunned them—when they crossed an invisible frontier. In our contemporary Gesellschaft world, however, these unofficial agents are not always available, and even when they are, may be told to mind their own business. Instead, there has been an attempt to provide a political alternative. The police and courts, along with norms of political correctness, have become the arbiters of acceptable behavior. Yet too great a drift in this direction is hazardous. It injects an impersonality into personal relationships, infecting them with the litigiousness so prevalent in present-day politics. As a result, the parties can become intransigent and fail to reach accommodations dependent on mutual sensitivity. In the place of informal, often unspoken adjustments, they demand demeaning public apologies that are more likely to alienate than ameliorate. As a result, in converting normal heterosexual antagonisms into a political warfare, gender Marxists have roiled already troubled waters.

Given all this damage, the question that leaps to mind is: Who benefits from radical feminism? Someone must gain something. Sadly the biggest winners in the gender wars seem to be those who are not invested in heterosexual intimacy. The most energetic of the radicals are not family oriented, often being indifferent to personal relationships with members of the opposite sex.[71] As Marcia Cohen[72] revealed in *Sisterhood*, many are openly lesbian and/or are primarily devoted to attaining public acclaim. The history of the feminist movement is replete with activists who have promoted the dissolution of traditional gender roles either because they covet aspects of the masculine identity or because they harbor an antipathy toward men. What is clear is that they advocate for everyone what they are convinced will work for themselves.

Nor do these reformers pursue their objectives with moderation or an appreciation of social complexities.[73] As committed moralists, they have blinders on. When men, women, or children protest that this new gender order inflicts hardships, they are reassured that all, in the end, will be well. In organizations such as the National Organization for Women (NOW), these messiahs gather to strategize on how to win, not on how to detect the deficiencies in their ideals. With as much as half of their membership gay, such associations tend to reinforce a disparagement of traditional gender roles.   An independence of family attachments persuades them that dismantling these patterns is equivalent to the attainment of personal autonomy.   Though there is surprisingly little documentary evidence of the pivotal role that lesbians have played in sustaining the radical feminist vision, a revealing glimpse into their contributions has been provided by Nancy Whittier.[74]   Her groundbreaking study of the informal networks, peer supports, and political affiliations of women's groups in Columbus, Ohio demonstrates how their personal dedication and socialist leanings have supplied both the backbone and the configuration of the movement.

In making these observations, I am, of course, acutely aware that I open myself to charges of bigotry and discrimination, to say nothing of being ad hominem.   Saying out loud that sexual orientation provides the incentive for a radical feminist commitment will assuredly convince many that I must be anti-lesbian.   However much I may protest, they will conclude that I am eager to persecute this beleaguered minority.   But pointing out the source of others' values when values are at issue, or being pro-heterosexual in a world where heterosexuality is still the norm, is not the same as to being anti-homosexual.   I am simply casting doubt on an extravagant, and ill considered, ideal that has impaired millions of lives.   The fact is that moral disputes of this sort are a species of polarized negotiations that, as such, are apt to be both emotionally charged and held hostage to simplified images.   In essence, they constitute a game of normative stickball that is being played for keeps—thus the tendency to get nasty.   Radical feminism, as a moral crusade, is no different from similar crusades.   When its central values are at stake, it is predictable that passions will rise, accusations fly, and the temptation to hurl invectives will become overwhelming.

Chapter 6

Extreme II: Radical Civil Rights
(Reform without Context)

THE ONE-WAY CONVERSATION

Shortly before his death, Mike Royko got into trouble. In one of his last columns for *The Chicago Tribune*, he made an egregious error. After having mentioned the unusual first name of an African-American athlete, he went on to ask, "What is this thing with black names anyway?" For raising this question, he was almost immediately pilloried by a media-wide posse. Crusading and outspoken critic though he had always been,[1] within two days he was forced to issue a retraction wherein he begged forgiveness for his indiscretion. To suggest that there was something peculiar about black names clearly had to be due to an unconscious bias. It implied that there was something wrong with them and this was an impression he wished to rectify.

Despite Royko's apology, something curious was happening here, something about which even many blacks felt ambivalent. This unease was first brought to my attention by a student who had pulled an unattributed piece up off the internet. Under the banner of the Commonweal Foundation, its author lamented, "At thirty-one, I am a member of the last generation of black Americans whose parents didn't give them names like Shaquana and Chaico. I grew up in predominately black Washington, D.C., around older relatives with names like Pamela, Harry, and Catherine." Shortly thereafter the writer qualified his disapproval by asking, "So, should I have restrained myself from laughing at the oddness of the name Shaquana? Or been surprised at the fact that I immediately identified the race of the person it belonged to?" To which he quickly but equivocally responded, wondering why people shouldn't be able to name themselves whatever they wanted while at the same time recalling how hard he had laughed at a *Saturday Night Live* sketch that poked fun at Scottish customs. Next he mused, "I once had a Jewish friend who chuckled over the fact that he'd met a woman named Israel. When he said something to the effect of 'Guess we know what she is, huh?,' my friend's smile indicated something more than his amusement: a certain pride, a certain identification: Those people are mine!" This led the author to ponder why blacks should not also be able to feel pride in being identifiably unique. After all, "A deprived group that gives its children made-up names rather than bending to tradition and choosing Anglo-derived ones must be tough, resourceful, and proud."

Certainly, most Americans are aware of how distinctive and arbitrary black names can be. When I was a vocational counselor, one of my clients admitted that she had baptized her child after a bathroom product because she admired its resonance, while a second explained that she had simply put sounds together until they appealed to her, and a third admitted that she had appropriated the official title of a Southeast Asian country precisely because it was different. More recently a white student confided that she had been the classmate of someone named Shithead (pronounced Shi-theed). With a smirk on her face, she wondered aloud if the girl's parents had thought ahead as to how this spelling would be received. When I related this incident to Lana Wachniak, a sociological colleague whose specialty is deviance, she assured me that this was an urban legend that she too had heard reported as if it were a first-hand experience. Assuming that this is correct, it is eloquent testimony to the underground resentment of many whites who do not feel free to comment on black naming practices more directly. For them, the example typifies the tendency of many black parents to misspell given names whether from ignorance, inadvertence, or a desire to be creative. Even so prominent a person as Oprah Winfrey, christened in honor of a Biblical personage, had the letters of her name reversed; the original was "Orpah."[2]

In their book, *The Language of Names*, Justin Kaplan and Anne Bernays[3] devote an entire chapter to what they term the "controversial issue" of black names. They observe that the "pattern keeps unraveling." "We are now seeing the latest form, in which a unique name, a neologism, often a daring and imaginative coinage...is created for each baby that comes along. Alexicor, Bogumila, Calendula, Daamanl, Eddleavy, Fontella, Gonorleathia, Hurie, Iniabase, Jivon, Kenee, Latif, Malakah, Najja, Olithyn, Pelissar, Quadrinea, Rasheena, Salonla, Tajuan, Unise, Vaneal, Wardsworth, Xtmeng, Yuriel, Zikkiyyia—these twenty-six first names were culled from a printout roster of children enrolled in the public schools of Chicago, zip code 60609. Some are more euphonious than others, but each one is sui generis, which in turn suggests that the child which bears it is also one of a kind...."

How different this practice is from that of the larger society can be judged by comparing it with the Jewish tradition. East European Jewry has for centuries chosen both secular and biblical names for its offspring. These are customarily derived from deceased relatives whom the parents wish to honor. In my case, I was named for two great-grandfathers, my Yiddish names being Moshe, Motcha, and Lazar, which were in turn derived from the Hebrew originals for Moses, Mordecai, and Lazarus. In English these were rendered Melvyn Leonard, which are themselves old-English names standing respectively for "legendary hero" and "like a lion." In other words, they all have a history. I realized how significant this can be when a cousin telephoned to say that he was contemplating naming his firstborn son after his father. He wanted to check whether this was a good idea, which prompted me to explain that doing so would be equivalent to wishing his still living father dead. Immediately he chose another name that was consistent with the tradition. How firmly these conventions are implanted was further exemplified by the reaction of the Commonweal writer's Jewish friend. I am willing to bet that when he smiled at the name of a woman called Israel, it was not because he felt a secret pride, but because Israel is a man's name; indeed, it is a fairly common male name. Assigning it to a woman was therefore as big a faux pas as would be calling her husband Sue. That a literate black writer should be blithely unaware of this speaks volumes about the lack of intercommunity contact.

Many European, African, and Asian kinship groups have patterns comparable to those of Jewry. Thus Catholics have historically named their children after saints, members of the British aristocracy have doted upon hyphenated surnames, and Russians have utilized patronymics as middle names. The question then arises as to why blacks are so different. Leonard Pitts,[4] writing for *The Miami Herald* suggests that his people "want...a name that reflect[s]...creativity and individuality," whereas the poet Sonia Sanchez[5] has proposed that some of these appellations provide a pseudo-African identification. They "may not be truly African, but they have the same polysyllabic flavor." Still, the question remains, why be different, creative, or African?

Unlike most Americans, those of African heritage were violently torn from their roots.[6] Their ancestors did not cross the Atlantic voluntarily, but were jammed together as slaves in the holds of merchant ships engaged in the triangular trade.[7] Upon arrival, they were further degraded by masters who beat them into submission and compelled them to adopt customs that facilitated their bondage.[8] Rather than having their own naming traditions respected, they might at the whim of an overseer be given peculiar first name such as Pompeii or Mopsey. For the most part, the slaves were completely stripped of last names. The result—as Malcolm X was wont to complain—was that after the Civil War many adopted the surnames of their former proprietors. That these are today eschewed as being slave-names should not come as a shock. Also understandable, with their historic ties to Africa traumatically cut, have been frantic attempts to revive the past and/or to replace it with a newly minted facsimile. The consequence has been a vivid expression of a people's flexibility, but also of its continued drift. Though a confirmation of pride and resilience, it also bespeaks an ambivalent separateness that DuBois characterized as "double-consciousness."[9]

All this is highly suggestive and extremely relevant to making sense of the position of African-Americans in this country. To be enjoined against discussing it, as Royko was, is therefore to impose an artificial ignorance. Yet this is our situation today. Explicitly verbalizing facts—however valid—if they are interpreted as derogatory, is taboo. It is taken as evidence of an indirect desire to demean the vulnerable and to return them to their previous condition of servitude.

For decades politicians and social activists have been calling for a dialogue between blacks and whites—presumably to clear the air. Whenever a troubling racial incident erupts, someone piously intones a summons to talk things out. George Bush did so after the Los Angeles-Rodney King riots; Bill Clinton did so after the first Simpson verdict. Clinton also called for a dialogue in conjunction with his race initiative. One of the devices he used for achieving this was a national town meeting. Yet despite repeated calls for candor, and a passable imitation of Phil Donahue, what emerged was a one-sided lecture on the evils of prejudice. When Abigail Thernstrom,[10] the single invited dissident, contradicted his position on affirmative action, Clinton badgered her into silence with a demand for a Yes or No response. Pleading for a discourse has, in fact, become a political ritual. Though the anticipated progress never seems to materialize, the true objective may be appeasement, for whenever the precipitant disappears, so does the rhetoric.

The reality—which we are not supposed to mention—is that there are many things one is not permitted to say in public. Opinions considered racially offensive are particularly liable to fall into this category. Although a dialogue is theoretically a two-way process—with people swapping their respective positions in an effort to achieve harmony—in racial matters one side is allowed a veto power over the other. Once it judges an assertion as unacceptable, it can call "foul" and the other must beg forgiveness. Just as women have become the final arbiters of rape, so African-Americans are now the unimpeachable experts on racism.[11] Nor is this lack of symmetry open to examination. Merely to mention it constitutes a foul. Indeed, not to make too light of the issue, but the situation is comparable to the toilet seat norm, with a "Don't ask, don't tell" policy prevailing in both.

Much to my distress, I encountered this situation while teaching my first college course on the sociology of education. Offered during a summer semester at Queens College, and ostensibly non-controversial, one of its few points of contention was the so-called "IQ controversy" wherein scientists, for over a century, have been arguing over whether biologically based differences can account for variations in racial achievement levels. Since I was familiar with the literature, I knew its potential combustibility. I resolved, therefore, to present the question as objectively as I could. With little fanfare or comment, I described the research and allowed my students to draw their own conclusions. In summation, I did, however, point out that there were no compelling data to support a belief in physiological disparities in reasoning. Culture could explain the patterns found and was, therefore, the most parsimonious explanation.

Two weeks later a note from the college president appeared in my mailbox. After a few pleasantries, it demanded to know what I was teaching in my sociology class. I was astonished and confused. Where I had been under the impression that things were moving smoothly, he wrote that complaints had been lodged that required a response. Two of my black students were apparently dissatisfied with the IQ lesson and had gone to their advisor who, in turn, bucked the matter upstairs. Their accusation—which was never brought to me—was that I had made slurs against black intelligence. Evidently, I was expected to denounce, with vigor and thoroughness, all intimations that there might be disparities. By attempting to be even-handed, I had, in their eyes, sided with the bigots.

The term ended before anything could come of this, but the impact was devastating. As a novice teacher, I was insecure to begin with. To discover that mentioning controversial topics might bring reprisals sent tremors down my spine and had a chilling effect.[12] If I could lose my job for uttering the wrong opinions, it was obviously wiser to divulge none. Discussions of race thereafter became out-of-bounds. Whether or not I had something meaningful to impart, it seemed more prudent to concentrate on less volatile areas. Indeed, not until years later, after I arrived at Kennesaw State University and was assigned to teach a *Race and Ethnicity* course, was this to change.

The challenge to my reticence occurred when, a scant two weeks into the term, I was approached by an apprehensive young student. Pretty and earnest, she button-holed me before I could enter the classroom. Because I had indicated that class participation would be factored into the final grade, she feared that keeping quiet would jeopardize her average. As she tremulously explained, this placed her in a bind, since her opinions were such that if she aired them, they might be construed as racist. While she did not believe they were, she was certain that others—especially blacks—might reach this conclusion. Could she, therefore, be given a special dispensation?

Much to my chagrin, I was soon to discover that hers was not an isolated case. Many of my Caucasian students maintained a polite reserve during our deliberations, fearing that whatever they said would be unacceptable. Like men caught in discussions of feminism, they tried to remain invisible, or failing that, muttered something tepid and insincere. Eager as I was to elicit a genuine dialogue, this presented a predicament that I for years afterwards struggled to address. Eventually, much to my relief, I did find a solution. It entailed self-revelation. Since it was obvious that a majority of students felt unsafe, I decided to expose my own vulnerabilities. If I were willing to put myself on the line, perhaps this example would enable them to do likewise. In marked contrast with the usual pedagogical practice of assuming an air of removed superiority, I would not claim to have personally risen above the perils of racism. On the contrary, I would acknowledge my humanity with all that this implied. In particular, I would offer myself as a model of how we all begin life with a parochial perspective that we only gradually, and partially, outgrow.

After a disclaimer about how easy, and therefore dangerous, it was to moralize, I commenced my discourse with a review of my own childhood. Far from having been born with a sociological textbook in hand, my Brooklyn upbringing exposed me to few African-Americans. The only one I could recall was the daughter of the janitor of an apartment house down the block, but she moved out in less than a year. Most of the others were either domestics or laborers, who were plainly regarded as different and inferior. Prejudice and discrimination might be spurned within the Jewish community, but this didn't signify an acceptance of intimate friendships with blacks. They were simply not on the same level. It was also apparent that they were physically threatening. In high school, for instance, they were the kids from the Coney Island projects who shook us down for our lunch money.

Nor, upon entering adulthood, did I immediately discover that blacks were fully human. In my imagination, I might have wanted to treat them as individuals rather than representatives of an exotic out-group, but my experience was not up to the task. This was why when I began working for welfare my attitude was paternalistic. As a poor benighted people, they obviously needed the benefit of my college education to surmount their squalor and ignorance. It thus came as a shock when they did not regard me as a long-awaited savior. It was even more humbling to discover that most of my clients knew more about dealing with life than I did. The embarrassing fact was that I was desperately naive, barely knowing how to balance my own checkbook, never mind how to help them cope with poverty.

Nor was I free of invidious stereotypes. One day while walking down Broadway, I spotted an interracial couple. Whereas I had previously seen pairs in which the man was white and the woman black, in this case the reverse was true. Suddenly the conjunction seemed incongruous. What was a white woman doing in this sort of relationship? Didn't she realize that he was probably exploiting her for sex? Then quite suddenly I recognized what I was thinking and it brought me up short. All at once my guileless prejudice was more appalling than anything they might have been doing. Clearly, if I were to be faithful to what I thought were my convictions, I would have to investigate this lapse.

Moral purity, I quickly ascertained, was more scarce than I had originally imagined. Most people might believe themselves guiltless, but few were. But more than this, to assume one's own rectitude took no special talent; it was candor regarding one's limitations that bespoke courage. As strange as it seemed, a sincere fealty to righteousness required a willingness to learn, which itself entailed an ability to entertain unwelcome lessons about oneself. Though these were uncomfortable, they were indispensable for a productive inner dialogue and a profitable outer one. Uncritical idealists, I came to realize, required people to be something more than human. For their proposals to work, they had to be saints. But neither blacks nor whites are. As biological and social creatures, we all have our limitations. Culture bound and hierarchical, we are invariably to some degree both foolish and unfair.

Because so much about race needs to be publicly deliberated, a broad-minded attitude is applicable well beyond the classroom.[13] In particular, recent research has revealed a substantial divide between blacks and whites on a host of issues. In their extensive study of racial politics, Donald Kinder and Lynn Sanders[14] (professors of political science at the Universities of Michigan and Chicago respectively) have documented a plethora of divergent opinions. Analyzing surveys conducted between 1986 and 1992, they found that 89.8% of blacks expressed a belief that the government should ensure equal employment opportunity, while only 46.2% of whites thought so. Similarly, 82.9% of blacks responded that the government should end school discrimination, though a scant 35.6% of whites agreed. Time and again, blacks indicated a positive attitude toward increased social spending and affirmative action, whereas whites were skeptical.[15] Even questions about something as apparently neutral as the desirability of capital punishment elicited contrary responses, with 36.9% of blacks being opposed as against a paltry 14.4% of whites.

If these oppositions are to be resolved, an authentic dialogue might prove useful. But to be fertile, it would have to be honest, with all sides attempting to tell the truth—about themselves and others. It would also profit from acknowledging disagreements without demanding immediate capitulation. Paradoxically, an uncritical idealism interferes with progress by insisting that the truth is already known. Other potentially useful viewpoints, instead of being regarded as plausible alternatives, are treated as noxious substances and side-stepped.

THE CIVIL RIGHTS IDEAL

African-Americans, without doubt, have been the victims of flagrant injustices. Some of these have been so barbarous that their consequences have been fatal, whereas others have been so subtle that their continuing presence is mistakenly disavowed. Nonetheless, millions of white Americans are aware of these inequities and wish them undone. They would like nothing better than to terminate the second-class citizenship of blacks and sincerely desire a color-blind society in which race is irrelevant. Many of these same persons do not, however, subscribe to the "radical civil rights agenda." This latter is more narrowly conceived than the restoration of justice to those deprived of it and hence is not the course they prefer.

Radical civil libertarians maintain two central tenets. The first is that virtually all the disabilities from which blacks suffer are attributable to white prejudice. A corollary of this is that were racism to disappear, blacks would immediately be on a par with everyone else. The second is that meaningful government interventions are essential for achieving this end. The federal government, in particular, is held liable for creating and enforcing civil rights guarantees. For the activists, "civil rights" is an omnibus term that subsumes any public intervention believed appropriate. In their view, whatever is necessary to ensure minority dignity constitutes a "right," and whenever a right must be governmentally enforced, it is a "civil" right.

Described more than a decade ago by Thomas Sowell[16] as the "civil rights vision," those who favor this agenda form a loose, but broad, aggregation of civil rights organizers, liberal politicians, members of the establishment media, and humanist academics. Although they regard themselves as dealing in common sense, they are really idealists who have converted a policy dispute over the best way to achieve racial integration into a moral jihad. In the process, however, they have grievously undermined the prospects of determining what is best. Hiram Warren Johnson[17] once said, "The first casualty when war comes is truth." The same, unfortunately, applies to moral warfare. In racial politics, because a take-no-prisoners spirit prevails, what is not already believed is never seriously contemplated.

One of the more impassioned advocates of the civil rights perspective is Andrew Hacker.[18] A political scientist (oddly enough) from Queens College, he is the author of the best selling *Two Nations: Black and White, Separate, Hostile, Unequal.* This one-time philosophy major has taken an ethical approach to racial issues, which continues to draw rave reviews from the civil rights establishment. Hacker begins his analysis by innocuously observing that, "America bears the mark of slavery. Even after emancipation, citizens who had been slaves still found themselves consigned to a subordinate status." He continues, again unobjectionably, "Something called racism obviously exists. As a complex of ideas and attitudes, which translate into action, it has taken a tragic toll on the lives of all Americans." Indeed, it is "an incubus that has haunted the country since Europeans first set foot on the continent....transcend[ing all efforts to eradicate it], largely because it arises from outlooks and assumptions of which we are largely unaware." Having cranked up his indictment to a fever pitch, Hacker goes on to raise it further by implicating this allegedly invisible source (i.e., racial prejudice) as the primary cause of a host of evils, including the racial income gap, differences in employment patterns, variations in educational achievement, school segregation, disparities in criminality, and inequities in law enforcement. White racism, in short, is responsible for most of the afflictions bedeviling the black community.

Answering Hacker's allegations is difficult because to deny them sounds as if one is denying that there are any problems. Nevertheless, in the interests of balance, an answer is required. One person forthright enough to do so has been the social critic Alan Wolfe.[19] Commenting upon Hacker's thesis, he has remarked on the huge range of phenomena that is attributed to racism. As Wolfe tells us, Hacker believes that even "hypertension, asthma, and AIDs—all of which affect the black community disproportionately—are 'not simply due to poverty' but also reflect 'the anxieties that come with being black in America.'" Hacker also argues that "'The strains that come with being black put extra burdens on a marriage' and therefore contribute to high rates of female-headed households and out-of-wedlock births." Wolfe, however, has reservations. While affirming the reality of racism, and the impairments thereby produced, he observes that, "The argument for white racism as the cause of what has gone wrong among the urban poor increasingly wears thin as social scientists investigate the complexity of human behavior."

Complaining specifically of "too intense a focus on white racism," Wolfe goes on to examine the actualities of crime and affirmative action. First of all, he suggests, it is often reality factors, and not mere bias, that shape the attitudes of Caucasians. "If there is any one reason why whites distance themselves from blacks, it is because they fear violent crime. In 1990, according to Hacker, 61.2 percent of all arrests for robbery, and 54.7 percent of all arrests for murder and manslaughter, were of blacks. This means that blacks were arrested five times more than their percentage of the population for one crime and four and a half times more for the other." Ever the circumspect sociologist, Wolfe notes that it is true that "Arrest rates do not measure crime per se, for not all criminals are arrested, and police forces generally show a tendency to arrest blacks more willingly than whites. Still, surveys of victims in general match the arrest ratios for the most violent crimes (except rape); 69.3 percent of those surveyed by the FBI in 1989 said those who robbed them were black, while 53.1 percent of all murders committed in 1990 were by blacks."

Wolfe sums up his position thus: "It is obviously a manifestation of racism for a white person to believe that every black male walking toward him is going to commit a robbery or a murder. But is it racism, given these differences in the racial composition of crime, to choose to live in a neighborhood that has a reputation for safety—even if in choosing a mostly white neighborhood, one abandons the worst areas in the inner city primarily to poor blacks?" To put this another way, when stereotypes are used to condemn an innocent person without so much as a trial, they are the handmaidens of bigotry. When, however, they help us calculate risks in the absence of more specific information, they can be valid.[20]

Contrary to what many people believe, stereotypes are not exclusively a consequence of ignorance or malice. As generalizations about groups of people, they are not transmitted undigested from one generation to another. In fact, they tend to be tested against the real world, and when found wanting—as was the old chestnut about blacks not being smart enough to be football quarterbacks—are often jettisoned. Moreover, not all stereotypes prove groundless. Although a grossly unflattering characteristic, random violence has become associated with African-American males because it summarizes some very sad facts. Even so ardent a defender of black rights as Jesse Jackson had to admit that he was relieved when one dark night he looked behind him to discover that the footsteps he heard belonged to a group of whites, not blacks. He too, along with a majority of both whites and blacks, was aware of the latter's reputation for brutality. As Wolfe confirms, stereotypes are not, of themselves, indicators of prejudice. It is only when they are used indiscriminately, without any effort at particularization, that they become oppressive.

Some devotees of the civil rights ideal have even enlisted science in their attempt to obscure this fact. Kinder and Sanders provide an excellent case in point. While commencing from the relative objectivity of social surveys, they proceed to stack the deck in favor of their desired thesis by ingeniously manipulating some basic concepts. In a chapter none too delicately entitled "Subtle Prejudice for Modern Times," they begin by proclaiming their belief that "Animosity toward blacks is expressed today less in the language of inherent, permanent, biological differences, and more in the language of American individualism, which depicts blacks as unwilling to try and too willing to take what they have not earned." "Defined this way," they continue, "racial resentment plays an important and expansive role in white public opinion." Moreover, "Wallace, Nixon, and Reagan, among others, helped to create and legitimate a new form of prejudice...., [which] rather than blatant...was that blacks should behave themselves....[and] work their way up without handouts or special favors in a society that was now color-blind."

Instead of acknowledging that conservatives might sincerely disagree with them about the causes and cures of racism, Kinder and Sanders launch an effort to demonstrate that they are trying to conceal what amounts to a flagrant bias behind a facade of virtue.[21] They begin by quoting the pioneering social psychologist Gordon Allport,[22] who defined "prejudice" as "an antipathy based on a *faulty* and *inflexible* generalization." [italics mine] This formulation is then employed to lay the foundation for a charge that contemporary conservatives treat individual blacks as members of a pariah group by impugning their character rather than their physiology. According to Kinder and Sanders, this new version of prejudice is more sophisticated than, but every bit as insidious as, its predecessor. They then attempt to prove this by suggesting that the manner in which whites answer survey questions demonstrates a secret hatred of blacks.

Among the items used to create an index tendentiously labeled "racial resentment" are:

Irish, Italian, Jewish and other minorities overcame prejudice and worked their way up. Blacks should do the same without any special favors.

Generations of slavery and discrimination have created conditions that make it difficult for blacks to work their way out of the lower class.

It's really a matter of some people not trying hard enough: if blacks would only try harder they could be just as well off as whites.

Besides these indicators, Kinder and Sanders detect a "subtle hostility" against African-Americans when respondents agree that many blacks could get along better without welfare or when they deny that they have "gotten less than they deserve." In their eyes, all of these are *faulty* and *inflexible* generalizations. "It would not be hard," they declare, "to make the case that the assertion 'if blacks would try harder they could be just as well off as whites' is wrong, just as it is wrong to deny that generations of slavery and discrimination make it difficult for blacks to work their way out of the lower class." According to them, Caucasians *mistakenly* "believe that blacks are less hard-working than whites, that blacks are more violent than whites, and that blacks are less intelligent than whites," all of which, in their view, are manifestations of bias. What is worse, those upholding these calumnies compound the injustice by continuing to endorse them despite decades of exposure to more accurate information.

But are these convictions really wrong and do they constitute proof of racial resentment? A case can be made that the patterns Kinder and Sanders deplore actually reveal a *responsibility orientation*. For starters, believing that blacks are more violent than whites is surely not mistaken.[23] As even Hacker's data demonstrate, African-Americans disproportionately perpetrate murderous assaults. The issue here is thus not what, but why—for the facts on the ground are incontestable. Similarly, it is not immediately apparent why a belief that blacks are less hardworking is faulty. As the research of William Julius Wilson reveals, blacks themselves attribute the economic failures of their compatriots to laziness. Indeed, Paul Sniderman and Thomas Piazza,[24] in their review of racism, cite a 1991 poll by the National Race Survey to the effect that more blacks than whites believe that other "blacks are lazy." Though these researchers dutifully identify this as a negative stereotype, it is evidently widespread, with fully 39% of black respondents subscribing to it.

In fact, when I worked for welfare, both my black and white colleagues agreed almost unanimously with this assessment. Although they would not have admitted it publicly, lest they be accused of bigotry, after numerous experiences with clients declaring an eagerness to work, then finding trivial excuses for not showing up, it was difficult not to arrive at the conclusion that their work ethic was deficient. The same point was made in a piece presented by Leslie Stahl[25] on *60 Minutes*. She revealed that trainers at STRIVE, a singularly successful job placement service for the chronically unemployed, insisted that their clients had difficulty obtaining employment, not because of racism, but because of their own inadequate work habits. Undoubtedly not all cultures have the same work ethic, indeed, Max Weber[26] is celebrated for the proposition that Protestantism produced an intense dedication to work. Why then should it be inconceivable that one of the legacies of slavery might be a desire not to labor too intensively for the benefit of "the man"? As so exalted an authority as W.E.B. DuBois[27] wrote in his comprehensive ethnography *The Philadelphia Negro*, "This is without doubt to be expected in a people who for generations have been trained to shirk work."

Even if it were wrong to believe that blacks are meaningfully more violent, or less work-oriented, these convictions are not ipso facto irrational.

Whatever their truth, those on both sides can, and do, make reasonable defenses of their positions. Surely, to give credence to the disfavored side cannot, in itself, be what Allport meant by "faulty." In judging what is acceptable, it is crucial to acknowledge that were honorable mistakes automatically branded as prejudiced, it would soon be impossible to determine the truth. Since both science and ordinary common sense are dependent on a willingness to take chances, including a willingness to explore ideas that might prove erroneous, we would quickly be left blind and dumb.

But let me venture into what I know to be shark-infested waters. When Kinder and Sanders declare that those who believe "blacks are less intelligent than whites" are flatly wrong, they also distort the evidence. For almost a century IQ tests have displayed a consistent pattern. When average scores for whites and blacks are compared, a fifteen point spread emerges.[28] This represents a full standard deviation and is, therefore, significant. Moreover, achievement tests in reading and math also a show large race-associated disparity, with blacks, as a group, persistently scoring several grade levels below others. None of this is in dispute. While it is unflattering, as John Adams[29] is celebrated for having pointed out, "Facts are stubborn things." For whatever reason, on average, blacks *are* performing at lower intellectual levels. If this leads some to conclude that they are inherently less intelligent, it is unfortunate, and almost surely in error, but not irrational. Rationality and truth are not the same; neither are rationality and niceness.

What is actually in dispute is whether measurable differences in IQ scores are the result of heredity or environment.[30] Yet, as even Kinder and Sanders admit, few whites today hold biology responsible and are more inclined to blame cultural factors. Nonetheless, these scholars refuse to accept such avowals. When current research, for example, that of Sniderman and Carmines or Schuman, Steeh, Bobo, and Krysan,[31] indicates that whites affirm a genetic equality, they suspect them of responding to external pressures and predict a resurgence of racism when these are removed. This, lamentably, is asserted with little corroboration.

But let me go further. To agree that blacks should follow the lead of the Irish,[32] Italians and Jews and work their way out of the lower class,[33] is not to deny that blacks have had, and continue to have, a more difficult road to traverse.[34] Reading this construction into affirmations that success is possible for them is unfair and casts unwarranted aspersions on those with an allegiance to personal responsibility. "Hard," they would surely aver, does not mean "impossible," nor is it an excuse for evading a bona fide effort. To turn Kinder and Sanders' accusations on their head, a disposition to emphasize the difficulties inherent in African-American upward mobility may itself be interpreted as suggesting a lack of ability to succeed. This, in turn, could be viewed as a form of paternalism.[35]   Though the obstacles thrown up by slavery, and by subsequent patterns of discrimination, have obviously been more pernicious than those encountered by voluntary immigrants, why should we assume that they can never be overcome?   In fact, Kinder and Sanders' inclination to interpret a responsibility orientation as indicative of racial antipathy seems arbitrary and a matter projecting an assumed negativity onto their opponents.   I find myself sympathizing with the reaction of Angela Oh.[36]   The only Asian appointed to President Clinton's race advisory board, when accused of minimizing black-white frictions she responded, "I don't believe that all white people are evil....[This] is not only false, but at some level, morally dishonest."

For better or worse, those who believe in the civil rights ideal are incensed by anyone who questions the destructive potency of racism. Whether they doubt the ubiquity of intolerance or challenge its capacity to prevent achievement, these others are depicted as heartless and ignorant. Illustrative of this tendency is what happened to Dinesh D'Souza.[37]   For the temerity of writing a book called *The End of Racism*, he was roundly denounced.   D'Souza naively thought that being nonwhite—he is of Indian extraction—would shield him against charges of bigotry, but this proved an illusion.   The title of his work not withstanding, he did not deny the existence of racism or of its deleterious effects.   He merely argued that much of what is taken as racism is actually a rational response to disquieting experiences, and that, in any event, racism is no longer the principal factor in holding blacks back.   If, for example, cab drivers fail to pick up black males, as Cornel West[38] correctly complains, it is because they legitimately fear the violence to which they might be subjected.   Similarly, if blacks refuse to pursue mainstream economic success because they expect to encounter prejudice, as Janet Mancini Billson[39] alleges, this is more their fault than that of those who discriminate against them.   Such observations, however, were utterly lost in the furor over his alleged thesis that racism has become anachronistic.   Not only were his qualifying comments not discussed, but typical of the response was that of one of my colleagues.   For the most part, a careful and compassionate scholar, when asked what he thought of D'Souza's contentions, he raised one arm straight overhead, flicked his wrist as if tossing out a piece of trash, and declared, "Oh, he's an idiot!"   Asked if he had read D'Souza's book, he replied that he had not, but that this didn't matter because he had seen reviews that made it transparent that he was "idiotic."   Anyone who thought racism a thing of the past obviously had to be.

Similarly censured for his nonconformist views has been Shelby Steele.[40] His essay on race relations, *The Content of Our Character*, has been perceived as an act of betrayal by many blacks. Though not previously considering himself a conservative,[41] he acquired this reputation once he proposed that some blacks used racism as an excuse for not taking advantage of the new opportunities available to them. In his view, harping on the sins of whites was an attempt to elicit guilt and thereby extract additional benefits. Rather than take the chance that they might flounder at endeavors in which they had no experience, many seemed to prefer portraying themselves as innocents of whom it was unfair to demand the same standards as applied to others. While Steele perceived himself to be a beleaguered truthteller, and a follower of Martin Luther King, in challenging the primacy of prejudice, he consigned himself to the status of an Uncle Tom.

But we have not yet finished with the civil rights ideal. Its second, and co-equal, proposition maintains that prejudice can be eradicated only by means of active governance. Representative of this position is Elliot Aronson.[42] A highly influential social psychologist, this one-time Harvard University professor is the author of *The Social Animal*, a premier textbook in his specialty. In its chapter on prejudice, one subsection makes the provocative assertion that "Stateways can change folkways." Phrased somewhat differently, its thesis is that government interventions can, and must, alter personal conduct.

Aronson begins his explanation by observing that "social psychologists at [one] time...believed the way to change behavior is to change attitudes." This, however, was a mistake. Subsequent research clearly demonstrated that exhortation did not work. As with mere information campaigns, the message was easily blocked by those who didn't want to hear it. The secret to real change lay the other way around. To quote Aronson, "What social psychologists have long known, but have only recently begun to understand is that *changes in behavior can affect changes in attitude.*" [The italics are his.] Indeed, a concrete test of this can be provided "if blacks and whites [are] brought into direct contact, [and] prejudiced individuals...come into contact with the reality of their own experience, not simply a stereotype.... [This] eventually...lead[s] to greater understanding," (assuming, that is, that they come together under conditions of equal status). These conditions are said to have been met in a housing project studied by Martin Deutsch and Mary Ellen Collins,[43] with the results being as expected. Specifically, the Deutsch investigation is claimed to have confirmed that racism declines once blacks and whites reside in adjacent apartments.

The secret to success is, according to Aronson, arranging the situation so that the desired behavior is *inevitable*. Direct contact in the here and now turns out not even to be necessary, for "if I know that you and I will inevitably be in close contact, and I don't like you, I will experience dissonance. In order to reduce [this] dissonance, I will try to convince myself you are not as bad as I had previously thought.... Accordingly, the mere fact that I know I must at some point be *in close contact* with you will force me to change my prejudiced attitudes about you, *all other things being equal*." This is why "children who [believe] they must inevitably eat a disliked vegetable...convince themselves the vegetable wasn't as bad as they had previously thought." Translated into public policy, the argument is that government programs—backed by the force of law—can compel integration and eliminate discrimination. In the end, by obliging people to live and work together, the barriers between them must fall.

Out in the real world, this philosophy helped launch the civil rights revolution. Initially directed at dismantling legal restrictions, and spearheaded by organizations such as the NAACP, the movement persuaded the federal government to integrate the Army, to rule that separate schools systems were unconstitutional, and to protect the voting rights of minorities. Bold leaders such as Martin Luther King,[44] accompanied by a myriad of intrepid acolytes, challenged Jim Crow legislation requiring blacks to sit at the back of the bus or to eat at colored-only lunch counters. Presumably, with the power of the state no longer holding the races apart, people of all shades would soon rub shoulders in bathrooms, classrooms, and at the ballot box where they would quickly discover that they had a lot in common, that they were all just people.

In recent decades, however, this strategy has been supplanted by a more activist one. Although politicians such as Hubert Humphrey pledged never to impose quotas, these eventually came into favor. The theory was, as Lyndon Johnson so eloquently expressed it, that a people who for centuries were held back needed a "head start" if they were to compete on equal terms. Besides the elimination of restrictive legislation, it was essential to institute programs that gave them a leg up. Set-asides, race-norming, educational benefits, and direct preferences in hiring would thereby place them in positions from whence they could acquire the skills to hold their own. Whites would then realize they had nothing to fear and would embrace their darker brothers.

Yet this is not what happened. As numerous surveys have indicated, most whites, and many blacks, resent affirmative action.[45] Thanks to these practices some minority members have attained jobs they might not have otherwise, but the price has been public acrimony and an impression that blacks are not sufficiently competent to be hired without special relief. Aronson, it will be recalled, judiciously commented that his projections would work only with *all other things being equal,* but apparently they never were. Had he been more cognizant of history, he might have realized that people tend to resist involuntary manipulation. In Deutsch's housing project, where proximity led to acceptance, this was not a problem because the residents signed up of their own accord. Military integration has also worked because its recruits have been volunteers. The forced busing of school children has not, however, and instead resulted in white flight. Nor has placing unprepared black students in elite colleges prevented them from dropping out at rates greater than average. This might have been predicted had it been noticed that seventy years of coercive rule did not communize the souls of the Russian people; nor did three centuries of slavery convince the progeny of African freemen that bondage was in their interest.

There are limits to what constraints can do. In the case of the civil rights ideal, these collided head on with the realities of democracy and the marketplace. The latter's competing values of equality and merit demonstrated an attractiveness that it was difficult for governmental paternalism to match. To allege that the radical civil rights agenda has been a tragic blunder is perhaps a bit strong, but it is not too much to state that its devotees are promoting a simplified and dangerous solution to an agonizing predicament. As do most idealists, they disregard truck-loads of troublesome evidence. Most Americans, including myself, would surely agree that in its initial incarnation the civil rights movement was not only justified but also essential; yet the questions we confront today are: Is the civil rights ideal the most effective way of improving race relations? And: Can it facilitate color-blindness or interracial assimilation? The answers to these are less than clear cut.

THE CULTURE OF SLAVERY

By overemphasizing the role prejudice plays in race-based rifts, civil rights radicals dangerously omit the most potent causative factors. For starters, they neglect the numerous cultural elements that contribute to the dismal status of American blacks. "Culture," as the term is employed by social scientists, refers to a comprehensive, learned, and shared way of life. Language, art, beliefs, values, technologies, and social norms are all subsumed within its domain. What the members of a society jointly think important, beautiful, or real turn out to be largely defined by predispositions transmitted from one generation to the next. Besides guiding how individuals react, because these proclivities are unconsciously internalized, they tend to be perpetuated, often over millennia. As a result, why a person acts as he or she does, usually cannot be established without delving into his or her cultural heritage.

Almost no one denies that culture is a powerful determinant of human behavior, but strangely, when it comes to race, there is a tendency to underestimate its impact. Sowell[46] has argued that culture is typically more important than biology in determining national differences, but all bets seem to be off when it comes to explaining the relative standing of whites and blacks in the United States. Some aspects of culture, however, are not controversial. Prejudice is one such phenomenon. Most people readily agree that this learned attitude toward blacks can be traced to the institutions of the antebellum South. Most also acknowledge that it has had deleterious effects. Similarly, as Spike Lee's[47] movie *School Daze* argued, many African-Americans judge each other's status by the lightness of their skin. This too is obviously a cultural artifact derived from slavery, but one more operative within the black community than the white. The difficulty seems to be in accepting that some black cultural legacies, might, in part, be responsible for their social failures.

Cultural incapacities can nevertheless have devastating consequences. What once enabled people to cope with a hostile social environment, may, under altered circumstances, become a liability.[48] To be more specific, some customs that were utilitarian when African-Americans were chattel slaves are dysfunctional in today's more supportive milieu. As a matter of history, and for understandable reasons, there evolved a "culture of slavery" that no longer fits in a world where slavery has been abolished. This, however, may be hard to swallow. Dinesh D'Souza seems to have ensured his renegade status by attributing black disabilities to what he described as "cultural pathologies." Though both Gunnar Myrdal[49] and Kenneth Clark[50] preceded him in the use of this pejorative label, in proposing that "illegitimacy, dependency and crime" derive from long-established black patterns, he was accused of stepping over the line and "blaming the victim." In contemporary parlance, as he was to discover, to designate something as a "pathology" brands it as "sick," which is a code word for "crazy." By choosing the appellation he did, D'Souza thus implied that blacks were morally defective and that their culture, more than being lamentable, was a voluntary, and irrational, decision for which they were culpable.

Yet whatever the moral ramifications of a particular term, to paraphrase Cornel West,[51] culture does matter. As is true of every other ethnic and racial assemblage, preferred patterns of behavior among African-Americans do have consequences. This assertion, however, needs to be placed in context. Cultures are not arbitrary inventions. They tend to evolve slowly in response to exigent circumstances. The simplest way to encapsulate this non-obvious process is to observe that *social structures produce cultures that in turn perpetuate social structures.* As here employed, "social structure" refers to a persistent pattern of relationships within a group. Hierarchies, family alliances, and intimate friendships all qualify. So does slavery. Indeed, who is bossed around by whom, and the methods by which this occurs, are central to the meaning of social structure. This last pattern, that is, slavery, for obvious reasons, places enormous stress on those at its receiving end.[52] As a result, they tend to adopt coping strategies that are passed along to their offspring—usually unconsciously. Unfortunately, once cultural models are established, they can impel people to reproduce dysfunctional modes of interaction. As Robert Park,[53] a leader of the Chicago School of sociology, put it: "Customs persist and preserve their external forms after they have lost their original meaning and functions." A simple illustration is the habit of obedience that a despot can install in his people. Stalin was so successful in this that after his death many Russians were nostalgic for his heavy hand. More to the point, the bowing and scraping of slaves, though these once prevented dreadful whippings, when replicated by their grandchildren reduce their opportunities to rise in society.

A less artificial example of the structure-culture-structure connection, and of its potency, are on view in the contrasting experiences of Italian-[54] and Jewish-Americans.[55] Both groups migrated to the United States during the same time frame, but their histories of economic mobility diverged markedly. Much of this can be related to their respective valuation of education, which, in turn, can be traced to their homelands. Three millennia ago, the Hebrews found themselves under attack by stronger powers, that is, Egypt and Assyria. Living at the crossroads between African and Asia, their tiny state was at the mercy of these aggressive conquerors. The solution to this structural dilemma was to take refuge in a cultural adaptation. Religion, and specifically a faith based upon a written text (i.e., the Bible), became their solace. But to maintain this, they needed to be literate, and hence to value literacy. Thousands of years later, this same orientation is evident in the Bar Mitzvah ceremony in which Jewish boys make their transition to manhood by proving to a congregation that they can read the Torah. In the capitalist United States, this inclination was readily transferred to secular studies, where it had a huge payoff in terms of professional advancement.

Italian-Americans, in marked contrast, had a different experience. South Italy, from whence most of them came, is also a crossroads. It lies in the middle of the Mediterranean where it is accessible to invasion by almost any power with a navy. Although today poor, historically it was an agriculturally prosperous region that made a tempting prize. As a result, it has been one of the most conquered places on earth. Virtually everyone has ruled it, except the indigenous people. Their primary defense was in the family. It, and not the government, was owed one's fundamental loyalty. Since education came from above, it was shunned and ordinary people turned their efforts to their small plots of land or their fishing boats. In America, this meant that even though free secular education was available, it was not utilized. The dream for one's children was that they graduate as quickly as possible, then get a paying job and contribute to the family coffers.

This difference, and its repercussions, are discernible in miniature in an anecdote related to me by my sister Carol Schwartz. While employed as a middle manager at a large corporation, she chanced upon the older sister of a childhood friend. During lunch together, the latter disclosed that she owed my sister a debt. Somewhat incredulous, Carol asked why. The response was that while her Jewish friends knew from their earliest days that they would some day go to college, this possibility had never occurred to her. A dutiful Italian daughter, after high school, she took the job expected of her. It was only the experience of her non-Italian peers that induced her to contemplate higher education. Much against the wishes of her family, but fortified by values appropriated from these others, she obtained a Bachelor's degree and entered upon a professional career. She had, in essence, modified her cultural legacy by adopting theirs.[56]

Returning to the situation of African-Americans, it is unimaginable that they alone among ethnic groups should have escaped enculturation or eluded its sometimes injurious consequences. A *culture of slavery* was obviously created by their condition, and just as obviously, had an impact that remains detectable. The exact nature of its components, or influence, may be debatable, but something clearly happened. Among the candidates for inclusion in such a culture are the following: a proclivity toward violence, family fragility, an intense emotional religiosity, a paternalistic orientation toward authority, an impaired work ethic, and a devaluation of education. This is, no doubt, an incomplete list, but it is a good place to start.

The *violence* inherent in the black community has been documented ad nauseam. Not only are its crime rates disproportionately high, but so is the tendency toward self-abuse. Much of this can be attributed to family patterns that, in some cases, go back to before the Civil War. In one celebrated instance, the journalist Fox Butterfield,[57] tracked a tradition of violence in the Bosket family to its roots in South Carolina. Beginning with Willie Bosket, an unrepentant multiple murderer, who at fifteen claimed to have committed two thousand crimes, including twenty-five stabbings, Butterfield trailed him, his murderous father Butch, and his abusive grandfather James back to the poisonous plantation system from whence their tendency toward intrafamilial aggression emerged. Willie became a celebrity when he shot two men to death on the New York subway and after his incarceration plunged a homemade stiletto into a prison guard's chest. At his trial, he defiantly admitted his guilt, but excused it because, in his view, he was "only a monster created by the system."[58] Butterfield concluded that the toxin went back further than this, to Edgefield county, whose white residents were locally renowned for being "pugnacious, reckless and prone to shed blood," and who cheerfully visited this propensity on their slaves. Sadly, this generated a way of life with the power to reproduce itself.

Similarly, Leon Dash,[59] also a journalist, entered the lives of a Washington, D.C. mother and her family to try to comprehend why they were so self-destructive. In *Rosa Lee*, his account of the life and times of Ms. Rosa Lee Cunningham, he painfully recapitulates the drug abuse, prostitution, and crime that were bequeathed from one generation to the next. Going back to Rosa Lee's poverty-stricken sharecropper roots, her conflicts with her own mother Rosetta, and her struggles to survive in a world that offered few avenues of success, he makes it clear that misery and self-hatred can be inherited. In one particularly poignant episode, Dash recounts how Rosa Lee cajoled her adolescent daughter to have sex with an older man in exchange for drugs for herself. The ruinous impact of this is also described, as was the girl's difficulty in surmounting it.

Even more readily demonstrable have been the consequences of servitude on attitudes toward *education*.[60] Where Italian peasants deliberately avoided public schools, preemancipation slaves were forbidden, on pain of death, to learn how to read or write. For them, education was a distant dream, that, in their inexperience, they had difficulty in instilling in their children. Despite lip service to what was intellectually understood as advantageous, many, especially the young, came to treat learning as if it were a white enterprise, successful students being ostracized as "oreos," that is, black on the outside and white on the inside. Less easy to demonstrate has been a culturally transmitted outlook toward *authority*. If slaveowners were paternalistic in regarding their property as overgrown children, many of their victims responded by expecting to be cared for. Not having obtained permission to exercise initiative, they grew dependent upon the good will of others. This currently finds expression in the paltry number of black entrepreneurs and the high number of black activists petitioning for government relief.

Perhaps the most important of the cultural antecedents impacting blacks have been those associated with their *families*.[61] Many early observers of the African-American condition, some of them black, had no doubts of this connection.[62] DuBois,[63] for one, after investigating slave family roles, concluded that their constitution had traumatic outcomes. Donna Franklin's[64] survey of the black family, *Ensuring Inequality*, describes him as believing that "slavery had a crippling effect on the slave father, who lacked the authority to govern or protect his family. In [his] view, 'his wife could be made his master's concubine, his daughter could be outraged, his son whipped, or himself sold away without [his] being able to protest or lift a preventing finger.'" Nor could the black male's family regard him as their provider, for they understood upon whose sufferance their daily bread depended—and he knew that they knew. The result, as reported in *The*

Philadelphia Negro,[65] was often "temporary cohabitation and the support of men" by their women. John Blassingame[66] too emphasizes the destructive repercussions of slave status, noting that "after marriage, the slave faced almost insurmountable odds in his efforts to build a strong stable family."

More recently Kenneth Clark, the black social psychologist whose research on the damaged self-esteem of African-American children helped persuade the Supreme Court[67] that "Separate was inherently unequal," also concluded that the black male, and his perceived role, were systematically degraded by slavery. "He was compelled to base his self-esteem instead on a kind of behavior that tended to support a stereotyped picture of the Negro male—sexual impulsiveness, irresponsibility, verbal bombast, posturing, and compensatory achievement in entertainment and athletics." In sum, he could not be regarded as a strong, dependable father figure.

Nor did the slave mother and her descendants fare significantly better. Although she could fulfill her function as a woman by bearing children, she had almost as little control over them as did her mate. As Frederick Douglass[68] observed in his autobiography, she was also at the mercy of the master; hence it was generally the physically less productive grandmother who oversaw the young. Nor did the black woman's culturally prescribed status meaningfully improve with freedom. Subsequent to slavery, it was frequently she who, with greater ease than her more threatening spouse, could obtain employment. For this, she was castigated as an emasculating matriarch. Despite the fact that the responsibility for supporting their children often lay on her shoulders, she was viewed as too strong and too independent.[69]

The structure-culture-structure model reached its apogee with the Moynihan Report,[70] officially entitled *The Negro Family: The Case for National Action*. Initially compiled during the Johnson administration, where it was intended as the foundation of a new approach to lifting blacks out of poverty, it quickly became a cause célèbre. Franklin[71] summarizes it as asserting that: (1) "the deterioration of the Negro family is clear from these facts: (a) nearly a quarter of urban Negro marriages are dissolved; (b) nearly one quarter of Negro births are now illegitimate; (c) as a consequence, almost one fourth of Negro families are headed by females; and (d) this breakdown of the Negro family has led to a startling increase in welfare dependency...., (2) The 'roots of the problem' lie in slavery; [and] in the effects of Reconstruction on the family, [etc.]," and (3) these defects are manifested in "an unstable family system," "a matriarchy," "higher rates of delinquency and crime," a personal "withdrawal" especially among males, and "higher rates of drug addiction."

Because Johnson[72] wanted to ensure black support for programs intended to strengthen their families, he vetted these conclusions with African-

American leaders. Encouraged by an initially favorable reaction, he was later caught off guard when a firestorm of protest erupted. Moynihan and Johnson had the misfortune of floating their culture hypothesis at the height of the civil rights era, just as it was about to tip over into a crusade for black pride and to flare out in sanguinary urban riots. Hordes of newly mobilized zealots could not accept what they perceived to be the defamation of their race. For them, it was insulting to ascribe black problems to an inherited familial defect. What was needed was stress on the ability blacks had demonstrated to endure the unendurable. It was the positive, and not the negative, that had to be accentuated.

Within short order, most black activists were insisting that African-American families should be applauded for their adaptability. Rather than the government, and its scientists, providing credence for a shopworn stereotype, they should be seeking to dissolve it. Were they not to do this, they would be reinforcing social prejudices. William Ryan, a civil rights leader, gave voice to this opinion by asserting that, "If we are to believe the new ideologues, we must conclude that segregation and discrimination are not the terrible villains we thought they were. Rather, we are told that the Negro's condition is due to his 'pathology,' his values, the way he lives, the kind of family life he lives,"—which is utterly unfair. To accuse black men, however inadvertently, of abandoning their families, or black women, however casually, of being castrating matriarchs, were execrable slurs that must not be tolerated.

Still and all, whatever the larger truth of the Moynihan thesis, there is something unquestionably unique about the black family. Its history has proved to be remarkably distinct from that of others. Moynihan's critics must thus do more than protest the demeaning aspects of his hypothesis. They need, at minimum, explain why events subsequent to the 1960s corroborated the institution's peculiar vulnerability. No other group, whatever its racial or ethnic origin, has experienced a meltdown of such proportions. Today, more than half of all black families are female-headed and almost 70% of all black children are illegitimate. This being so, it is virtually impossible to avoid the suspicion that there was something detrimental in their original make-up—something probably generated by slavery.

In concluding her richly nuanced exploration of the black family Franklin[73] almost concludes as much, but in the end observed that, "The 'institutional' and 'cultural' paradigms that have been utilized to explain this phenomenon are limited in that they cannot explain the differential effects societal changes have had on the family structure of black families over time." In this she is correct. To maintain that culture alone, and only a culture derived from slavery, can account for all that has transpired would be absurd. Other social structures, for example, economic ones, have also contributed to the situation, as has white culture. Whatever the original destructiveness of the plantation system and the coping mechanisms it spawned, subsequent reactions to Reconstruction, Jim Crow legislation, the welfare system, dual-tier labor markets, and white hypocrisy have all produced independent effects. Our complex world is riven with both structural and cultural causes that themselves have interactive effects. That said, the ongoing repercussions of a culture of slavery remain central to understanding what has happened to blacks. The internalized feelings, beliefs, and norms it generated remain with us, as do the burdens of white intolerance. To leave them out grossly distorts our picture of reality.

EMPOWERMENT

One of the aspects of social structure without which the status and fate of African-Americans cannot be deciphered is the distribution of personal power. Not only did slavery strip its victims of a way of life, but it also thrust them onto the bottom rung of a hierarchy not of their own devising. Few people have less control over their destinies than do chattel slaves and few are as subject to arbitrary maltreatment from above. That they should have resented this, and, having attained their freedom, desire a radical revision in their rank, was inevitable.[74] Their standing, unlike that of women, is a genuine stratification predicament. The question that needs to be addressed is, therefore, whether the civil rights ideal offers a practical route toward its rectification.

Proponents of the radical civil rights solution believe that with the proper legislation, those who have had to endure undeserved abuse can attain positions commensurate with their gifts. Rather than being tread underfoot, they will thereby obtain power and a fair share of social goods and interpersonal respect. The concept used to describe this strategy is "empowerment." The government, and all fair-minded people, are, as it were, urged to bestow what centuries of servitude denied. Whatever the feasibility of this objective, it is true that if blacks are to rise above the wretched circumstances to which they were once consigned, they must achieve more clout. But the question persists as to how this is best accomplished. The civil rights ideal, as is admitted by proponents such as Harold Cruse,[75] assumes that authority must be equally distributed throughout society. Indeed, it insists that elementary morality depends upon it. Yet this may not be possible. If human beings evolved as hierarchical creatures—as there is reason to believe they did[76]—then in seeking personal advancement, they will create iniquities, regardless of laws to the contrary.

And if they do, a world in which everyone is equally influential is a fantasy. The concept may be lyrically beautiful, but its attractiveness does not imply achievability.

To be plainspoken, empowerment is a hoax. It is a refined confidence game perpetrated by opinion leaders who may believe in it, but who should know better. Power is not something within the province of anyone to bestow, never mind in equal proportions. People compete for power; they assert power. It is not an unencumbered gift to be given, but something that must be earned and exercised. It is also something that can be lost. In contests for hierarchical supremacy, there are winners and losers. Those who would gain command need to be capable of behaving in certain ways, not merely of being passive receptacles. More to the point, to retain their spoils, they must successfully defend them from others who covet them as much as they do. Power struggles are a fact of the human condition that cannot be wished out of existence because they happen to be unfair. As crude as it is to admit, hierarchical winners are compelled to defeat others who are themselves no pushovers. Their own power is always relative to these others and always open to challenge.

Life is pervaded by what are best described as "tests of strength" in which individuals measure their ascendancy against others. Just as male rams butt heads and baboons threaten each other with their canine teeth, human beings discover who is more powerful in trials of strength that are no less real for being more subtle or more effectively disguised. Many of these contests may be symbolic, but they are jarring nevertheless. Who has better skills, more allies, or greater persistence is often determined in activities that allow these to be displayed. Just as a game of tennis can make it clear who has the better backhand, a political campaign, a rivalry for promotion, or a marketing plan can reveal who is the "tougher" competitor. When someone wins in such endeavors, especially if this is decisive, he thereby acquires a reputation for power that translates into further power. As a consequence, people seek visible victories so that they will no longer have to keep fighting.

Yet when it comes to race, many idealists believe that these rules are suspended and they subscribe to what may be called "the rich father-in-law" theory of power. The myth that animates their hopes is of the poor but earnest young man who meets, falls in love with, and marries the daughter of a wealthy businessman. This magnate, who, as it happens, heads a huge corporation is so taken by his new son-in-law that he raises him to dizzying heights by appointing him its chief operating officer. Usually the scenario ends there with the assumption of a happy ending in which the young man makes a smooth transition to business tycoon. In the racial version of this allegory, the father-in-law is a rich uncle, namely Uncle Sam. Presumably, the government, in selecting deserving individuals for advancement, thereby makes them more powerful. No follow-up is envisioned, for it is taken for granted that once a person has power, it is his thence forward.

All this, however, is sheer fantasy. It falls within the same realm as the conviction of young children that if they are appointed the "boss," others will automatically do their bidding. The empowerment fable nonetheless commences with something that might happen. Heads of large organizations generally do possess an ability to promote people regardless of merit. As long as they are authorized to hire and fire, their decisions are likely to be honored, even when they are poor ones. But what happens when the person so selected appears in the office? A title on the door does not suffice to make him boss. A son-in-law must demonstrate that he deserves to be obeyed. If he has neither the gravitas, nor the expertise, to uphold his position, he will rarely be respected. Despite an initial show of deference, he is likely to slide into figurehead status.

Several decades ago, Alvin Gouldner[77] did a study of succession within organizations in which he discovered that subordinates do not reflexively comply with the orders of a new superior. Once a person has assumed an unaccustomed position, his work first begins. If he (or she) does not possess the resources to command deference, it will be withheld. In Gouldner's case, an inexperienced leader floundered after having been designated the head of a gypsum plant. His predecessor, though unloved by the central office, had the dedication of his subordinates, which they were unwilling to transfer to a stranger. When the new man issued orders, these were evaded. Deeply frustrated, he sought to enforce his mandates. One of the techniques he chose was close supervision, but this was so resented that his underlings ridiculed him for being like a little mouse who was forever popping up from a hole. Another strategy he used was strategic replacements in which he fired popular subordinates and substituted his friends. This, however, was so clumsily handled that it had little effect. Eventually the new manager sought the backing of his superiors, but his pleas became so insistent that they too lost confidence in him. His insecurity showed through so vividly that, in the end, no one found him compelling.

In the case of race, the requirements for upward mobility have not been repealed. Anyone who wishes to have his higher status respected must be able to inspire compliance. Those with greater power than themselves, be they individuals or social institutions, can delegate leadership via hiring policies or college scholarships, but they cannot make these stick.[78] Ordinary people resist manipulation by proxy. Once they recognize that a superior does not have the qualifications to operate independently, they tend to sabotage him. Indeed, they will almost certainly test him to determine if he has the mettle to survive on his own. In this case, all a person's sponsor can do is to place his designee in a position where power is available, then serve as an ally when others challenge him. But a godfather, however well intentioned, cannot handle all the provocations to which the person will be subjected, nor imbue him with leadership qualities he does not possess. It is often assumed that after a redistribution of authority, those raised to positions of command will learn by doing. Maybe so—but certainly not always. The tactic can just as easily backfire and create grievances that fester until there is an explosion. In fact, those raised beyond their competence, or the continual protection of their sponsors, frequently resort to dictatorial policies, with all the deleterious consequences this implies.

In truth, power struggles are interminable and result in a circulation of elites that sometimes develops as idealists desire, but sometimes not. Moralizing about these matters can make a difference, but only a modest one. During the 1970s, when I worked as a reporter for a northern New Jersey newspaper, I encountered these limits in action. The War Against Poverty was at full tilt and community organizers were struggling to erect local centers of power. As part of their strategy, they invited poor people to participate in instituting advocacy groups that would get them heard at city hall. In conjunction with my reportorial duties, I attended several of these meetings. They were an eye opener. Although the term "empowerment" was bandied about, what was in evidence was chaos. People shouted at each other, threw punches, and, on more than one occasion, called in the police to restore order. In retrospect, they resembled nothing so much as the vulgar free-for-alls now on display during daytime television talk shows.

At the time, among the most persuasive advocates of grassroots bootstrapping were Richard Cloward and Frances Fox Piven,[79] who argued that it was the most effective means for teaching people how to participate in the political process. They trumpeted many ephemeral successes, but several vital ingredients were always missing, first and foremost among these being self-discipline and self-direction among their erstwhile beneficiaries. The truth is that people who hope to exercise power in a middle-class society require skills for which slavery, segregation, and poverty have ill prepared them.[80] Assuming that slavery does propagate a unique culture, the attitudes thereby established and the abilities thereby stymied can make it difficult to exercise power. A lack of initiative, for instance, can preclude taking the risks that will demonstrate one's abilities, while a tendency toward violence can instigate reprisals that undermine one's interpersonal alliances.

When I worked at the methadone clinic, many of my clients also exhibited these deficiencies. Good persons though some were, most lacked impulse control and therefore indulged in behaviors that alienated others. Indeed, many carried razor blades in their shoes and walking sticks that doubled as clubs. They were also notorious for engaging in crude deceptions when trying to get extra methadone. A favorite ploy was to claim that a grandmother had recently died and it was necessary to attend her out-of-state funeral. This, however, was frequently professed well past the normal complement of four grandparents. The upshot is that no one, neither their peers nor their counselors, regarded them as candidates for leadership. Their evident lack of trustworthiness, and propensity for indiscriminate violence, deprived them of the respect they sought.

More specific to the African-American situation is so-called "black rage." It too interferes with the effective implementation of power. Those who cannot control their anger find themselves at a disadvantage when trying to be assertive. Both riots and temper tantrums are notoriously ineffective at influencing others. Because they betoken weakness and not strength, in a mass society, if all that is known about a person is that he is prone to explosiveness, he is unlikely to be taken seriously. Those who undertake positions of authority must, therefore, have sufficient self restraint not to blurt out whatever comes to mind. Uncensored emotion rarely promotes mastery. Yet the indignities of slavery initiated anger of massive proportions. The very impotence experienced made rage all but inescapable. Franz Fanon[81] recognized this decades ago, as has Ellis Cose,[82] who recently documented the same proclivity among successful African-Americans. Though the latter have good jobs and nice homes, many nurse resentments toward a world that keeps asking them to prove themselves.

Besides self-discipline, success is facilitated by self-direction. Would-be leaders must be able to make difficult decisions independently. This world is full of uncertainties; hence the potentially powerful have to be capable of figuring out the best course on their own. As Melvin Kohn[83] has shown with respect to social class, people in the upper reaches of society value aptitudes such as being able to determine how and why things work. They also possess a willingness to take calculated risks in an environment where things can go wrong. These dispositions, however, do not come naturally. They take competencies rarely acquired by those who grow up surrounded by others who constantly tell them what to do—which is exactly the situation at the bottom of the pecking order.

Unfortunately, developing the requisite orientations can take decades, even centuries. Because they entail emotional proficiencies, individual adjustments occur with agonizing slowness. People do not simply decide to be different and then follow through; they must often turn their guts inside-out before any movement is detectable. In some ways, African-Americans, as a group, are at an adolescent phase of development. This must not be taken to imply that individual blacks are immature, but as a group they often demonstrate tendencies toward unsophisticated patterns of self-assertion.

The term "adolescent" is meant to evoke the strategies teenagers use when they assert autonomy. Surely, black Americans, just like adolescents, are seeking independence after an extended period of subjugation. And just as surely, they are doing so against determined resistance.

Older adolescents, of course, are notorious for being prickly and for making their parents' lives miserable. Despite remonstrances not to, they stay out late, are disrespectful of their elders, and behave like shameless know-it-alls. Pointless defiance is their stock-in-trade, as is pompous inexperience. But herein lies an irony. Their obnoxiousness has a point. It is essentially a conspicuous assertion of power. To be accounted as real, strength must be proven, and to be proven, it must be exercised in the face of disapproval. Only when a child prevails in the teeth of parental opposition can he, and others, be certain that, in this area at least, he has greater power than they. This is, in other words, a test of strength that helps define relative power.

When it comes to racial stratification, there is a comparable need to demonstrate potency despite the desires of others. Although whites may graciously confer responsibilities upon their former inferiors, these remain symbolic, mere tokens, as long as they depend on the goodwill of their donors.[84] Without the resources to protect themselves from gratuitous slander, vengeful lynchings, or capricious sellouts, blacks have the appearance, but not the substance of power. Real power is present only when others cannot snatch it away on a whim, hence the stridency, the I-dare-you-to-do-something-about-it tone, and the extravagant demands that accompany many black initiatives. Witness the so-called "cool pose" as investigated by Richard Majors and Janet Mancini Billson[85] and by Elijah Anderson.[86] Most of us are familiar with the strut, the braggadocio, and the feigned indifference of the streetwise black male. Fonzies-with-an-attitude, they dare the white community to be offended. Their carriage shouts from the rooftops that they will be what they want to be regardless of what their detractors think. In their own world, at least, they will be worthy of respect.

Perhaps the most egregious recent example of this need to say "No!" to whites was demonstrated in the first O.J. Simpson trial. When a mostly black panel acquitted Simpson of what most white observers regarded as an horrific crime, they, in essence, engaged in jury nullification.[87] In effect, they told the world that "We are the jury, and, like it or not, we will decide the issue. Even if this entails interpreting the law to suit ourselves, there is nothing you can do about it." The cheer that went up among black TV audiences across the nation was a rousing endorsement of their stance. That white audiences were shocked by their glee was a bonus. It demonstrated a relative impotence, and brought many African-Americans a sense of solidarity that enhanced their feelings of victory.

All of these considerations, of course, run counter to the civil rights ideal, which conspicuously ignores the effects of both culture and social structure. Those who subscribe to it seem to believe that if they insist on its adequacy, some day their faith will be vindicated. What is more, since those who oppose them are obviously bad guys, they must be demonized. Not only need they be given no credence, but their ideas do not have to be studied. As William Julius Wilson[88] has suggested, many liberal scholars have "shied away from researching behavior construed as unflattering or stigmatizing to particular racial minorities." In the name of giving the deserving a break, they quietly abstain from a rigorous analysis of the proposals made on their behalf.

Yet the danger in this course, and its potential for disaster, lies in failing to recognize when one has entered upon a dead end. Just because a society has embarked on a policy intended to improve the lot of a portion of its citizenry does not ensure this will succeed.[89] The efforts made may make no difference, or worse still, harm the predicted beneficiaries. Moreover, in choosing one direction over another, more promising policies may be prevented from seeing the light of day. If the observations made earlier regarding slave culture and social hierarchy have any validity, dramatic changes may be expected to come gradually. Though trying to speed things along is psychologically understandable, it can actually slow them down. In the final analysis, ideologically based ventures make people feel better by giving them a sense of doing something, but sadly may also delay the arrival of a longed for utopia.

Chapter 7

Extreme III: Radical Medicalism
(Excuse Abuse)

ONE FREE MURDER

The blood must have been everywhere. A shotgun at close range is not a delicate instrument. It sprays dozens of pellets that can rip into the flesh, tearing open innumerable capillaries, veins, and arteries. Moreover, the weapon's blast is such that it can splatter shards of hair, flesh, and sinew over huge areas. Not withstanding all this, not even withstanding the fact that their final shots came from muzzles placed firmly against their parent's heads, the Menendez brothers, and their lawyers, were able to persuade several jurors at their first trial that this was not murder. Amazingly, although these decision-makers had seen photographs of the devastation (even if some were suppressed as too inflammatory), they still maintained that it was not the fault of those who admitted pulling the triggers.

At the time of the shooting, the Menendez boys, Lyle and Eric, were college-age adults, but they were portrayed as harmless juveniles, compelled to defend their lives against brutal, almost omnipotent parents. Despite having methodically planned the killing, despite having exchanged buckshot for less lethal birdshot prior to doing the deed, they were not regarded as voluntary agents. A wealth of details may have suggested that they were, but neither having earlier gone on a family outing and pretending nothing was amiss, nor bursting in upon their unarmed parents and firing and reloading and then firing again—some fifteen times in all, nor cleaning up after themselves, including picking up the spent cartridges, nor arranging an alibi that involved purchasing movie tickets beforehand was held against them. Neither was subsequently lying to the police, going on a spending

153

spree, or inducing friends to perjure themselves. Both cumulatively and individually, these were discounted because the brothers plausibly claimed to have been the victims of sexual and emotional abuse. As such, they were adjudged not responsible.

In court, Lyle and Eric strove to appear sympathetic. While sitting at their table, they looked clean-cut and concerned; while on the witness stand, they sobbed and seemed distraught. It quickly developed that the core of their defense was an assertion that they were merely protecting themselves. Their parents, though wealthy and powerful, had allegedly bullied and sexually intimidated them for years. Witness upon witness testified that Jose was an overbearing father who reveled in humiliating his sons, while Kitty was a depressed and pill-popping mother who rarely came to their rescue. That sexual exploitation had occurred was not, however, irrevocably established, for the allegations depended mostly upon the tearful recollections of the defendants. It had, nevertheless, been placed on the record. According to the attorneys, this established grounds for a plea of "imperfect self-defense." Decades of appalling behavior had obviously induced the brothers to fear for their lives. Just as the victims of traumatic stress may feel under attack half a lifetime after the precipitating event, so they sensed that their parents were about to murder them and that they needed to take action. Whether or not this was true, their sincere belief provided an excuse. Yes, they pulled the trigger, but, as with anyone provoked to self-defense, they committed no crime.

Yet these were adults—adults who presumably had other ways of protecting themselves. No one had required them to reside in their parents' home. Instead of driving to San Diego and using false identification documents to buy shotguns, they could have rented an apartment across town. And rather than depend upon their parents' for financial support, they might have obtained jobs. This would, of course, have forced them to live more modestly, but no one would have died. Nor did they have to shoot their mother or make sure that she was dead after she was down. Even if they were terrified of their father, their mother was no threat, especially after she had been wounded. Nor were they in imminent danger of attack. Ordinarily self-defense is justifiable because the danger comes up so suddenly that the intended victim has to act immediately and without calculation. In their case, the peril, if present, existed in the minds of the defendants, allowing them days, weeks, or months to deliberate. To suggest that they had no options was bizarre.

Most observers, even those who did not follow the trial, sensed that something was going wrong. James Q. Wilson,[1] an expert on criminology, detected this in the questions he was being asked while on the lecture circuit. Typically these had been about gun control, drug legalization, or the death penalty. But, as he has reported, "In 1995 that all changed. The first—and for many people, the only—question was, How could the Menendez brothers have gotten off?.... Two rich boys had executed their parents for financial gain, and the criminal justice system could not convict them of what they surely deserved, first degree murder. My audiences were profoundly upset about what they—and I—regarded as an indefensible outcome."

So why did the jurors not have the same reaction? How could they have been sold on the proposition that the defendants had no control over their actions? Apart from the sympathy generated by a graphic recapitulation of what the boys allegedly experienced, how, when so many alternatives were available, could they have appeared to be hapless pawns of fate? Part of the answer must be laid at the door of science. At the first trial, Judge Stanley Weinberg was induced to permit a bevy of expert witnesses to testify that the Menendez brothers could not help themselves. For biological reasons, they were powerless in the face of overwhelming pressures. Had almost anyone else been in their shoes, they too would have perpetrated the same grizzly deeds.

The notion that all human beings are at the mercy of a host of irresistible forces has gained broad currency. Rather than fostering a perception of ourselves as masters of our own destinies, science, in uncovering the causes of behavior, is purported to have discovered that we cannot make independent choices. Although we may feel in charge, events themselves take priority. One widely endorsed instance of this belief is the so-called "battered woman syndrome." Its most prominent advocate, Dr. Lenore Walker,[2] a Denver psychologist, has actively sought to persuade the courts, and ordinary people, that women who have been abused lose their ability to act rationally; that after years of traumatic beatings, they are forced into mute submission. Where less terrified others might find the means to remove themselves from harm's way, they perceive no exit, and hence remain loyal to an abuser who continues to subject them to violence.

The battered woman's syndrome has been invoked to explain many incidents of women killing their tormentors. Though a wife may have, in the middle of the night, while he was fast asleep, stabbed her husband in the chest or blown his head off with a pistol, it was not her fault. As the victim of the tragedy, she was suffering from a diminished capacity and hence was not culpable. Just as it would be inappropriate, and unavailing, to blame a schizophrenic individual whose delusions impelled him to throw a television set out the window, so it would be absurd to penalize her. For those in the grip of a mental defect, albeit a temporary one, ordinary sanctions do not apply. What is needed is not incarceration, but psychotherapy so that they can regain control. Put another way, only the scientific treatment of a scientifically established disorder is suitable.

To shift gears to another domain where science has declared its preeminence, the causes of and attempted "remedies" for homosexuality are likewise controversial. Whether this orientation is normal, and morally defensible, has in recent years been heatedly debated. Historically, different societies have dealt with the proclivity very differently. Same sex behavior seems to be universal, but whether it is condemned or condoned varies dramatically. As the proponents of homosexuality are fond of pointing out, in some societies, such as ancient Greece, it was not only accepted but also celebrated. Men of stature, when they composed poetry in praise of their lovers, generally did so of young boys. Indeed the Greeks seem not to have made a distinction between homosexual and heterosexual love. Thus, the sociologist David Greenberg[3] tells us, "It was said [approvingly] of Alcibiades, Athenian politician and general in the last half of the fifth century B.C., 'that in his adolescence he drew away the husbands from their wives, and as a young man the wives from their husbands.'" We even have accounts of bisexuality in reference to Socrates and the Homeric heroes. And as late as the second century A.D., a book by Artemidorus Daldianus includes a passage on sexual dreams that indicates, "Having sexual intercourse with one's servant, whether male or female, is good; for slaves are possessions of the dreamer, so that they signify, quite naturally, that the dreamer will derive pleasure from his possessions...."

Many preliterate societies have also taken a tolerant approach toward same-sex coupling. Thus among the Tiwi[4] of northern Australia, young men frequently appeased their lust with other young men. In their community, fathers traditionally betrothed their daughters at birth to adult male allies. As a result, when these marriages were consummated, the husbands were ordinarily much older than their wives. This left a long period during early adulthood when men were unattached and forbidden to have intercourse with nubile young women already belonging to others. Not surprisingly, out in the bush some cheating between heterosexual couples occurred, but so did homosexual alliances within the bachelors' camps. Much as today's incarcerated heterosexuals turn to "fresh meat" for solace, so did they, only they did this voluntarily. There have also been cases, as among the Cheyenne,[5] in which men uncomfortable with the warrior role have been allowed to dress, and live, as women. Not only was this accepted, but they were even thought to possess special spiritual qualities.

We, however, are the heirs to a Judeo-Christian tradition.[6] The Bible, as most of us know, frowns on homosexuality, and so do most churches. In their view, sexuality should be reserved for procreation. Even heterosexual lust is scorned. How much more sinful then is copulation that can never be fruitful. In addition, its concurrent promiscuous and extramarital character makes the orientation a threat to the family. As a consequence, in the West a ban on homosexuality has extended through medieval times right up to the present, with Christian denominations as diverse as fundamentalist Protestants and Roman Catholics discouraging it. Among their allies has also been the Orthodox Jewish rabbinate, which likewise has vociferously lobbied against the extension of same-sex liaisons.

In the modern era, attitudes toward homosexuality have been similarly, and as decisively, shaped by the development of psychiatry. Foremost among those who brought the orientation to the attention of the medical community was the secular Jewish physician Sigmund Freud.[7] Living and working in Austria, one of his preoccupations was childhood sexuality. Not only was he interested in demonstrating that very young children have sexual impulses, but he also believed that these were modified in significant ways as they matured. Initially, all children were thought to be polymorphously perverse. Since gender specificity was irrelevant to them, they had both homosexual and heterosexual desires. When, however, their sexual development proceeded normally, they ultimately reached a critical turning point during the Oedipal period. The five- or six-year-old boy, in particular, after experiencing an intense love for his mother, discovered in his father a strong and implacable rival whom he at length pacified by giving up his claims to the woman they both coveted. As a substitute, he identified with his father in the expectation that when he grew to be a man, he too would be able to have a woman of his own.

In the case of homosexuality, this sequence supposedly went awry. Greenberg summarizes the alternative Freudian dynamic as follows: for the future homosexual too "strong [an] attachment to the mother makes involvement with other women difficult. By pursuing other men, the son notifies his father that he will not compete with him for the love of his mother and reassures his mother that he will not abandon her for another woman. Identifying himself with her, he chooses partners he can love narcissistically, imagining that he is the partner, receiving the love he wants from his mother." In this view, if the oedipal crisis is not successfully resolved, the boy is unable to assume his role as an adult male and substitutes a quasi-feminine one in its stead.

The good news, according to the Freudians, is that psychoanalysis can help a person work through this fixation. Although all men retain a latent homosexuality, revisiting the scene of childhood traumas can enable the sexually neurotic to redo their previous relationships and, at long length, move past them. To be therapeutic, this experience has to be emotionally profound, but, with guidance from a professional helper, success is possible. Given the mid-century influence of the Freudians, this conviction came to be enshrined in the official handbook of the American Psychiatric Association. In the second edition of its *Diagnostic and Statistical Manual* (DSM-II),[8] which in 1968 attempted to define all recognized psychiatric conditions, there, under the heading of sexual deviations, appeared "homosexuality." Classified as a neurosis, it, along with other sexual disorders such as fetishism, pedophilia, transvestitism, voyeurism, and sadism, was provided with no further elucidation, save the overarching one that it involved "sexual interests...directed primarily toward objects other than people of the opposite sex, toward sexual acts not usually associated with coitus, or toward coitus performed under bizarre circumstances as in necrophilia, pedophilia, sexual sadism, or fetishism." As such, it was recognized as being a candidate for medical treatment, that is, for a psychiatric cure.

By the 1970s there was already a call to revise this evaluation. At the time, psychiatry was seeking a more sophisticated and biologically informed image. Its rapid growth and burgeoning prestige appeared to require a redefinition of its basic diagnostic categories to make them more precise and empirical—if for nothing else than to appease the insurance companies who footed most of their bills. As importantly, it seemed prudent to cut the discipline's ties to a specific theory, which, after all, might prove wrong, and which, in any event, was going out of style. The Freudian concepts earlier so prominent had to be removed and replaced with more descriptive ones. In the end, the amended volume contained many more categories, each of which was elaborated in far more detail. Where the DSM-II contained a mere 134 short pages, the completed DSM-III[9] stretched to 494 larger ones and was accompanied by a variety of supporting documents that explained how it was compiled and how it should be employed.

When this revision project was launched, there had been no expectation of modifying the criteria for diagnosing homosexuality, never mind eliminating them.[10] But this was the 1970s, and agitation had developed among gays to have their rights respected. This was to lead, in 1972, to a chance encounter that would revolutionize the status of homosexuals within the medical community. It occurred between Dr. Robert Spitzer and representatives of a dissident medical faction. A member of the APA Committee on Nomenclature and Statistics that produced the DSM-II, Spitzer was delegated to supplant it. Although appointed chair of the task force assigned the project, he was not an expert in the area of homosexuality, nor had he intended to become one. Nonetheless, as he was later to explain, "I went to this conference on behavioral modification which [a] gay lib group broke up. I found myself talking to a very angry young man. At that time I was convinced that homosexuality was a disorder and that it belonged in the classification, I told him so." This, however, was to change.

Spitzer had found himself challenged to defend his position. In the words of his primary accoster, Dr. Ron Gold, "He said he [Spitzer] believed in the illness theory. I said, all right, who do you believe? And he hadn't read any of it" (referring to the professional literature). Apparently being face-to-face with an earnest fellow professional who adamantly opposed the orthodox position made a profound impression. Confronted with his own ignorance, Spitzer capitulated. As early as the next year, he modified his stance and was converted into one of the most ardent critics of the Freudian legacy. But more than this, given his organizational connections, he was able to shepherd a reworked diagnosis through to its inclusion.

First, he arranged a meeting between the activists and the new Committee on Nomenclature and Statistics. Later he wrote an influential position paper that, although not calling for the recognition of homosexuality as fully normal, now described it as a form of "irregular sexual behavior." Spitzer reasoned that "If psychiatry was to broaden its diagnostic system to include 'suboptimal' behaviors as mental disorders,...it would have to recognize celibacy, religious fanaticism, racism, vegetarianism, and male chauvinism as diagnostic categories." Eventually this approach was to bear fruit. The redone manual would not list homosexuality per se as a disorder. Instead, in the chapter on psychosexual conditions, under the heading of "Other Psychosexual Disorders" appeared a residual category called "ego-dystonic homosexuality." No longer applying to all homosexuals, it was "reserved for those homosexuals for whom changing sexual orientation is a persistent concern." In other words, only those whose excessive loneliness, guilt, shame, anxiety, or depression made them profoundly unhappy qualified. Otherwise same-sex patterns were deemed within the normal range.

Because an unusual amount of discomfort accompanied this shift, those politicking for it organized a referendum among the entire membership of the APA. They wanted to make certain that there was sufficient backing for the radical alteration they proposed. Although they had moments of anxiety, ultimately the vote was not close. Fifty-eight percent of the returned ballots favored deleting homosexuality from the new DSM, whereas only 38% voted against. Just how remarkable this event was can be gauged by imagining doctors being asked whether chicken pox is a disease. Science, in this case, was being decided, not by the emergence of new evidence, but by how a group of professionals evaluated one type of human behavior. Theirs, in short, was a moral, not a medical, determination.

This brings us back to the link between homosexuality and the Menendez case. What they have in common seems to be a desire to reconceptualize moral dilemmas as medical ones. Living, as we do, in an age of science, it possesses a cachet that is difficult to repudiate. Surrounded by television sets, automobiles, space travel, computers, and CAT scanners, people are hard-put to deny that they are the beneficiaries of enormous technological advances. As a result, science, and those associated with it, have acquired a credibility that often extends past their areas of expertise. Previously, we saw how Margaret Mead used the authority of anthropology to lend credence to a romanticized interpretation of Samoan sexual customs. Bertrand Russell performed a similar alchemy when he equated sexual liberation with modernity. Why, therefore, shouldn't the status of particular criminal or sexual behaviors receive the same treatment and be redefined as scientific, rather than moral questions?

The trouble with this course is that these really are moral issues. They are about rules of conduct, not about objective facts, about social negotiations, not unbiased discoveries.[11] The medicalist innovators may abhor this wrangling, and wish to eliminate it by jumping straight to indisputable truths, but this is disingenuous and fundamentally irresponsible. Morality, though most of us might like to think otherwise, is inherently fraught with uncertainty. Hedged in, as it is, by contending factions forever jockeying for an advantage, it boasts of no secure resting place. But this can be terribly uncomfortable for the participants. As do we all, they crave dependable answers, especially to important questions. These were once furnished by religion. It offered a set of absolute beliefs that could presumably be verified by checking a sacred book or by consulting with spiritual experts. Yet while some fundamentalists still find these channels convincing, a growing number of us find them wanting. This is where science has stepped in and why, as the custodian of "objective" truth, it is often invoked as the arbiter between rival factions.

But science cannot provide definitive prescriptions. If it could, it might be able to settle the differences between the players. Unfortunately, moral judgments are not truisms. People may subscribe to them as if they were, but this does not change their actual status. In point of fact, though science can legitimately influence which standards individuals choose to support, it cannot foreclose the process of deciding. With scientific discoveries always subject to reinterpretation, identical observations may even furnish data for diametrically opposed conclusions. This means that despite the tendency of moral protagonists to assert their conclusions as if they were certain, this is usually a ploy to induce others to refrain from attack. Those involved know that if something is an empirical truth, it is difficult to deny. As we shall shortly see, this tactic is so effective that it has been applied to homosexuality, imperfect self-defense, and the battered woman syndrome alike.

THE MEDICAL MODEL

At the node between science and morality, the medicalist ideal has surfaced as the primary explanation of why some forms of conduct are more acceptable than others. Though the consequences of this gambit are frequently as disastrous as those of radical feminism or radical civil rights, its perils are not as universally recognized or as passionately debated. This "medical model"[12] of human problems has, however, come to the attention of sociologists who fault it for reconceptualizing deviant[13] behavior as a biological condition.[14] They note that what was formerly regarded a moral failure is now considered a disease.[15] Even so, the medicalist link to personal irresponsibility is not fully appreciated. In many ways, its rereading of moral problems has come to seem so normal that its effects are rendered imperceptible. When it is challenged, people actually wonder why.

The growing pervasiveness of the medical perspective is even detectable in the language we use. Nowadays, people often express approval by calling something "healthy."[16] Whether talking about a food, an attitude, or a way of life, this term denotes something to be aspired to. Conversely, our lexicon has become crowded with medicalized terms of opprobrium. That which we wish to reject may be stigmatized as "sick," "pathological," "psycho," or "mental." Where once our ancestors perceived the devil's footprints in abhorrent conduct, we today suspect a "chemical imbalance" or a "genetic disorder." This proclivity is so prevalent that instead of declaring something "bad," we dismiss it as "toxic," "tainted," or "disordered."

But we need to be more precise. The medical model, that is, the medical ideal as applied to personal problems, has several features. As physicians have uncovered more physical causes of illness, the conviction has grown that all human behaviors, good and bad alike, have a physiological substrate.[17] Moreover, since these behaviors are regarded as occasioned by antecedent events—much as a fever is provoked by a bacterial infection—they are deemed to be no more within the control of the afflicted individual than would be a medical symptom. Everyone recognizes that people catch colds, that they do not voluntarily decide to sneeze or to run a fever. As a result, when ill, patients are not blamed for their inability to perform up to everyday standards. Rather than forcing them to go to work or to drive to the store, we instead provide them a "sick role"[18] that encourages staying home, drinking fluids and watching TV.

When this pattern is applied to forbidden behaviors, some interesting inferences emerge. Whether we are talking about interpersonal aggression, substance abuse, or unusual sexual appetites, recurring negative conduct must now be construed as beyond the command of the individual. Because all these behaviors are *caused*, some by genetic influences and others by inept child-rearing, he must presumably not be held accountable. Rather, his or her dispositions have to be accepted as a given. Put another way, since he, and what he does, are not equivalent, he cannot be personally reproached. Indeed, as a sovereign individual, he has to be accorded the same leeway as someone suffering from cancer. If anything is done to him, it should be to provide a referral for the appropriate professional help. Psychiatrists, psychologists, social workers, family therapists, and personal counselors, as the agents best situated to reinstate optimum functioning, must immediately be called in.

This perspective casts moralists in the role of villains. Their tendency to punish that which they believe to be immoral is interpreted as a vestige of older, more superstitious times. Today, with science leading the way, such cruelty is thought superfluous, whereas insights into why people behave badly are believed to be the key to identifying the optimal means of effecting change. Moreover, those with the clearest discernment, namely the helping professionals, are in a favored position. It thus behooves the rest of us to delegate them responsibility for regulating problem behaviors. If this seems extreme, it should be realized that their elevation is believed a logical extension of our shared desire to achieve rationality, a token, as it were, of our intention to be reasonable. As a bonus, because these designees are professionals, they are considered more humane than the average layman. Idealistic, dedicated, and pledged to do good, besides utilizing their expertise, they are publicly committed to eschewing injury—witness the Hippocratic Oath, wherein doctors swear, above all, to do no harm.

Waving the banner for this agenda are, first and foremost, the physicians, who for years have propagandized in favor of an expanded role in shaping societal decisions. Today many unabashedly provide advice on career choices, family discipline, and social abuse. The Centers for Disease Control,[19] for instance, recently launched a campaign to reduce interpersonal violence, designating this an aspect of "preventive medicine." Everything from programs to quit smoking to the conduct of foreign policy seem now to have fallen within the medical purview. Moreover, other, subsidiary, medicalists from a variety of backgrounds have added weight to this movement. Jurists, feminists, and racial activists have all climbed aboard the bandwagon. Medicalism is, in fact, so elastic and so persuasive a means for escaping blame that opportunists of every stripe have found it expedient to claim it as their own. Even the man on the street enlists it when convenient. Its who-me, I-couldn't-help-myself, pose is just too tempting to pass by.

Yet the medical model is a frail reed that does not sustain scrutiny well. Indeed, several of its cornerstone theses fail the rationality test. First, as is elaborated upon later, evidence of causality does not of itself eliminate personal responsibility. Since all human actions are caused, were culpability derived exclusively from an absence of antecedents, this would imply that no one is ever responsible for anything. Second, the disease model of personal moral lapses is flawed. While some unacceptable behaviors may be a consequence of physiological breakdowns, others surely have a different source. Because they are not all purely biological, thinking primarily in terms of a cure can be counterproductive. Third, helping professionals, and more particularly, psychiatrists, are not necessarily the best equipped to control what needs controlling. They are neither the paragons of virtue they sometimes pretend to be, nor are they invariably the best situated to intervene as needed. In sum, the medical ideal may seem plausible, but only when not examined too closely.

Let us take a more intimate look, beginning with the disease theory of personal problems.[20] Its definition of normal functioning turns out to be a disguised form of moralizing. Operating behind a screen of medical authority, it condemns some forms of conduct as pathological, not, as one might imagine, because their etiology falls within specific biological boundaries, but because a significant proportion of the medical community has agreed to proscribe them. The impression given is that a person's body, or mind, is not operating properly and that this must be rectified if he or she is to be prevented from doing something untoward. Yet this is misleading. Often there is no evidence whatever of a biological disturbance. Even more strangely, when this lack of an identifiable physiological cause is recognized, as it sometimes is, the condemned behavior is not categorized as nonmedical; it is merely relabeled as a "functional" disorder and treated as if it were physical anyway.

Most people assume that the word "disease" has a precise medical meaning, but this is an illusion. Physicians use the word in the same sense as do most laypersons, that is, as referring to "a condition in which bodily health is impaired." In ordinary discourse, they rely on a vague, intuitive sense of impairment, whereby corporeal weakness, a life-threatening tumor, or a disfiguring rash each qualifies for inclusion. When pursuing scientific accuracy, however, they substitute the concept of a "disorder."[21] All of the DSMs define the conditions they cover as mental disorders, not diseases. The introduction to the DSM-III[22] handles the matter as follows: "Each of the mental disorders is conceptualized as a clinically significant behavioral or psychological syndrome or pattern that occurs in an individual and that is typically associated with either a painful symptom (distress) or impairment of one or more important areas of functioning (disability)." It will be noted that this explication, though attempting to be comprehensive, is not specifically physiological.

The outcome of this tactic is that many behavioral patterns that ordinary people would not consider diseases routinely show up in the DSMs. For instance, early in the DSM-III, there occurs a set of conditions identified as "conduct disorders." Applied exclusively to children, their essential feature is "a repetitive and persistent pattern of conduct in which the basic rights of others or major age-appropriate societal norms or rules are violated." But wait! How was that again? A repetitive and persistent pattern of conduct that violates norms? If this is not a moral judgment, I, for one, am not certain what would be. The condemnation of rule-breaking here is not merely implicit; it is overtly stated. Though the manual goes on to assert that this "conduct is more serious than the ordinary mischief and pranks of children and adolescents," it still refers to conduct. This fact is later reaffirmed when in considering diagnostic criteria, the document cites behaviors such as "violence against persons or property," "thefts outside the home," and "repeated running away." It is apparent here that these indicators are different from those that would be applicable to, let us say, psychoses. Unlike schizophrenia,[23] in which hallucinations, delusions, and a loosening of logical associations are prominent, with conduct disorders there is no inkling of a biological malfunction.

But the DSM-III is not finished. Among the other non-organic childhood conditions it enlarges upon is "separation anxiety." This is described as entailing "excessive anxiety on separation from major attachment figures or from home or other familiar surroundings." In other words, if a young child becomes "unduly" distressed when his mother leaves the room, this is bad. Who would disagree? But does this constitute a disease? And what of some of the categories reserved for adults? Among these are the "adjustment disorders." These entail "maladaptive reaction[s] to...identifiable psychosocial stressor[s]." Thus an "impairment in social or occupational functioning," coupled with an "excessive" reaction to a stressor, is said to indicate their presence. This means that when, for instance, a person gets seriously depressed or seriously anxious, he or she can be diagnosed with such a condition. But who is to decide what is maladaptive or excessive—two incidentally blatantly evaluative modifiers? Why, the psychiatric community of course. Likewise, it determines the presence, and inappropriateness, of the "personality disorders." These are coded on a separate axis from the medical ones, but their appearance in the same volume ensures that, in practice, they are regarded as forms of craziness. Among these are the histrionic, the narcissistic, and the antisocial personality disorders. The last of these refers to persons who engage in criminal activities, are terrible parents, or have difficulty sustaining love relationships. Also prone to a lack of impulse control and habitual lying, they are not exactly nice people. Nor, according to the APA task force, are histrionic personalities.[24] Largely women, they tend toward self-dramatization, an overreaction to minor events, and irrational, angry outbursts that are difficult to live with. Likewise, narcissists, who are apt to be men, are singled out for their grandiosity, fantasies of unlimited success, and interpersonal exploitativeness.

Even as the APA was amassing this compendium, many competent observers understood that most of its entries were not diseases in a conventional sense. Since few were occasioned by infectious organisms, genetic malfunctions, or dietary deficiencies, and, in most cases, there were no detectable anomalies in anatomy or physiology, they were clearly different from the traditional ones. Distress and discomfort might be present, but why these were considered medical indicators was never fully explained. At the time, Theodore Blau,[25] then President of the American Psychological Association, was so exasperated that he protested against the whole exercise. In his view, it represented an imperialistic foray by physicians into psychological territory, and in a letter to the president of the APA he objected to describing mental disorders as a subset of medical disorders, noting that "Of the 17 major diagnostic classes, at least 10 have no known organic etiology....and some were obviously acquired through learning experiences."

But the authors of the DSMs were subjected to pressures from friendly critics as well. The nonphysiological character of most psychiatric disorders exposed the compilers of the DSM-IV[26] (which when published in 1994 had swollen to some 886 pages) to intense lobbying. Lenore Walker, as might be anticipated, engaged in aggressive efforts to have her battered women syndrome included, but so did civil rights organizations who wanted racial prejudice to be so designated. Although Robert Spitzer had thought it bizarre for "racism, vegetarianism, and male chauvinism" to be viewed as mental disorders, the partisans of these new categories had no such qualms. They understood that officially labeling an opponent as "defective" rather than "bad" dug him a hole so deep that extrication might prove impossible. Thus, if being prejudiced or anti-feminist were truly diseases, those inclined toward these attitudes needed a cure, not a respectful hearing. Much as the North Vietnamese sent their opponents to forced reeducation camps, political zealots equipped with an official psychiatric imprimatur could summarily refer their adversaries for corrective "therapy."

Fortunately, the authors of the DSM-IV saw fit to sidestep this quagmire. Some revisions were made, but these were relatively modest. Among the new inclusions were premenstrual conditions and among the deletions the passive-aggressive personality disorder. This latter had previously been characterized as involving a tendency to resist adequate functioning by engaging in procrastination, dawdling, or stubbornness. Its reevaluation was apparently occasioned by a realization that to stigmatize those trapped in coercive social environments as responding inappropriately when they were conducting themselves in the only way possible was unfair. Certifying them, rather than their oppressors, as candidates for treatment was the ultimate insult.

If the solidity of the definitions of mental disease is less than inspiring, so, it develops, are the sterling qualities imputed to those doing the judging. The expertise, moral rectitude, and compassion of medical persons are generally no greater than that of other persons and surely are not sufficient to merit a privileged status in applying moral norms. Like most professional bodies, psychiatric ones have been prone to mythologizing their founders as culture heroes.[27]   In the same manner as sociologists, geologists, chemists and physicists, they have concocted official histories that confer demigod standing on their forebearers. This, however, can be embarrassing, for the realities are otherwise. When, for instance, the textbooks[28] inform us that two centuries ago it was physicians who struck the chains off the insane, they are engaging in a deception. In the standard version of events, Dr. Philippe Pinel is supposed, during the French Revolution, to have totally reformed the management of the insane. As the physician in charge of the Bicetre, a large Parisian insane asylum, he is depicted as literally unlocking his patient's manacles and setting them free. Yet it was physicians who historically oppressed the mentally ill. Religious fanatics may be singled out for blame, but Bicetre, and Bedlam in England, were in fact administered by doctors. Ironically, many of the innovations for which Pinel is credited were actually pioneered by the religious activists.

Indeed, medicine itself has not been particularly humane. Accustomed as we have grown to medical interventions that save lives, it is easy to forget that not long ago these were habitually unavailing. Often it was the infliction of pain that certified a treatment's legitimacy. One has only to glance at the kings of yore to see how radical their remedies were. For example, when Charles II of England developed seizures, the royal physicians were called in. The year was 1683, a mere three centuries ago, but as his biographer Antonia Fraser[29] explains, "The poor King's body was purged and bled and cauterized and clystered and blistered. Red-hot irons were put on his shaven skull and his naked feet. His urine became scalding through the lavish use of canthrades. Cupping-glasses and all the weird resources of medicine at the time were applied. They all had one thing in common: they were extremely painful to the patient." The inescapable conclusion is that not only was the king made to suffer, but that his death was hastened.

Nor did patients with psychiatric diagnoses fare better. George III got all the retribution any American patriot could have desired when late in his life he was seized by "madness." It was not the king's enemies who administered this revenge, but his physicians.[30] As the Countess Harcourt reported, "The unhappy patient...was no longer treated as a human being. His body was immediately encased in a machine which left no liberty of motion. He was sometimes chained to a stake. He was frequently beaten and starved, and at best he was kept in subjection by menacing and violent language." The historian William Bynum also notes that, "He was in addition blistered, bled, and given digitalis, tartar emetic, and various other drugs." Those who have seen the movie "The Madness of King George" will recognize that his attending "mad doctors" sought to dominate their patient, even though he was a king.

Fortunately, at about this time, Samuel Tuke[31] was working to improve the treatment of the insane. Tuke was no physician, but a Quaker layman who believed in kindness and morality. At his York Retreat, chains did not exist. He believed in walking and talking with his erstwhile madmen. A real-life good Samaritan, he was convinced that if these poor souls were treated as people, they would respond by rejoining the sane world. He called this a "moral treatment" and it seemed to work. Indeed, reformers trekked to his sanitarium from all over Europe in hopes of emulating his methods. For awhile, kindness actually became the rage. Ultimately when mental asylums were introduced in countries such as the United States, it was in frank imitation of his techniques.[32]

Many other stories of medical indifference and secular compassion could be told. Physicians, it should not be forgotten, were responsible for the snake pits of late Victorianism[33] and the prefrontal lobotomies and insulin shock of modern times,[34] while it was humanitarians, such as Dorothea Dix,[35] who fought to get the insane released from confinement in jails and dank cellars. Merely swearing an oath, or being restricted by a code of ethics, does not in itself bestow decency or common sense. Doctors are, after all, human. Like the rest of us, however much they may know, their wisdom is limited and their motives mixed. Clearly, a specialization in medicine is not tantamount to moral training. It may even be argued that regular exposure to distress, as part of one's occupation, can be desensitizing. For some people, at least, it may make them less qualified to identify what is morally acceptable. Why, therefore, would nonprofessionals wish to abdicate their independent judgment to medicalists who disingenuously stake out a privileged role?

Finally, the logic exemplified in the medical model is itself questionable. Whatever the advances of modern medicine in treating psychosis, their relevance to moral issues is doubtful. This, however, tends to become obscured because during moral negotiations the parties seek whatever advantage they can, including the concealment of awkward facts. If logic threatens to interfere with making a point, it will be jettisoned. Understandably, this tactic is not openly declared. Instead, that which is persuasive is dressed up as if it were logical. Because there is a flexibility to moral reasoning that can be breathtaking, the outlook for innovation is almost unlimited. Ironically, a ready illustration of how even contradictory arguments can be made to appear plausible is provided by the debate over homosexuality. In this contest, medicalized arguments occur with equal fluency on both sides of the dispute. The effect is to allow the parties to believe whatever they choose to believe.

To grasp how this is possible, we must begin by recognizing that moral reasoning is often conducted by way of analogy. The same, parenthetically, is true of the law.[36] In comparing one case with another, attorneys typically seek to demonstrate that because their salient characteristics are identical, they should be decided in the same way. Thus, if this is an apple and that an orange, because both are fruit, the corresponding statute must apply. This places a bounty on stressing commonalities, with embarrassing points of contrast systematically excluded. No one, for instance, need know that an orange is high in citric acid content and that an apple is not, if this would disturb the conclusion. The same sort of tactic appears in morality with tedious regularity. Because its rules are also founded on examples, there is a bias toward arguing by way of them. As a result, specific exemplars are compared, reshuffled, then pasted together to fit the needs of the moment.

In the case of homosexuality, the challenge is to supply analogies that prove the orientation either is or is not moral. As it happens, when the protagonists get down to business, their favored examples tend to come from the redoubtable nature-nurture controversy. What is especially curious is that either side of the nature-nurture divide may be scavenged for evidence favoring either verdict. Both a medical interpretation that insists homosexuality is biologically caused and a humanist one that favors a social origin are interchangeably employed either to defend or to censure it. Naturally, whichever argument is made, its proponents, with conviction, claim to have humanity and/or science on their side.

Let us see how this contest goes, beginning with nature-based arguments. If it is assumed that homosexuality has a physiological underpinning, for example, that gay brains are demonstrably different from straight ones, those who favor homosexuality will contend that because this is so, the behavior is beyond the control of its victims, and therefore it is absurd to blame them for what they cannot alter. In their view, it makes as much sense to rebuke biologically compelled sex as to castigate the diabetic for requiring insulin. At first blush this seems credible, but the game in not over, for the other side has yet to be heard. Interestingly, it too can agree that homosexuality is biological, but will exploit this for the opposing purpose of demonstrating that it must be proscribed. This faction simply resorts to portraying the condition as a genetic taint. Just as Cesare Lombroso[37] once argued that some people must be incarcerated because they are "born" criminals, those who scorn homosexuals can regard them as "bad seeds" who need to be separated from the rest of us. Nowadays this latter argument is out of fashion, but it is no less *logical* than the alternative.

Moving to the nurture half of the controversy, there appears to have developed an amnesia regarding the application of environmental explanations to the justification of homosexuality. Not long ago it was actively contended that if homosexuality were learned—as when little boys grow up with dominating mothers and passive fathers—a homosexual outcome could not entail culpability. Having no choice about who his parents were, or how they would raise him, the child could not possibly control how he would turn out. If anyone were responsible, it was therefore his parents, for they were the ones who shaped his behavior. Yet here too there is a counter-argument. Those who believe that homosexuality is a sin can agree that it is learned behavior, but still condemn the practice. All they need do is assert that what is learned can be unlearned. Children may have no choice regarding how they will be raised, but as adults can determine how they will live. When a person finds himself enmeshed in a homosexual lifestyle, it is thus his responsibility to take corrective action. If he does not, he is culpable.

The medical model, much to the chagrin of its proponents, offers no guidance in escaping this labyrinth. Though its idealization of biology places it squarely at the disposal of some options, it cannot corroborate any of these. All it can do is provide facts, yet as David Hume[38] emphasized, what *is* cannot, of itself, determine what *should* be. As seriously, an unexamined faith in circumscribed data can discourage an examination of the position of homosexuals in the larger heterosexual society. To be more specific, a dedication to proving the rectitude of gays has produced a plethora of information about brain chemistry and cultural diversity, but little regarding why tensions exist between heterosexuals and homosexuals. Though this is a conflict of long standing, its investigation, not being of advantage to either side, is egregiously neglected.

ROLE PROBLEMS

As with radical feminism and radical civil rights, there are alternative ways of conceiving the problems and, therefore, the solutions addressed by the medicalization ideal, alternatives that, not incidentally, entail less personal and social disruption. The medical model has proved its mettle in dealing with heart disease and the measles, but this is not automatically transferable to personal problems. Unfortunately, those dazzled by medicine's accomplishments are not inclined to envision other possibilities. Yet these too need to be considered.

When most people contemplate psychiatry, they conjure up images of the psychoanalyst's couch. Freud may be out of professional favor, but his technique for probing deep into the psyche to identify childhood traumas retains its sway over the popular imagination.[39] Because the average person suspects that if he ever needs a psychiatric intervention, it will entail coping with personal despondency, a technique oriented in this direction is appealing. The medical model, in contrast, is fixated on the problems of the psychotic. Its emphasis on chemical imbalances and genetic dispositions literally evolved from an effort to understand, and to relieve, conditions such as schizophrenia and manic-depressive illness. Comparing these with ordinary diseases proved heuristically fruitful, but doing the same with personal suffering is dubious. To call it "a disease like any other" is not only wrong; it is potentially debilitating.

Personal unhappiness is a common part of the human condition. In the Jewish community it is sometimes referred to as "michigas," that is, as a "little craziness." Once, when Freud[40] was asked to explain the goal of psychoanalysis, he described it as restoring a person to a state of "normal unhappiness." This captures the essence of his belief that we are all a tad off center regardless of what we publicly pretend. It turns out that this personal strangeness, and its attendant distress, is often related to our social roles. When these, rather than our brain physiology, go wrong, we experience the sort of discomfort that may require a professional consultation. Yet this phenomenon is so little understood that it feels mysterious, and because it does, people are inclined to assign its effects to something more tangible, such as brain chemistry.

We have already encountered social roles when discussing gender. There the division of labor between men and women was at issue, but here the question is broader. Social roles come in many guises; some are associated with gender, some with the jobs we perform at home or at work, some with our personal relationships. It is these last that concern us here. To be technical, roles are complex patterns of persistent interpersonal behaviors that are associated with specific social tasks or positions.[41] In the case of "personal" roles, these patterns are associated with us individually.[42] Each person, in growing up, gains a reputation for behaving in predictable ways. Partly this is thrust upon us by others in accord with their needs; partly it derives from our own preferences. The variations engendered are enormous, with all of us eventually enacting multiple overlapping roles. Among the possible blueprints are: the *family clown*, the *smart one*, the *scapegoat*, the *black sheep*, the *artist*, the *born leader*, the *family hero*, the *great beauty*, the *baby*, and the *rebel*.

Often these roles are confused with personal traits. It is assumed that a person's having an identifiable quality or talent is both the necessary and sufficient condition for the ascription of a role. But neither supposition is true. A person can have the quality and not be imputed the role, or not have it, and it may be ascribed anyway. In my own family this was manifest in the roles my sister and I were assigned. From our earliest days, I was known as the *smart one* and she the *dumb one*. When company came over, it was my responsibility to show how bright I was, while it was hers to do something foolish over which everyone could chuckle. Conversely, she was the *athletic one*, while I was the *klutz*. It was she who first demonstrated how to ride a bicycle and I who could not master the rudiments of using a hammer. Yet none of these characterizations derived unambiguously from who we were. They became, as it were, our niches in the family division of labor. A complex broth of abilities and desires emanating from all members of the family had contributed to erecting them. Moreover, they served important system functions, addressing our parents' needs, as well as our own. They were, in any event, misleading. My sister, for instance, was not, and is not, dumb. Nor am I so physically inept that I cannot tie a shoelace. There might have been some truth in how we were perceived—I was smart and she athletic—but our actual capacities were distorted so as to justify the way we were treated.

Many of these personal roles are rewarding to those enacting them. To be acclaimed for one's artistic ability or intelligence can be gratifying. Others, however, are crippling. *Scapegoats*[43] and *black sheep* are habitually excoriated for sins they never committed. A person trapped in such a role may, as a result, be unable to meet his needs and will probably be unhappy. The persistent character of his role assignment will consign him to unsatisfying activities and acrimonious relationships. Sadly and counterintuitively, despite his recognizing the repetitive nature of this distress, he will probably have difficulty in extricating himself from it. For reasons originating with the demands of his role partners and his internal emotional commitments, effortless change is virtually impossible. To describe him as being trapped in a "dysfunctional" role is, therefore, not a stretch. If this is true, also implied is a need to address, and replace, the defective role so as to achieve the tranquillity for which the person yearns.

Some years ago when I wrote *Role Change*,[44] I began with a thumbnail sketch of a former client I called Angela. One of the personal roles in which she was ensnared was that of a *rejected child*. Having been banished from her mother's company following an out-of-wedlock birth, once her mother married and had additional children, Angela was recalled from the exile she had endured at her grandparents' home. But even within the bosom of her reconstituted family, she remained an embarrassment who was never completely welcome. No matter what she did, she was blamed for deficiencies she could not seem to correct. Later in life, Angela passed through a series of unsatisfying relationships. Sooner or later, each ended when whomever she decided might make an appropriate partner rejected her. From her perspective, the reason for this was transparent; there was something wrong with her—something that made her anathema to other human beings. In therapy, however, it became apparent that she was sabotaging her relationships. Having previously assumed the mantle of the rejected child, she now behaved in ways that enlisted others in reenacting her family history. Angela was distressed by the rebuffs, but could not seem to prevent herself from precipitating them.

A familiar example of this apparently irrational tendency was also displayed by former president Richard Nixon. It is always dangerous to analyze someone from afar, but his self-destructive disposition has been so richly documented that is cries out for interpretation. With the caveat that the succeeding details may be in error and/or oversimplified, we can begin by observing that Nixon always seemed to get into scrapes from which he needed deliverance. He himself endorsed this interpretation in his book *Six Crises*.[45] In it, he recounts the dramatic events surrounding the Hiss case, the Checkers speech, and his 1960 campaign for president. Garry Wills,[46] in *Nixon Agonistes*, also examined these incidents, but did so from the interpretive context of a self-made man struggling to create an identity for himself. Neither of these chronicles, of course, included the most significant crisis in Nixon's career, namely the Watergate affair and its aftermath. Few human beings have had to overcome as huge a collapse, yet, remarkably, he did. By the time of his death, many observers marveled at how he had rehabilitated himself and appropriated the mantle of elder statesman.

If we step back from this roller coaster ride, and away from the partisan politics of recrimination and counter-recrimination, the repetitiveness of his adventures is startling. Buried amidst the historic paraphernalia is evidently the dysfunctional personal role of a sometimes tortured human being. To put a label on it, we might say that Nixon was the quintessential "*outsider*." But he was an outsider with a twist. He was an outsider who got to be on the inside, but was never comfortable there. Many commentators have been astonished at how so obviously a private man could have sought, and become successful, in so public a profession. Yet there he was, ill at ease with strangers, not given to small talk or gruff affability, clawing his way into the corridors of power, being knocked off course, often ejected from the ring completely, but coming back, time and again, against all odds and the fondest wishes of his enemies. The contrast with his arch-rival, Jack Kennedy, was stark, and to Nixon, galling. He too wanted to be a well-liked and charming insider, but, however much he tried, he could not. Neither he, nor his detractors, allowed his many victories to be definitive.

As with all of us, the roots of Nixon's *insider-outsider* role lay in his childhood. The second son of Quaker parents, he grew up in modest circumstances in southern California. His mother Hannah was a reserved, hard working, and religious woman. In his farewell speech at the White House, Nixon tearfully described her as a "saint." Apparently she was regarded as one by other people as well. She believed in doing the right thing, but doing it quietly. Nixon biographers, such as Stephen Ambrose,[47] relate few vivid stories about Hannah. As he says, no one "mentioned much joy in her life, there were no funny stories, no memory of pranks or laughter." Prepared to make sacrifices for others, she seems to have had difficulty in sharing herself emotionally. One of her outstanding qualities, however, was an ability to make others feel guilty. In adulthood, her children recalled with awe how much more fearful they were of being talked to by her than yelled at by her husband.

Nixon's father Frank was cut from very different cloth. Born into the Methodist church, he did not convert until he moved into predominantly Quaker Whittier, California. As a consequence, the calm, let-us-reason-together tradition of the Quakers did not come naturally to him. On the contrary, he tended to be "boisterous, argumentative, and much too loud to suit the Milhous girls," all save Hannah, that is. Initially a laborer, then the owner of a hard-scrabble lemon grove, then the proprietor of a more prosperous gas station and general store, he was an upright man and a pillar of the church, but also an abrasive one who had to be kept away from his customers lest he offend them. A far more vivid character than his wife, his passion lay in arguing politics, mostly of the Republican persuasion.

Though oddly matched opposites, Ambrose describes their union as "hugely successful," with "Hannah's calm ways, her compassion for others, her peaceful thoughts...a nice balance to Frank's excitability, his inability to see someone else's point of view, and his aggressive nature." Offered this harsh choice, Richard became his mother's son. Though he often debated politics with his father, and was deeply influenced by him, he was not one of the boys the way his brothers were. On the contrary, to quote Ambrose again, "There was a lot of noise and violence in the Nixon home, with Richard and his mother trying to keep the peace between Frank and his other two sons." Indeed Nixon later described himself as having developed an "aversion to personal confrontations" which he managed to dodge by immersing himself in daydreams and reading. A bright and competitive child, he was good at school, where his unusually sharp memory brought him notice. By the time he entered high school, he was active in school politics, the drama club, the debating society, and even tried dating. At one point, he had a steady girlfriend, but was neither "personable [nor] sexy with girls." According to Olga Florence, "he was smart, [but] set apart." By the time he graduated, and was offered a scholarship to Harvard, "He knew everyone in Whittier High, but had no real friends." Much to his disappointment, for financial reasons, he had to turn down Harvard, but after four years at Whittier College, was able to enroll at the prestigious Duke Law School and compete successfully while there.

Later on, of course, Nixon was to become an officer in the Navy, a United States Congressman, the Vice President of the United States, and President of the nation, but he was always set apart, never quite belonging. Ever eager to fit in, he was respected, and voted for, but rarely well-liked. Even Dwight Eisenhower, who raised him to presidential stature, seems to have harbored personal reservations. The pattern was thus similar to that of his school years in which he was admitted to insider positions because of his talents and energy, but once there, remained uncomfortably apart. Significantly, this pattern was also evident within his family of origin. There can be no doubt that Richard Nixon was loved. But the way in which he was loved placed him in an awkward position. He was not part of his father's company of boys, but the ally of his more emotionally remote mother. In a sense, he was an insider with her, but an insider without the sort of nurturance that usually accompanies being included. This must have been confusing and disharmonious, leaving the young Nixon feeling like a foreigner in his own home, uncertain about what, if anything, he could do to fit in—a conundrum he was never to resolve.

Nixon's *insider-outsider* role sprang from many sources. Though no one consciously mandated it, it was negotiated among a variety of parties. One source was unquestionably his parents, whose mode of relating to each other and to their children set the stage for the tasks he would find available. Another was Nixon himself. Were he less intelligent, competitive, or shy, he would not have selected the solutions he did.[48] They simply would not have been congenial. Though he apparently shared many temperamental traits with his parents, these would have found different expressions had he not had the opportunities he did.

What is nevertheless striking is the repetitive nature of his behavior. In essence, a role constructed in childhood survived to configure his most sophisticated adult relationships. Sigmund Freud spoke of a "repetition compulsion." He noticed that many of his patients recapitulated their earliest interactions later on in life. Indeed, they seemed not to be able to help themselves. Quite unconsciously they stumbled into the same dilemmas they had previously vowed never to repeat. Women who had been abused by their fathers married husbands who abused them. Men whose confidence had been undermined by insensitive mothers found jobs with bosses who likewise undermined their confidence.

A social role interpretation explains these sorts of incongruity quite handily. Virtually all personal roles, the helpful and the harmful, are learned early in life and repeated later on. As part of someone's identity, they are recapitulated because they are integral to who the person is. Moreover, unless replaced by other roles, they are destined to be recycled, often unto death. But another wrinkle must be acknowledged here. As Freud stressed, that which is too painful to be experienced will be repressed. No longer apparent, it does not disappear, but operates at an unconscious level. This, in fact, is the standard fate of dysfunctional roles. They are so deeply submerged that the person enacting them tends not to recognize them. To her, they signify a mystery. On the surface, she may understand that, as her friends have been telling her, she should avoid falling in love with a man as violent as her father, but when she begins courting, she will feel certain that this new man is sensitive and gentle. Only after the wedding will his real self gradually become apparent. But as this realization sinks in, it will make no sense to her that she did not notice it before. The only answer that does will be that there is something wrong with her. She must be defective. Perhaps she suffers from a physiologically based personality disorder that requires medical treatment. Such recurring troubles are nonetheless the signature of role problems. They epitomize a person's obsession with reworking interpersonal patterns that have never worked as desired.

But a person's problems will not end here. The distress she has to endure will extend beyond that associated with the dysfunctional role itself. Its inability to meet her requirements for love and respect may be agonizing, but the process of moving on to something better will also be painful. As a component of her personal identity, the role, no matter how uncomfortable, cannot be lightly sloughed off. Neither good nor bad ones permit themselves to be dropped or covered over; they must be relinquished. Because their host is invariably attached to them, just as when a loved one dies, these personal roles have to be grieved over and imperceptibly allowed to recede into the past. The physician Elizabeth Kubler-Ross[49] is responsible for explicating the requisite sequence with respect to death. Several stages, including denial, anger, bargaining, depression, and acceptance must be endured before equanimity returns. Yet when a role, as opposed to a deceased relative, is to be relinquished, these phases tend to be prolonged and obscure. Because roles are inherently less observable than death, it is difficult to tell when they are irretrievably lost. As a result, a denial of their failures is more troublesome to penetrate and the need for social support less manifest. Ironically, the medical model, by concealing these factors, only intensifies the difficulty.

Resocialization—for this is what role change is officially called—though the appropriate mechanism for overcoming a dysfunctional role, can drag on for years. When it is accomplished with the assistance of a helping professional, it is typically referred to as psychotherapy,[50] but it can also occur unobserved and unremarked. In any case, the more central a role is to a person's sense of self, the more angst, turmoil, and sadness that can be expected. Yet, as with the dysfunctional role itself, the origin and purpose of these symptoms can be enigmatic. The tendency is, therefore, to convert them into a more substantial form by interpreting each as a separate problem and labeling it a "disorder." This, however, is no more than a manifestation of the fact that an allegiance to the medical model predisposes people to attribute their discomfort to physiological afflictions. Unhappily, this, in turn, makes it more likely that they will rely on medications and less likely that they will utilize their own resources.

When resocialization runs its course undeflected by medical obstructions, a person's ability to construct more satisfying roles is enhanced. In the end, she has a greater chance of gaining mastery over her life and of becoming what she has the capacity to be. As importantly, from a role perspective, self-control is decidedly possible. As negotiated products, her behavioral patterns, while not strictly within her control, are subject to her influence because she actively participates in their creation. Although she may be unable to short-circuit the steps needed to bury a failed role, she can consciously resolve to engineer its replacement. If desirous of more satisfying roles, she can commit herself to enduring the intense emotionality of role change and to developing the competence of a successful renegotiator. None of this is intrinsically less scientific than the medical alternative. It is simply a different way of understanding what goes wrong, and might—just might—be superior.[51]

SOCIAL CONTROL

The radical medicalization ideal has also be used to supplant a whole range of social controls. Taken to its logical conclusion, it virtually excludes personal responsibility and most collective modes of social discipline. And yet, say the medicalists, this is required by the alternatives. The real danger, according to them, comes from chants and spells, incantations and trances, voodoo dolls, and sheep entrails.[52] Such magical forms of control are not only uninformed, but also a potential source of flagrant abuse. Even today, in parts of the Pacific, Africa, and South America, thousands of private individuals use witchcraft to summon the spirits of the dead to afflict those who have offended their sense of justice or their desire for ascendancy.[53] When a favorite tool is stolen, a wife seduced, or a crop fails, they seek to punish those responsible. To modern minds, the vagueness, subjectivity, and inefficiency of this policy is alarming. Its vulnerability to maltreatment and error leaves them trembling with dread and searching for a superior option.

Many find their salvation in a combination of biology, chemistry, and the philosophy of Jean-Jacques Rousseau. In their view, as long as a person's body, and more specifically his brain, is functioning normally, there is no need for external controls. Just as Rousseau[54] assumed that human beings are born pure and then corrupted by civilization, they are convinced that physiologically healthy people instinctively make sound choices when they are not constrained to do otherwise. If they do something immoral, it must be because their systems have been thrown out of kilter. Fortunately, when this does occur, control can be restored by disinterested medical specialists who have been trained to recognize what has gone wrong and know how to rectify it.

Yet this self-proclaimed scientific analysis offers as gross a simplification as its more primitive competitors. Ensuring conformity with important social rules is one of the most complex of all human endeavors, possessing as it does many dimensions that may be invoked in a host of different manners. Those who assume that there is only one best way to enforce moral behavior engage in a perilous fallacy that, at its worst, encourages a concentration of authority in too few hands. Still, making a choice regarding how to intercede in a control situation can be bewildering. When trying to determine the most effective mechanism in a particular case, among the alternatives from which one may choose are: (a) the religious versus the scientific, (b) the formal versus the informal, and (c) the reward versus the punishment.

Thus the religious versus scientific antithesis enjoins people to decide what causes rule breaking and therefore what can best prevent it. If engaging in evil results from being manipulated by the devil, then spiritual experts should be consulted, with priests, shamans, and prayer books being the most appropriate instruments of amelioration. If, however, hormonal imbalances are at fault, medical experts are more fitting, with therapists, drugs, and hospitals taking precedence. This dichotomy, however, leaves out some significant options. There is, for instance, what might be termed the civic alternative.[55] Families, business organizations, and governments all seek to proscribe certain behaviors. While their theories of causality may be less refined than those of the theologians and scientists, their methods are more so. Modern political states have, in fact, evolved an immense panoply of control devices. Their police forces apprehend wrongdoers, their court systems determine who has broken the law, and their penal institutions prevent the commission of further crimes. Indeed, these modalities continue to become more elaborate, with new laws, fresh precedents, and alternative punishments emerging on a regular basis.

The formal versus informal dimension, in contrast, requires a choice between official or unofficial enforcement agencies. Are professionals, a bureaucratic hierarchy, or written regulations indispensable for control or can it arise locally and unconsciously? Formal mechanisms are usually easy to identify—proclaiming themselves with buildings, uniforms, and legislative assemblies—but, for all that, they are not necessarily the most effective. The natural, and unplanned, disapproval and ostracism of friends and relatives are also potent, if frequently underestimated, instruments. Paradoxically, we typically fear them more than we do a jail term.

Punishment versus reward also requires decisions. Are positive or negative sanctions more effective? Almost everyone agrees that some form of external sanction is essential to enforcing moral rules, but should people be praised or blamed, have their self-esteem enhanced or undermined, or be incarcerated or allowed out on their own recognizance? Opinions are divided. Some are for penalties; others for additional supports.

Devotees of the medical model, as might be expected, have no difficulty in deciding. Their ideal certifies that the science, formal, and reward poles of these dichotomies are always to be preferred. Science is equated with truth, formalism with organization, and reward with compassion. Anyone who would choose otherwise must, therefore, do so from ignorance or malignity. Whether or not they appreciate it, they would thereby abet falsity, confusion, and depravity. The medicalist vision assumes that once upon a time society was mired in a dark age from which it emerged only with difficulty. Having since then moved onto broad enlightened uplands, for us to sustain this progress, it is essential to cling to rationality and decency. Civilization is too fragile an achievement to be left undefended.

Yet there are dissenters. James Q. Wilson,[56] who emphatically identifies himself as a social scientist, vigorously contends that there is a difference between judging and explaining. Science may identify causes, but causes in themselves cannot assign responsibility. As he observes, "One can concede—indeed, if one is an especially ambitious social scientist, one will proclaim—that all human behavior is caused." But if "caused" means to be beyond the control of the actor—which, in fact, it does not—then as Michael Moore[57] affirms, this would inevitably lead to the absurd conclusion that "Nobody can be blamed for anything." With regard to moral questions, this is unacceptable. What is at stake is accountability, not a dispassionate description of which action instigates what outcome. As Wilson explains, the goal is first to send "a message to people who are learning to behave that they ought to acquire those habits and beliefs that will facilitate their conformity to the essential rules of civilized conduct, [and] second, [that] a strict view of personal accountability [should convey] a message to individuals choosing between alternative courses of action that there are important consequences that are likely to flow from making a bad choice." The scientific study of behavior can help determine who should be held responsible, but this is not the same as holding them responsible. To conclude that science is the exclusive repository of social control is therefore an unscientific mistake.

Wilson himself has helped clarify the crucial role of civil institutions in maintaining social order. By highlighting the "broken window effect" he has called attention to the fact that if a society wants its standards observed, it must enforce the little ones as well as the big ones, and it must enforce these promptly. If broken windows, graffiti, or derelicts sprawled in cardboard boxes are allowed to persist unhindered, they will not only endure, but also send a signal that more serious infractions too will be tolerated. The validity of Wilson's hypothesis has, in recent years, been confirmed by the dramatic decrease in major crime experienced in New York City once it began cracking down on minor violations.

Rational dissent regarding too narrow a reliance on formal control mechanisms is also possible. Morality, in fact, is more dependent on informal controls. To judge from contemporary biases this might not be suspected, for wherever one looks, there has been an explosion in formal regulations. Statutes, administrative guidelines, and legal precedents have multiplied beyond the capacity of anyone to keep track. The police, for instance, though officially charged with executing the law, can no longer be sure of its details. They haven't the time to read its many incarnations, never mind to reconcile the disparities and contradictions. Philip Howard,[58] in his *The Death of Common Sense: How Law Is Suffocating America*, has cataloged this proliferation. His thesis is that in an effort to reduce ambiguities, and to ensure equity, official rules have been applied to almost every aspect of life. As a result, the courts are clogged with cases and administrative enforcement agencies, such as OSHA, have arrogantly demanded compliance with a horde of trivial, and often irrelevant, ordinances. Bricks are defined as hazardous substances, guard rails are required be exactly 42 inches high, and nuns are forced to install elevators they cannot afford into buildings where they will not be used.

This impulse is also visible in the APA's *Diagnostic and Statistical*[59] manuals. Their burgeoning number of ever more exquisitely defined categories theoretically makes for more effective treatment, but in reality generates confusion, disputes, and false precision. Moreover, the increasing application of medical interventions to personal problems has resulted in psychiatrists invading elementary schools after a madman shoots down students, in college counselors advising married students to divorce so that they can "find themselves," and in social workers plucking infants out of their homes because a disgruntled neighbor has filed a complaint. While it cannot be doubted that the professionalization of helpers has brought improvements, these have not been uniform. Nor would ensuring them a monopoly better the situation. What happened during the 1950s is instructive. Educators at the time proclaimed that parents must not interfere with teaching their children how to read. As the experts, teachers demanded exclusive rights to the task for themselves. But this turned out to be a serious mistake because, for as we today know, parental involvement is the single best predictor of educational success. The methods Mom and Dad employ may not derive from pedagogical theory, but they work nevertheless.

The fact is that morality is largely a matter of unconscious and unregulated interventions. These may be informal, but they are emphatically not inept. One of the main elements of morality, it will be recalled, is its intense emotionality. Anger,[60] guilt, shame, and disgust are vital to how it functions, being, among others things, its first line of defense in assuring compliance with accepted principles.[61] Official rules, with their exact statements and designated enforcement agents, contribute to preventing murder and thievery, but have neither the coverage nor the internal access of moral emotions. Feelings, in contrast, are everywhere and in everyone. They can be overheard in the chatter of gossiping friends and observed in the storm-tossed sleep of the remorseful adolescent. Medicalists might like to believe that a potentially infallible internal moral compass resides within every healthy person, but it could not, and would not, be present without the prior operation of these emotions.

What is more, informal moral sanctions depend heavily on praise and blame. When a child does the right thing, he sees it in his parents' sparkling eyes, and when it's wrong, in their furrowed brows. Angry blame does not have to shout to be heard. Nor does it have to follow a person around or fling him into a castle dungeon. Because it is converted into guilt that the person carries internally, it is extraordinarily efficient and extraordinarily difficult to evade. Similarly shame, which seems so modest an instrument, can be excruciating to endure. People will change the way they dress, how they talk, and whom they befriend rather than bear it. This means that social norms enforced by emotional sanctions are often more strictly observed that those dependent on fines or imprisonment. What good is it to a thief to have eluded detection by the police, if his friends and relatives will not allow him to buy them a drink because they do not want to be tainted by his ill-gotten gains?

While disregarding the power of either civil or informal sanctions can be disastrous—each is too integral a part of social control to be dismissed—the most egregious error of the medical model is in neglecting punishment as a legitimate form of restraint. Its reverence for reward in instilling desired behaviors is not only excessive, but also misplaced. Besides discarding a potent tool, it opens the floodgates to "excuse abuse." Though its adherents seem not to realize it, when an abhorrence of punishment becomes too great, it facilitates an evasion of responsibility.

The modern era has witnessed a veritable stampede away from punishment. In area upon area, it has been denounced as superfluous and inappropriate. First, in religion, the movement has been from a vengeful God to a merciful one. No longer do preachers hurl fire and brimstone from the pulpit; instead they remind their congregations that heaven belongs to the sensitive and loving. In philosophy, a comparable trend is discernible in its extolling the gentle art of excuse making.[62] J.L. Austin,[63] one of architects of analytic philosophy, wrote an article literally entitled "A Plea for Excuses" in which he argued that these could not be minimized when conduct is challenged. Extenuations, palliations, mitigations, partial justifications, as well as simple excuses, were, in his view, all legitimate responses to attack. Sociologists too have followed this lead and reinforced it. In a critically acclaimed article called "Accounts," Marvin Scott and Stanford Lyman[64] suggested that words can be used to elucidate why something apparently blameworthy is really a blameless accident, a biological inevitability, or was compelled by a third party. Erving Goffman[65] in his book *Relations in Public* likewise elaborated upon this theme, expanding it into the larger domain of "remedial work" which he reported to include accounts, apologies, and requests. Sociologists have similarly promoted "labeling theory"[66] which alleges that crime and mental illness are caused by identifying people as criminal or psychotic. Locking them up in prisons or mental hospitals is what, in fact, produces their deviant persona. The implication is that ordinary people must refrain from inflicting what Goffman[67] called "stigma," lest they create a self-fulfilling prophecy. The overall effect has therefore been to legitimize rule breaking and to provide loopholes for escaping chastisement.

Academic psychologists too have been active in derogating punishment. In an exemplary summary of their positions, John Staddon[68] offers the views of B.F. Skinner as representative. Among the propositions Skinner has vouched-safe are that punishment is ineffective, that it is dangerously subject to counterattack, and that reward is always a more profitable option. Staddon demurs. According to him, laboratory tests with rats clearly demonstrate that punishment works and has persistent effects. Although it is often resisted, this is not always successful. Nor is reward particularly useful in suppressing behaviors—which incidentally is what morality aims to do. Indeed, it is a combination of reward *and* punishment that works best. As most people instinctively learn, carrots and sticks are preferable to either alone. Every now and then, one of my students who has taken a course in psychology authoritatively proclaims that violence is invariably wrong—that it never settles anything, but, as I hastily point out, the Civil War and World War II, each heavy on punishment, made huge, and lasting, differences.

Moving closer to purely medical excuses, one finds those derived from psychotherapy. Although a clinical psychologist, Carl Rogers[69] has been responsible for an outlook that has come to pervade all sorts of talking cures, including the psychiatric. Rogers claimed that successful therapeutic relationships depend on the clinician maintaining "unconditional positive regard" for the client. He or she has to be "nonjudgmental," clearly distinguishing between the person, who is basically good—in the Rousseauian sense—and what he or she has done, which may be bad.[70] Despite being dressed up as science, this essentially recapitulates the Christian injunctions to love thy neighbor as thyself and to turn the other cheek. It explicitly enjoins the clinician to abstain from blame.

Unfortunately, while often appropriate within a clinical setting, this stance has been applied to all sorts of other relationships. Everyone, we are told, deserves unqualified acceptance all of the time. In therapy, of course, overtly blaming a client is an excellent vehicle for alienating him and for terminating the collaboration. Typically, people who come for therapy feel vulnerable. Having experienced multiple failures, rejections, and frustrations, they are in a defensive posture. To point a finger at them at such a moment and bark out, "You scoundrel!" is thus almost guaranteed to provoke a negative reaction. Yet even here, withholding blame is not the same as making no judgment. I once had a client who murdered his wife. After he confronted her for cheating on him, she counterattacked by impugning his manhood. He then lost control and shot her. Decades later, he was still contrite. In this context, had I said, "It was not your fault," or "I accept you regardless of what you did," he would have perceived me as an amoral fool and our relationship would have abruptly terminated. Rather, we both agreed that murder was wrong and that he shouldn't have done it. All I needed to do to be therapeutically correct was to refrain from rubbing his nose in the act. In a nonclinical setting, a tactful honesty regarding moral judgments is similarly appropriate. There are situations in which overt blame is counterindicated, but denying the validity of making any judgment whatsoever only exacerbates problems. As most of us realize, when a person violates an important rule, passively accepting this is equivalent to condoning the behavior.

In medicine proper, punitive judgments are often circumvented by treating destructive behaviors as if they were physiological manifestations of disease.[71] Taught that diseases are responsive to chemotherapy, physicians hasten to prescribe drugs in a multitude of circumstances.[72] This they can achieve without any reference to the patient's moral status, with the result that legitimate blame is often replaced by a note to the pharmacy.

In the legal system, which has for more than a century been colonized by medical thinking, ostensibly physiological excuses have progressively gained ground. Starting with the M'Naghten Rule which canceled a person's culpability for murder if he did not "know the nature and quality of the act," it has introduced defeasibility for a hodgepodge of unusual mental states.[73] If someone's deeds are the product of a mental disease or defect, or if he lacks a "substantial capacity" to appreciate the wrongfulness of what he did, lawyers and judges have sought to relieve him of an oppressive prison term. Presumably, if he did not understand his behaviors, and could not regulate them, then punishment would be wasted. In a sense, his defect is punishment enough and does not have to be intensified through gratuitous discomfort.

But this is to beg the question. It assumes that negative sanctions are ineffective over a broad range of mental conditions. The real question, as Wilson states, is whether a legal system can "foster self-control by stigmatizing and punishing its absence." The point of enforced rules, it must be recognized, is to dissuade people from doing that which they are either tempted or predisposed to do. If those with mental abnormalities, whether or not these are caused by disease, can be influenced by moral restraints, then blaming or incarcerating them is a valid form of discipline. Currently, in cases of negligence, people are held liable when they fail to see that which is "in plain sight." Being distracted, when one should not be, is not considered an excuse. To ask that those with emotional limitations do likewise is, therefore, not to demand the impossible. On the other hand, inventing reasons for evading moral requirements, is not an indicator of civilization, but of a misplaced sympathy. Thus to a posteriori accept claims that a person is the victim of intoxication, a postpartum depression, excessive stress, years of battery, or eating too many Twinkies does not relieve her of the duty to exercise discretion. Nor does it demonstrate that her judge is especially sensitive. To reiterate, neither biological nor social causations themselves certify an inability to exercise control. If anything, their presence suggests that control is *more* necessary. It is, after all, the person born with a violent temperament who must be most vigilant regarding his anger and the one caught in the vortex of an urban riot who is most responsible for keeping his emotional distance.

The medical model by tilting overmuch to physiological explanations, formalized interventions, and nonpunitive sanctions deprives people of protections they not only deserve, but require. Historically, no society has survived without religious, informal, and painful sanctions. Radical medicalists, by insisting that they must—like other ideologues—foster a fantasy. In explaining personal responsibilities away, their favored ideal leaves out too much. What is worse, in promoting its exclusivity, they interfere with adopting more viable practices. Does this mean that medicine, professional control agents, or personal rewards have no place in the enforcement of moral standards? Of course not. Social control is sufficiently important, and complex, to benefit from a variety of approaches. What is needed is a comprehensive and flexible outlook, not an ideological straightjacket.

Chapter 8

Luminosity Blindness

THE SANTA CLAUS BETRAYAL

At five I had my suspicions, but by six I knew—there was no Santa Claus. My family might not have been Christian, but Santa visited our house too. Although there was no tree or fireplace, we hung stockings from the living room bookcases and early on Christmas morning a wealth of brightly wrapped packages were spread out beneath them. It was a magical time for us kids. My father was not a demonstrative man, but one of the ways in which he could express his love was by showering us with anonymous presents. There was always a wondrous variety of unexpected goodies. We children could barely contain our glee awaiting the morning and even before the sun rose would sneak out of our beds to reconnoiter the situation. Opening our gifts was always a thrill, with smiles and giggles punctuating the air, as we ripped the wrapping paper off the brightly colored boxes and then tested out our haul.

At first I did believe. The holiday was such fun that when my parents told me about this jolly old elf in a red suit who, once a year, rewarded good little boys and girls, I didn't question them. Even though they said he came down the chimney and we had no chimney, I still believed. So did my sister. Two and a half years younger than I, she did not fully understand what was happening, but loved it anyway. Indeed, as my doubts grew, her faith intensified. I'm not sure what first aroused my skepticism. It may have been hearing delighted noises coming from the living room one Christmas Eve after I had supposedly gone to sleep. Or it might have been something a classmate said. In any event, I do remember having cracked open the

185

bedroom door and caught my parents hunched over what looked like festive packages. The next year I went searching through the house before the appointed day and found toys squirreled about in a variety of out of the way places. The experience was eerie—exciting, confusing, and disappointing, all at the same time.

When I related this discovery to my sister, she was unimpressed. Although I now insisted that there was no Santa Claus, she refused to believe me. Certainly when on Christmas Day our parents reassured us that these marvelous playthings had come from him, there was nothing I could say that would dissuade her. She even taunted me with a: "See, I told you so." The next year I was better prepared. This time when I found the concealed presents, I brought her to the spot. There, at the top of the kitchen cabinet, once I had pulled over a step stool to reach them, were a doll, a truck, and several other items. One, a plastic trumpet, I was confident had to be for her because I was too big for it. Four or five at the time, she could barely bring herself to trust her eyes. When, however, on Christmas Day, these very objects appeared under the bookcases, she too was converted. She wasn't happy about the matter, but the proof was too strong. I wasn't happy either, but it was because the trumpet I thought for her had my name on it.

Every year, variations on this theme are played out across the globe. Millions of children who have learned to await the arrival of the mythic sprite—children who know the names of his reindeer and his wife by heart, children who have sent letters to the North Pole requesting specific gifts, children who pleaded to leave cookies out for him—are shocked when they encounter the truth. Many work overtime to deny its validity, but sooner or later, they too must capitulate. It is a rite of passage that few evade. Parents believe that the Santa myth brings joy to childhood and are convinced that refusing it to their offspring would cruelly deny them its proofs of love, fun, and protection, and they are right. The holiday's merriment is a wonderful, life-affirming elixir. But there is another, far darker message embedded within it. Eventually the myth is always shattered, and when it is, this is experienced as a betrayal. What children believe to be real is revealed to be an illusion, and what is worse, an illusion that was foisted upon them by people they thought they could trust.

The pain of finding out that Santa is not real is one of the formative disillusionments of life, one that may be resisted, but not proscribed. As the opening wedge of a long series of discoveries that demonstrate that the world is not what it seems, it can be alarming. It alerts us that there may be nasty surprises lurking inside the most commonplace occurrences. Ultimately we are all inducted into a massive game of social stickball where at any moment we can lose our way and fall on our faces. For better or worse, the uncertainty, strife, and disappointment intrinsic to growing up await us all. And yet it is essential that we begin the process of realizing that our idealizations are erroneous fairly early on. An ability to adjust to these shocks is just as imperative for our sanity as is a belief that the universe is a fundamentally secure place.[1] Still, no child can, all at once, absorb the complexities that must be mastered. The journey to enlightenment is always slow and tentative. Little by little, we are exposed to an expanding swarm of unpleasant revelations. Without anyone planning it, we are enticed to believe things that are untrue, then placed in circumstances where we cannot escape their disconfirmation.

Disillusionment, as we learned earlier, is normal. But this does not mean that it is automatic. We usually oppose the necessary disclosures with all our might. In the 1960s, the conventional wisdom had it that growing up invariably concluded with a person selling out and teenagers were advised never to trust anyone over thirty. Today, having grown to adulthood, this same generation has learned what their parents knew before them, that few things are simple and that even the "over thirty" injunction is an overgeneralization. These now grownups find themselves in a position analogous to that of Mark Twain[2] when, as an adult, he was forced to reassess his father's capabilities. In his teens, Twain recalled, he had been appalled by how little his father knew, but by the time he was in his twenties, he was amazed at how much he had learned in the interim.

Some specimens of disillusionment are, in retrospect, almost amusing. Most children, for example, imagine that their parents are too asexual to have ever engaged in intercourse. Their friends' parents may have lowered themselves to something so vulgar, but not theirs. Other fantasies are more serious. A belief that authority figures are inevitably well informed and benevolent is one of these. So is the conviction that important decisions are habitually made in a wise and orderly fashion. It can take decades to figure out that many determinations result from social negotiations in which no one is in charge. The fact is that politics are universal within human institutions. Large-scale enterprises are rife with individuals maneuvering for advantage and coalitions striving for dominance. Most people abhor the intrigues these involve and hope someday to find themselves in a more pristine environment, but they are destined to be disappointed. Although some organizations are more just, and tame, than others, none are without the irrationalities inherent in unplanned and passionate conflict.[3]

The irony is that despite their loathing of being fooled, most people cooperate in maintaining a variety of fictions. Because they continue to imagine that their idealizations can protect them from what they dread, they refuse to recognize these for what they are. In the 1930s Chester Barnard,[4] himself an executive, wrote a book, *The Function of the Executive*, in which he discussed what he called the "myth of supreme authority." In explaining why those who exercise organizational power are obeyed, he theorized that without the cooperation of their underlings, they could never impose their will. As insecure human beings themselves, they were often unsure about what would work best, and depended on those to whom they gave orders to assume that they knew what they were talking about. Fortunately for them, most of their subordinates enthusiastically conspired in unconsciously projecting powers onto them that they did not possess. These underlings assumed that their boss must have gotten where he was because he was smarter, tougher, and better informed than they. It could, therefore, come as a jolt to discover that some superiors are, to put it mildly, jerks. This might be so disconcerting that a subordinate would rather rationalize the situation by concluding that it was an exception. The truth is, however, that all bosses, no matter how competent, have their limitations. The notion that they are mysteriously efficacious is a soap bubble that can be burst by anyone with the courage to prick it. Few of us do, however, because we are emotionally invested in believing that someone is both willing, and able, to guard us against our own frailties.

More poignant by far are the disappointments experienced in quest of perfect love. These defeats too are initially denied by most of us. In popular mythology, love is supposed to conquer all and he who has the good fortune to achieve it, will, theoretically, be healed by it. Whatever frustrations one may have had to endure before that miraculous moment arrives will be cast aside and life become an endless sea of enchantment. Surely, every adolescent is convinced that the truly loved, and loving, walk on air, their heads befuddled by joy and their hearts overflowing with magnanimity. No wonder then that so many engage in the frenzied pursuit of the perfect relationship. But why, one must ask, do so few attain it? It cannot be from a lack of effort, for the collective investment is staggering. Curiously, those for whom love is an obsession often end up the least fulfilled. Instead of procuring the never ending infatuation they seek, they frequently enter relationships with partners who are insensitive, selfish, and unable to help them attain their innermost needs.

The desperation implicit in the love myth was glaringly apparent among patients at the Rochester Psychiatric Center. Schizophrenia[5] is an insidious disease. Its onset is usually in the late teens or early twenties, just when a person is getting ready to venture out into adult society. Though the victim has often been regarded as having a promising future, suddenly a dramatic break with reality in which he hears voices, imagines himself prey to a huge conspiracy, or, worst of all, is frozen in catatonic isolation, intervenes to derail his hopes. Whatever his symptoms, he is no longer regarded as normal or sought after as an attractive intimate partner. At RPC, many of these casualties wandered around like lost puppies. When they came to see me, they generally complained of having no future and no prospect of having someone of the opposite sex ever finding them deserving. Eventually many came to the conclusion that only someone suffering from the same disorder as they could care about them. Only such a person would understand their symptoms or recognize that these did not cancel out their humanity. The result was a rash of hospital romances. Despite their mutual condition, the light of love shown in the eyes of these twosomes. What was even better, they discovered a future. Like anyone embarked on a close relationship, they made plans for renting an apartment, seeking a job, or having a child. With each other's support, they were certain to find the strength to surmount whatever complications arose.

This, however, was not the cinema and happy endings were rare. The standard outcome was that after several months the relationship foundered. If they had moved into an apartment together, after awhile they returned to counseling protesting that their partner had deceived them. Much to their despair, he or she had proven neither understanding nor caring. Despite a solemn pact to meet each other's needs, this perfidious other had reneged on the agreement. As the aggrieved party explained in excruciating detail, she had begged for relief, often tearfully on her knees, but this had been ignominiously rebuffed. Rather incongruously, both parties told similar stories. Each was painfully aware that his or her needs were not being met and blamed the other for not coming through.

The difficulty was that each found his or her own issues more salient than the other's. Thus, when either turned to the other for help, this partner seemed oblivious to these entreaties. And the more each clamored to be heard, the more certain it was that the other would be too self-absorbed to respond. What neither realized is that a mutually supportive relationship depends as much on an ability to give as to benefit from receiving. Because both were extremely needy, although they wished to be supportive, they were unable to do so. Moreover, in their desperation, they became so insistent on securing relief, that their company was burdensome. Sadly, one of life's most tragic paradoxes is that those with the most to gain from love are typically the least apt to obtain it. Their very agony undermines the quest. On the other hand, those raised in loving environments, and therefore who already feel good about themselves, are more able to give love and, as a consequence, to elicit it.

This is not good news for those who idealize love. If they expect to be rescued, they are sure to be disappointed. In their imaginations, they may be confident that it will enable them to blossom, but it has no such power. Although this is grossly unfair, if they are to be saved, it is they who must do the saving. Yet the illusion of deliverance is so potent that it can be traumatic to relinquish. More than a betrayal by a specific individual, it can feel like a betrayal by life itself. Unfortunately, when hope depends on a fantasy, anything that threatens this will be experienced as a personal assault, which means that the impulse to oppose it can be astonishingly strong.

Just how emotionally devastating disillusionment can be has been candidly revealed by David Horowitz[6] in his often heart-rending memoir *Radical Son*. The child of 1930s era Communist Party loyalists, he grew up being taught that the salvation of mankind depended upon the outbreak of a socialist revolution that would convert everyone into loving brothers and equal owners of society's riches. So determined was he to fulfill his parent's fantasy, that he devoted the first half of his adult life to promoting it, even rising to become editor of the radical journal *Ramparts*. When, at last, he began to have doubts about the humanitarian consequences of his convictions—largely occasioned by the Black Panther murder of a woman he had recommended for employment—he not only experienced the agonies of no longer having a personal compass, but found himself shunned by colleagues who refused to allow their own beliefs to be challenged. Ostracized, slandered, and confused, he sunk into a depression that nearly paralyzed his professional life and for years threw his intimate relations into turmoil.

It becomes apparent why disillusionment is often regarded as a menace. Idealizations are not merely pleasant diversions, but integral elements in a defense against failure. People need hope. Though they cannot manipulate the world as they might wish, they can manipulate their representations of it. Because none of us is able to ensure that our needs will always be met, in our imaginations we can at least comfort ourselves with the conviction that some day they will. Deep inside all our souls we continue to believe that Santa Claus is alive and well, and living in a house just around the corner. But there is a danger in this. Unencumbered gifts are not the norm. Depending upon them to make reality bearable is to invite ruin. Indeed, too spirited a resistance to accepting life's boundaries sets one up for calamity. For one thing, too great a hunger after salvation makes one susceptible to chicanery—either from oneself or others. This explains why, in part, idealism can go too far and induce people to hold on to beliefs with no empirical foundation or prospect of such a foundation.

HARD TRUTHS

When I was a counselor, my clients and acquaintances would periodically recommend books they had found inspirational. One of the perennial favorites was M. Scott Peck's[7] *The Road Less Traveled*. It begins with a line that was quoted to me many times: "Life is difficult." The next paragraph continues, "This is a great truth, one of the greatest truths." "Yes," my confidants would solemnly intone, "Life is difficult! It is true!" Then they would patiently explain why this had been a liberating insight that relieved them of the fear that their own difficulties were unique and a product of personal deficiencies. Peck would surely agree. He too believed that only an acceptance of life's pains can make it less ominous; that only then are people freed from tilting with the inevitable windmills.

Yet the same individuals who cheerfully informed me that existence was difficult did not relish acknowledging its hard facts. Admitting that life, in general, was demanding was one thing, but confronting its particular dilemmas was quite another. Though people may vary in what they find daunting, a fair sample can be gleaned from what they use their ideals to conceal. We have already discussed a number of these cases. Disorienting modifications in the gender division of labor, the vulnerabilities inherent in intimate relationships, personal limitations arising from a dysfunctional cultural legacy, the vicissitudes in asserting relative power—especially where racial differences exist, the obstinate predicaments buried within our personal roles, and the world's need to exercise coercive external restraints to maintain social order have each proven too distressing for some people to endure. In fact, change itself can be difficult to withstand. The very process of making things different can be traumatic, involving as it does emotional upheavals and unfulfilled expectations. Because no one likes to lose, and because we all have weaknesses, the impulse not to examine that which we are unable to dispel is eternal.

In his *Marginalized in the Middle* Alan Wolfe[8] stresses the difference between realism and romanticism. As a sociological critic, he construes his responsibility to be the dispassionate examination of social realities, many of which he knows to be unpleasant. Various other critics, however, start from a very different position. As romantics, they "begin with the proposition that the existing society is so corrupt, its practices so decadent, its institutions so warped, that the only effective criticism is one of passionate rejection. The critic's vocation is to denounce and, in so doing, to express longings that will be visionary, imaginative, hopeful." Such critics "resonate with romanticism" looking as they do "beyond the injustice of today to the utopia of tomorrow."

Romantics can be both liberal and conservative—their attacks on "bourgeois" values coming either from the left or the right. The primary qualification for inclusion in their ranks is not a particular belief structure, but a tendency to dismiss that which exists in favor of that which never was. As Wolfe points out, most of these visionaries are self-involved. Their dreams, though ostensibly directed toward the future, are more indicative of personal fantasies. Whether these apparitions invoke a world of organic harmony, traditional values, or loving spontaneity, as a rule, they are likely to be more poetic than scientific. Often romantics are self-consciously theoretical, which means that they are also detached from reality; hence their recommendations are difficult to implement. Although the range of their proposals is enormous, these have been distressingly unproductive. As Wolfe enumerates, romantics, if they are "educational theorists...envision schools that will remake personalities[9]...[and if] enthusiasts for immigrants romanticize cultural differences. [Likewise,] unseemly realities such as pornography will be wished away....[and the belief propounded that] conflict and disagreement can be overcome by communitarian longings...."[10] This list of aspirations is long and seductive, but the evidence corroborating them surprisingly sparse.

Realists, in contrast, "try to understand the world around them, no matter how distasteful, politically objectionable, or immoral [it] may be."[11] They recognize that romanticism is a "slippery guide" to understanding the universe; that, for instance, if "political considerations compel [a person to] turn away from reality; merely to discuss pathological behavior among the poor [may be rejected as constituting] a form of 'blaming the victim.'" This may make the critic feel noble, but, if the destitute do, in fact, exhibit self-defeating behaviors, it will hinder attempts at helping them. Realists, on the other hand, pride themselves in being grounded in a particular place and time, with their eyes, ears, and fingertips all primed to gather information. They may not like what they perceive, but they are committed to employing it as their guide to action. For them, the mundane, the representative, and the tragic count for as much, or more, than the inspirational, exceptional, and imaginary.

Yet, as Wolfe concludes, "a commitment to realism is a commitment to being old-fashioned, in almost any of the meanings of the term. Realistic fiction and realistic painting are no longer in style. Legal realism speaks to the concerns of a bygone era. The idea that we can capture reality, even by the words we speak, is considered hopelessly naive by today's philosophical avant garde. Even in international relations, *realpolitik* is undermined...[by] an idealistic stress on moral and ethical foreign policy." Realism, however, does have advantages. Those "intent on dismissing the possibility of real knowledge, certain that the marginalized possess a truth unavailable to the conventional, attracted to literary theory rather than social science...lose [their] ability to persuade or explain." They also forfeit the benefits of genuine improvements in the lives of real people.

Indeed, the romanticism of the social idealist has a lot in common with that of the lovelorn. Some people seem to fall in love with love. They are so enamored with the idea of being in a magical relationship with someone of incomparable worth that they have difficulty forming enduring alliances with actual human beings. When they go out on dates, and even when they marry, they imagine that the person with whom they are involved is like the one of whom they have always dreamt; hence when this other reveals human frailties, they may use these as an excuse for rejection. Real human beings are not always emotionally available, do not give unconditional love,[12] and frequently fail to be understanding. Sometimes they throw their underwear on the floor, visit uncouth relatives, or have inconvenient headaches. If only a fairy tale princess, or a knight in shining armor, will do, the stage is set for disappointment and fiasco. Real loving relationships, as most adults learn, entail hard work, compromise, and an acceptance of limitations.[13]

Nevertheless romantic deceptions are popular. Whether in personal relationships, politics, or on the job, people often prefer the shining lie they can believe to the hard truth they must endure. They may insist that they want the truth, and believe it, but allow themselves to be deluded with dreary regularity. The fact is that they want to be bamboozled because life is too prickly to be digested raw. Glowing images are their substitute for, and shield against, dismal realities. Ironically, although romantic ideals seem to bespeak an optimism about the future, they actually reveal a pessimism about it. Those willing to settle for fantasies implicitly admit that they do not expect to be able to make a difference in their own lives.

We human beings are, of course, symbol users.[14] Our capacity to employ images and sounds to stand for other things is unique in the animal kingdom. Yet despite this being our glory, it is also our potential downfall. While signs permit us to manipulate what is not present, including the future, and therefore to develop and implement complex plans, they also allow us to live in fantasy worlds and set up housekeeping, as it were, in the midst of our delusions. In a sense we tell ourselves stories that we believe and that become substitutes for concrete facts.[15] When these stories are in accord with reality, they can be useful guides, but when they are not, they can lead us up to and beyond the edge. Unfortunately, that which can be used can also be abused. Unbeknownst to ourselves, we can become slaves to emblems of our own invention and grant them more authority than things we can touch and see.

"Equality" is such a symbolic invention. Not withstanding the influence bestowed upon it as part of America's civic religion,[16] it is a concept and not an unambiguous state of affairs. Although, in the mind's eye, it may feel absolute—perhaps being represented by congruent triangles or overlapping circles—in its social incarnation it is something utterly distinct. Actual human beings, after all, vary in innumerable dimensions, from height, wealth, and intelligence, to the things that make them happy and the relationships they are willing to maintain. Calls for equality can therefore represent very different things to different individuals. Ironically, because these disparities in meaning are always present, the romantics can perpetually uncover evidence that equivalence has not been achieved and therefore that society must be reorganized to attain it. No matter how fair a society, they can make it sound as if it were drowning in injustice merely by showing that not all people are treated in exactly the same way. But this is a shell game. In reality, the concept to which they and their listeners pay allegiance has been transformed to serve the purposes of the critic. Much as in the childhood game where one person says, "I am thinking of a number" and the other is supposed to guess it, the critic's interpretation is subjective and open to substitution so as to make his point.

In contrast to the faults they find with other people's realities, idealists, with distressing regularity, get away with guaranteeing the advantages of their own unrealizable visions precisely because these are impossible to check. As moral messiahs, they know that the future is always over the horizon and therefore amenable to portrayal in the rosiest of hues. As a consequence, when they hawk their wares, they do so with panache. Happily for them, they find a ready market for these promises. Some people simply feel so empty that they are prepared to swallow anything—and to swallow it whole. If an affirmation is massive enough, they ask no questions and hasten to pledge their troth. Of course there is a Santa, a feminist utopia, civil rights legislation guaranteed to work, and a perfect psychotropic medication. Should subsequent events place these in doubt, some individuals will continue to endorse them, for virtually any explanatory rationalization will be given credence by those who are primed to believe.

Which brings us to a strange, and previously unidentified, phenomenon. One of the maladies from which most human beings seem to suffer is "luminosity blindness." Ideals can be dazzlingly beautiful. Those dedicated to them typically present them in the purest of light, with their outlines crisp, their inner connections precise, and their benefits unambiguous. These glowing exemplars of the perfect future are, as it were, converted into crystalline structures with facets so immaculate that the sheen coming off of them overwhelms the eye. Unable to be scrutinized directly, the imperfections that blemish their surfaces and the structural defects that weaken their internal skeletons, are rendered invisible. One finds, as if one were staring at the sun, that such ideals possess a luminosity so phenomenal they leave an indelible impression at the very same moment that their details are being washed out.

As creatures who can peer into the future, we human beings dote on hope. We forever look forward to the day when our problems will be solved and our nagging discomforts will disappear. Our goal-oriented natures prompt us to aspire to that which is not only satisfying, but special. Hope is thus a wonderful balm. It converts what is currently excruciating into a mere inconvenience that can be weathered on the way to something much better. Fixing our eyes on what we expect will make us feel good; we somehow substitute this for what we actually experience. Creatures of faith, we literally surround ourselves with a universe of fanciful archetypes that we have no interest in dispelling.

Those who do not take stock in unrealistic ideals often find themselves accused of cynicism. They are reputed to be so bitter, so disillusioned by life's disappointments, that they will not believe in anything. Whenever someone suggests an improvement—any improvement—they are accused of disparaging it and insisting that it cannot work. Presumably, from their jaundiced viewpoint, happiness is impossible and reform an illusion. Realists, however, do not have to be cynics. They need not believe that life is uniformly bleak, merely that it has limitations. Nor do they have to conclude that improvements are impracticable, merely that they are difficult. They too can have hope, but theirs will be a hope tempered by reality.

Another species of contrary soul scoffed at by the romantics are the apathetic. Like cynics, they too are purported to be dropouts, but dropouts who lack the energy to mock the ideal. They simply don't care. Their pessimism is so ingrained that they see no point in protesting against anything. Again, this disposition does not have to apply to the realist. In actuality, he or she typically cares enough to confront that which is painful. Realists are, in fact, engaged, active, and innovative people. Most are committed to making the world a better place, but they will argue that this must be incremental. In other words, they are meliorists convinced that improvements come slowly and in small doses. If their gaze is not on some distant star, it is on the close by and accessible. Still, realists take chances. Like romantics, they can subscribe to Robert Browning's[17] admonition that "A man's reach should exceed his grasp, or what's a heaven for?" The difference is that they expect to attain that at which they aim or, at least, to discover why it is unattainable. If the apparently possible is disclosed to be unrealizable, they are also prepared to redirect their efforts along more profitable lines.

THE BEGINNING OF WISDOM

When I first encountered George Will's observation that disillusionment is the beginning of wisdom, it stuck me as true, but also that he had not provided directions for how to proceed from one to the other. The normal tendency of people to embrace their ideals in a death grip is so pronounced, and their ability to discern alternatives so feeble, from whence could wisdom derive? Apparently the world itself provides the impetus. The experience, and the shock, of colliding with that which one did not anticipate can have contradictory effects. On one hand, it can reinforce a desire to retreat into self-deception, and on the other, can fuel an appetite to explore unforeseen truths. Whether it is the world's complexities, or its unfairness, that one finds intimidating, each can be examined in the hope of developing improved coping strategies.

My own career provides an illustration of this phenomenon. In retrospect, I find myself having learned lessons many of my contemporaries did not. Like other children of the sixties, I had expected government programs to provide the basis for a more just and prosperous world. As part of a new breed of well-educated and well-intentioned activists, my peers and I would administer a system purpose-built to maximize interpersonal caring and to minimize selfish conflict. We would bring out the best in humanity by devoting ourselves to being the best that we could be. It was, therefore, with the greatest reluctance that I had to acknowledge I was on a collision course with reality. It took time and many small disillusionments for me to realize that we human beings, and the social structures that we create, have enormous limitations. Even today I remain shaken by the fact that I was forced to recognize the deficiencies of social programs in ways that others who have not personally experienced their operations have not. To my enduring surprise, I sometimes find myself wincing as I listen to politicians, clinicians, or educators project hopelessly naive solutions to important social problems. Don't they realize, I wonder, that these fantasies cannot work?

When I first obtained employment with New York City's Welfare Department, I was about as naive as it is possible to be. If life is awash with the unexpected, this was certainly true for me. Despite longing to make a significant contribution, I did not understand the nature of the problems I would encounter or what might constitute genuine progress. As decisively, like most young people, I was resistant to recognizing unwanted facts. My childhood idealism was very much intact and drove me to see what I wanted to see. One of the things I had idealized was social rules. As far as I was concerned, the rules were the rules. They were absolute and meant precisely what they said they did. Moreover, I was convinced that if these standards were not strictly enforced, the social order would instantly collapse and the world slide into a Hobbesian state of nature in which everyone would be at war with everyone else. Back in my school days, some of my fellow students had tried to bend the regulations to their own advantage, but we mature adults would surely be more like our teachers and take them seriously. It never occurred to me that specific standards needed to be interpreted in order to be applied or that they might be honored more in accord with the interests of those in authority than with some objective criterion.

The official structure of the welfare system at first seemed to confirm the primacy of the sort of rules I craved. It rested, after all, on a mountain of regulations administered by employees intentionally hired to enforce them. Indeed, I was one of these enforcement agents. My job was to make certain that its clients abided by its written dictums—which to me meant the same standards for all. Consequently, when ordered to cut a check for a woman who, according to the statutes, was not entitled to it, I felt betrayed. How could this extortion, for that is how I construed it, be allowed to succeed? Wouldn't someone notice that the rules had been bent and those responsible be brought to justice? The answer, as was soon apparent, was no. There was barely a ripple of disgust as this contravention proceeded through the system. The situation may have been perceived as atypical, but not as a violation of law.

This was my first indication that rules, despite being explicit, could be plastic. I had originally assumed that, particularly when formal, they were unambiguous, and furthermore, that those who administered them read from the same page. But here, when the unanticipated had arisen, consternation erupted among the middle managers. They literally had to think things through; things not recorded in any specific place. They also had to factor in what they believed the mayor—their boss—wanted. In the end, it was decided that it was better to prevent a riot than to be officious. To this day, however, I am not sure this determination was correct. Sending the message that blackmail can be effective was also dangerous. But it was a close call that gave me pause and made me realize that those in positions of responsibility had to weigh many consequences.

By the time I arrived at the methadone clinic, I knew there were things to be learned. It was also evident that in working with addicted clients the stakes were higher. The issue now was not so much rule consistency as therapeutic efficacy, with life and death, not mere money, on the line. Now I had to ask myself: What did I, as a presumably expert helper, owe my clients? Having in the interim raised my professional sights, I had begun to think of myself as a clinician and hence been sensitized to questions of professional ethics. The result was that, both at home and between interviews with my clients, I devoured books on counseling technique and on substance abuse. Among the factors upon which the authorities seemed agreed was that a therapeutic relationship was crucial and that counselor dedication was at its core. One had genuinely to care, for if one didn't, the client would detect this and the requisite trust would evaporate. Since I did care, the question was how to make this palpable.

My supervisor, however, had other priorities. The orderly functioning of the clinic concerned him more than did any particular clinical relationship. He feared that a lack of discipline could become contagious and undermine its integrity. Thus, where I fretted about Kevin's mental stability, he agonized over the example that Kevin was setting. Try as I might, I could not get him to worry more about Kevin as an individual. Conversely, he could not alter my commitment, but, given an opening, jumped at the opportunity to disregard it. Once more I felt betrayed, but more than this, that Kevin had been betrayed. After he was killed, this solidified into a conviction that he had virtually been murdered.

As a counselor, the therapeutic ideal naturally occupied my field of vision. It, and specific clients, took precedence over what happened elsewhere. As a consequence, it bothered me that my supervisor was not clinically sophisticated and I was convinced that a better educated person would come to a different conclusion. Nevertheless, he had a responsibility that I did not have and he took it seriously. The dynamics I believed operative within my client probably were as I imagined, but my ability to help was less than I supposed and more in line with what he thought. Who came closer to the truth must remain an open question, but the comparison between Kevin's needs and those of other clients had to be made, there being a larger picture than the one that preoccupied me. Once more the determination of what was best turned out to be more ambiguous than I initially realized.

Uncomfortably for me, being outstationed at the Rochester Psychiatric Center was again to enlarge my perspective. With all but my doctoral dissertation behind me, I was feeling pretty chipper when I arrived on the scene. Few people, I realized, had the combination of experience and academics that I did. Surely, I was now an "expert" who deserved to be treated as such. This, of course, did not transpire. RPC was the largest therapeutic institution with which I had been associated and it quickly became clear that it was held hostage to bureaucratic imperatives I had not suspected. Much to my annoyance, quoting Goffman[18] only convinced my more experienced colleagues that I did not know what I was talking about—which, as it turned out, I did not. But none of us, not I nor they, genuinely understood the organization's whys and wherefores. I may have relied on Goffman, and they on the weight of tradition, but neither of us was sure of why they were so elaborate. What was incontestable was that our insights were no match for the hospital's inertia. While in school, and under the illusion that knowledge was equivalent to power, I had imagined that if you understood how something worked, you could always alter it. It now dawned on me that sometimes you only learned why things couldn't be changed. Specifically, bureaucracies were apparently subject to a goal displacement that might not be open to repeal. Though their priorities often shifted before one's eyes, one might not be able to switch them back.

Given the legislative reforms then in progress, it had obviously occurred to others that what was wrong with the psychiatric infrastructure could not be remedied from within. But deinstitutionalization held its own perils. The ideals of some of the reformers were as out of touch with reality as were mine. Merely discharging patients and referring them for drug treatment would not bring the freedom that the optimists forecast. Still, I was to learn an even more nettlesome lesson. Good intentions brought together within an idealistic movement did not always terminate in a positive outcome. The power of a successful political combine could actually generate a momentum that worked against the interests of those supposedly to be helped. Clearly, even after it had become evident that the mandated discharge plans could not be effectively implemented, instead of their advocates reexamining this strategy, they redoubled their efforts to force them through. Neither a lack of group homes, nor an inability to compel outpatients to take their medications, had deterred them. Even when feedback from RPC indicated that defective plans resulted in rehospitalization, the reformers were unimpressed, blaming this on sabotage by unenlightened staffers. Their solution was to insist on discharge by fiat. Success would be ensured by the simple expedient of not admitting failure. And so it was. Although within months former patients were showing up under Rochester's bridges, this was attributed to homelessness, not deinstitutionalization. The explanation was a transparent rationalization—which should have been exploded by an enraged citizenry—but it slid by under the protection of those dedicated to liberating the mentally ill. The united strength of psychiatrists, administrators, politicians, journalists, and concerned parents proved sufficient to sustain a policy where words substituted for deeds and speaking the truth was taken as evidence of mean-spiritness.

Finally, there was my encounter with the hospital psychiatrist over Greg. One might be forgiven for imagining that after the many speed bumps that had rattled my confidence, I would not be perturbed by another reversal. But ideals die hard. My conviction that competence and commitment would ultimately triumph persisted in the face of massive disconfirmation. Though I had been working in the mental health system long enough to realize that credentials were often honored above ability, somehow I hoped that common sense and professional dedication would prevail. If I took the time to understand my clients, and the options available to them, and conscientiously coordinated my efforts with other professionals and the client, my recommendations would have to be respected. Besides, I was a Ph.D. which should count for something.

What I had not considered was that hierarchical seniority counted for more. Given my previous encounters, it should have registered that my competitor was a psychiatrist, which made him almost invulnerable.

Ostensibly, in meeting together, we were to discuss the merits of a particular option, but this was never in the cards. The psychiatrist needed to demonstrate who was in charge, even if this entailed insulting me, silencing the OT, or intimidating Greg. When I proved too stiff-necked to capitulate, he enlisted the cooperation of my supervisor to put me in my place. And while I saw this ploy coming, I was not able to counteract it. My reliance on candor and a hand shake to bind my supervisor to my cause terminated in ignoble failure. Eventually my anger at having been deceived was so great that in reaction I wound up in the agency's doghouse. Despite being a sociologist indoctrinated in the potency of social stratification, I made the elementary mistake of underestimating the solidarity of those in authority. Because, as Barnard[19] observed, bosses have personal limitations, they present a common front to their underlings. Much as parents unite against a child, they combine against obstreperous subordinates. The result was that my very intransigence became my undoing. Clearly, determining the best means of rehabilitating Greg had shrunk to insignificance when compared with the need to contain my insubordination. Whatever else happened, the sanctity of the hierarchy had to be maintained.

Having been on the losing end of this affair, it might seem that I should now denounce social ranking as a crass anachronism. But that, despite the temptation, would be the riposte of an unregenerate idealist. It would simply reassert that I was right and, therefore whoever was lined up against me was wrong. Since Greg did attempt suicide, as predicted, this might seem warranted, but the utility of overarching social arrangements is not always apparent. Dominance hierarchies are not only universal, they are also functional, enabling people to organize large-scale activities that coordinate complex tasks.[20] An argument can therefore be made that preserving the integrity of this specific hierarchy was more material than correctly deciding an individual case. In a sense, the practice of credentialing was itself on the line. Had the validity of my adversary's medical standing not been confirmed, professional usage could have been in jeopardy. In a calling where competence does not manifest itself in a precise batting average, threatening the authority of the professional degree could have left everyone adrift.

Perhaps this defense is overly energetic, but unexpected complications are the bane of the unrepentant idealist. Their exclusion from his calculations regularly creates gaps where land mines can be buried. Yet disillusionment is not fun. While a person's eyes can be forced open by colliding with failed expectations, this can also be prevented by refusing to see what is in plain sight. Only when someone is prepared to take risks is the experience of being contradicted by reality growth inducing. The world contains many lessons, but they are hard ones that require courage to assimilate. Among the most important are:

1. *Life is complex.* The part of life with which we are in contact is only a small piece of a larger whole. Individual discoveries may enlarge our awareness, but however glorious, they must not be confused with encompassing its entirety. There is always something lurking beyond the next bend that can add to the picture we have been constructing. Substituting a simplified vision cannot change this; it may merely dissuade us from looking further.

2. *Life is uncertain.* The surprises never stop coming. We do not understand much of what is out there, but even less of this is within our control. Ambiguity, change, and ignorance ensure that most of our predictions will turn out wrong. This can create anxiety, for that which is not under our control can be dangerous. Nonetheless, we must tolerate this uncertainty, making the best guesses we can and adjusting as necessary.

3. *We all have limitations.* Our abilities are finite and our capacity to attain coveted goals bounded. No matter how smart we are, someone else is smarter; no matter how skilled at making plans, others are more ingenious. No one has a monopoly on strength, beauty, knowledge, talent, or luck. Nor can any one of us make everything we imagine come true. Some things are physically impossible; others are merely improbable. Sooner or later, that which we had not counted on intervenes to upset our hopes and we must cope with the resulting loss and frustration.

4. *Life's conflicts never end.* Because valued resources are in short supply, and because there is a superabundance of those pursuing them, some will win and some will lose. In particular, because we human beings are hierarchical creatures, the number of places available at the top is always restricted. The result is that people fight to prevail and will fight hard. Not surprisingly, the ensuing clashes can be bruising. People may dream of a peaceful resting place, but there are constant challenges to be met.

5. *Mistakes will be made.* The perfect solution does not exist, nor does its perfect implementation. Limited human beings, in a complex and uncertain world, inevitably err. Entering upon novel situations with incomplete knowledge and unpracticed skills makes some stumbles inescapable. The near universality of conflict also ensures that some others will be glad to exploit these lapses. Yet it is only from making mistakes that people learn. Those who cannot recognize when they have failed, and make corrections accordingly, are doomed to repeat their blunders.[21] Admitting error, at least to oneself, is among the most painful things that anyone can do, but it is also among the most productive.

6. *Irrationality is inevitable.* Not only do people make mistakes, but they often refuse to recognize the reality of those they do make. The nature of

human hierarchies, social roles, and personal relationships is such that people cling to fantasies and adamantly reject logical plans of action. Instead of pursing their interests intelligently, they follow their emotions into defeat and unhappiness. Nor can education correct this when faith, revenge, or hope take precedence over experience.

7. *People will get hurt.* Life is full of pain, much of it necessary for discovering how to deal with its problems. Scraped knees are unpleasant, but they are a concomitant of learning how to walk. Yet some pain is gratuitously inflicted. Were we human beings stronger and better informed, we might be able to refrain from this sort of cruelty. But we are not. Much as we may rue it, we are not a band of angels; hence even though improvements are possible, and the pain can be reduced, it cannot be eliminated.

If hard lessons are indeed integral to wisdom, it is clear why wisdom is in such short supply. Mercifully, the capacity to acquire enlightenment is sufficiently beneficial that it continues to be held in high repute. Haltingly, and imperfectly, people do continue to stumble toward it. Complexities, of course, are easier to recognize than they are to integrate. Their complications are difficult to assimilate; hence new discoveries often sit cheek by jowl beside old verities. Similarly, the limitations revealed when we try to improve ourselves ensure that we rarely mature as much as we would hope. Our lingering ignorance and ineptitudes virtually guarantee that we will not be able to live up to our ambitions. Illusions, in contrast, are simpler to incorporate. These ideals may be fraudulent, and falsely purport to be uncomplicated, boundless, and infallible, but they always find disciples. In their very simplicity, they attract those who are intimidated by more valid goals.

PERSONAL RESPONSIBILITY

About a year after I began working at the Gold Star Mother Clinic, we moved from the ferry boat to a refurbished warehouse on Canal Street. The new building was more commodious and, for staff and clients alike, more comfortable. One day before lunch, a colleague suggested that we go across the Hudson River to a seafood place he knew in Hoboken. I had a newly purchased car available and our access to the Holland Tunnel was direct. After getting my little Volkswagen bug out of the parking lot, five of us crammed into it on the way to what turned out to be a delightful meal. When we returned, there were only two hours left on our shift. Someone in the back seat suggested that I not waste my money by pulling into a commercial lot, but take advantage of the no-parking zone in front of the clinic. With so little time before leaving, the car was unlikely to be ticketed. A chorus of voices assured me that this was so.

Within the hour, a client was knocking at my door breathlessly informing me that a meter maid was prowling outside. By the time I got downstairs, it was too late. There beneath my windshield wiper was a thirty-five dollar ticket. The air went out of my lungs as I stared at it in disbelief. This was my first parking ticket ever. What was worse, I felt as if my friends had failed to protect me. I immediately rushed back inside expecting them to commiserate and to offer help in defraying the cost. But no one said a thing. It was almost as if I had become invisible. Their unspoken attitude was that it was my car and my business, not that this had been a joint venture with the ticket part of our shared expense. I was dumbfounded. Here I had been the gracious host chauffeuring everyone to lunch and no one was grateful enough to come to my assistance.

The fact was that I was hurt, but I was also too embarrassed to say anything. Instead, I returned to my office where I angrily brooded over the lack of appreciation. It was several days later, while riding to work, that it occurred to me that it was my car, my decision to park it, and hence my responsibility. If I were to have control of the vehicle, and the benefits that accrued from this, I would have to accept the consequences of choosing where and how to drive it. That, I now realized, was part of being an adult. Support from others was nice, but if I were going to make independent determinations, I had to be prepared to stand by them. Even if these went against the grain, and I had to endure their consequences alone, I would have to be resolute.

The same holds true for ethical choices. To be an adult moral agent implies a willingness to take personal responsibility. Unless someone is ready to defend his or her actions, that person is behaving like a child. More to the point, to subscribe to a particular ideal is to make a moral choice. It is to endorse a discrete vision of the future, a vision that always has repercussions. Those who renounce the effects of what they underwrite, in effect, deny their role in determining what happens. Idealism sounds trouble free, as if it were too lofty to incur sinister baggage, but this is wrong. When ideals are in error, they, and their adherents, may have a great deal to answer for.

Few people regard themselves as irresponsible. Were they told that they had deceived themselves about a specific ideal, they would be aghast. They would certainly protest against accusations of being extreme or of having failed to examine what they stand for. Yet herein resides another irony associated with idealism. Idealists not only think of themselves as conscientious, but they also tend to be conscientious. However bizarre their objectives, and however much the damage inflicted, they sincerely believe themselves to be moral. They are likewise convinced that they try harder than other people—because they generally do. Should they become the butt of criticism, they are persuaded that this is because they are purer than others and are more prepared to go the extra mile. What their accusers interpret as extremism is, in their view, a reflection of these others' own laziness and capacity for compromise.

Historically, idealists have put considerable effort into complying with the standards they promote. Pythagoras founded a community that engendered a strict dietary code, St. Thomas More allowed himself to be executed rather than take an oath of allegiance offensive to his religious sensibilities, the Shakers abstained from sex even as their communities were shrinking, the Hitler youth volunteered for front-line service in World War II as Soviet arms rolled into Berlin, Chinese peasants scared tens of millions of sparrows to death on the word of a revered leader, and radical medicalists have allowed murderers to go free so as to remain consistent with their theories. When caught up in a chosen doctrine, an idealist's focus can be remarkably intense, with the effort expended on its actualization confused with its merit. Zealous partisanship is taken as a mark of honor and a refusal to consider alternatives as a sign of integrity. Although conscientiousness is admirable when its goals are worthy and are softened by flexibility, it is important to recognize that neither of these may be the case.

Closely allied with conscientiousness is faithfulness. Those intent on being moral often pride themselves on their loyalty. Life may subject them to many stinging betrayals, but they refuse to abandon that to which they are pledged. What their parents, church, or party taught them is proper, they will fight for with matchless vigor. Their energy does not flag, their guard does not drop, and apparently contrary evidence does not delude them into apostasy. Such steadfastness may be honorable, but, where blind, can also be a vice. It was, after all, what prompted German teenagers to hold out in the rubble of the Third Reich and what induced the followers of a Charles Manson to commit multiple brutal murders.

Idealism, despite its sparkling reputation, is not automatically moral. Though pursued in the name of what is right, it can be misplaced. It is, for instance, not always compassionate. There are the obvious cases, such as the Nazi manipulation of eugenics to justify the gassing of epileptics,[22] but there are less egregious examples too. Recently in the United States there was a debate over the most appropriate way to organize public welfare. Some believed that governmental support is an entitlement due every indigent person regardless of the cause of his or her poverty. They wrung their hands at the plight of innocent children born into squalor and schizophrenics living on street grates, and asked how anyone could be unmoved by their condition. Others responded that real compassion does not hand out money indiscriminately or without demanding a reciprocal effort. Along with Marvin Olasky[23] in his *The Tragedy of American Compassion*, they argued that making people dependent on charity was not compassionate and robbed them of their dignity and their ability to rise in society.

When working for welfare in the 1960s, it was this latter pattern I saw in operation. Statistically, this was the period during which national welfare roles expanded most dramatically. It was also a time when the authorities encouraged people to apply for public assistance. One of my duties was literally to distribute pamphlets that insisted welfare was a right and that if the poor did not avail themselves of it, they were being victimized by the system. During this same period, the City of New York almost implemented a reform in which welfare eligibility was to be determined solely through the written declarations of the recipients. Making home visits would cease, as would investigations of how clients spent their checks. Some cheating was expected, but, in retrospect, the colossally naive assumption[24] was made that this would be minimal and that any increased utilization would be temporary.

Common sense may call ideological projections into question, but their devotees do not. Their certitude, though frightening to those who do not share it, is for them reassuring. More distressing, in their eyes, is the prospect of being without an answer. That they might be mistaken, or have to endure doubt, are wholly unacceptable. As a result, they seek precision in formulae they can trust. When in a quandary, they demand uncomplicated phrases and procedures that can be reliably plugged into. Slogans such as, "All power to the people," "Liberty and justice for all," and "A chicken in every pot" seem to incorporate what is desired and become their guiding principles.

This demand for idealistic precision and simplicity has, since the Warren Court, infected American jurisprudence with a well-intentioned formalism that has brought the system to the brink of catastrophe. In an effort to make sure that no innocent person is ever convicted, and that no individual, however modest his circumstances, is ever abused, a train of protective devices have been put in place under the banner of due process. One of these is the Miranda rule that requires the police to read an arrestee his rights immediately upon being taken into custody. He must be informed that anything he says can be used against him and that he has a right to have a lawyer present whenever he is questioned. Should these privileges be abrogated, his case can be thrown out of court, despite the gravity of his crime or the preponderance of the evidence. Judge Harold Rothwax[25] in his *Guilty: The Collapse of Criminal Justice* wonders what is the point of discouraging felons from confessing. It is one thing, he declares, to respect their right not to incriminate themselves, but quite another to guarantee the presence of an attorney during their initial interrogation. This last only adds a person to the scene whose job it is to demand that the suspect not reveal anything.

For my own part, I am wary of the prudence of excluding evidence simply because it has been gathered in violation of some protocol. The logic behind this is apparently that it will discourage the police, and prosecutors, from infringing on personal rights. So far as I am aware, there is no empirical corroboration of this prediction. But much worse, the police are, in effect, being punished by forcing them to release the criminal into the community. Tragically, it is the man on the street, a person who has played no part in the legal proceedings, who pays the price by being exposed to further criminal predation. Rothwax too denounces this and similar blunders. Among these is the practice of ensuring a speedy trial by enjoining prosecutors to bring an accused to trial within a date-certain on pain of having the case dismissed. In some instances, this has allowed a defendant to argue successfully that his rights were being breached because after jumping bail he was not speedily apprehended and retried.

If moral rules are indeed informal, then to reduce them to exact recipes ipso facto does them violence. The resultant precision may seem ideal, but, in removing judgment from the process, the original intent and our ability to adjust the rules to fit fluctuating contexts are eliminated. True responsibility entails a refusal to be seduced by what seems unambiguous. Magical incantations should remain the province of the very young. Possessing neither the experience, nor the mental faculties, of adults, they are incapable of the critical thinking necessary for truly moral appraisals and hence can be excused for believing in Santa Claus. The chronologically mature are not so fortunate. They cannot plead incapacity. Yet they too have an appetite for fairy tales. When Princess Diana[26] of England tragically died in an automobile crash, the outpouring of grief was astonishing. A vital young woman, a loving mother, and, to all appearances, a basically decent human being, she was canonized for alleged contributions to world peace. Some even suggested that she be awarded a posthumous Nobel prize. But her real achievements, apart from the charity work performed by all royals, were few. Though her sense of style was better than her ex-husband's, her chief accomplishment was fulfilling other people's dreams by marrying a prince. Their ability to identify with her thwarted quest for a happy ending was what made her special. Sadly, this media-reinforced fantasy was more real to some than their own lives. When it came crashing down, they could scarcely contain their remorse.

But fairy tales are not life. Neither are they especially moral or responsible. Once naiveté becomes the ideal, the dangers are multiplied. Gullibility is not a virtue,[27] nor is a susceptibility to glittering appearances.

Because ideals are subject to manipulation, they are likewise subject to defilement. Those who too enthusiastically embrace them place the rest of us in jeopardy. No matter how innocent their intentions, they may become the unwitting allies of evil. This is a stark assessment, but equally grim is the fact that many people equate the juvenile with the upright. They celebrate youth for its own sake and a purity of heart for its artlessness. Unhappily for us, when these, rather than a judicious maturity, become the goals of most people, society is in mortal peril. Accountability depends upon a realistic idealism and a capacity to engage in sophisticated self-examination. These, however, are adult qualities, beyond the scope of the very young, for they require courage, perseverance, and an ability to tolerate disappointment.

Chapter 9

No Respect

WHICH SIDE ARE YOU ON?

"Everybody does it!"

As allegations of Bill Clinton's sexual indiscretions began to pile up, many ordinary citizens asserted that they were no big deal. Hadn't John Kennedy indulged his sexual appetites while in the White House? Didn't Franklin Roosevelt have a mistress? Weren't there even reports that the straight-laced George Bush had had an affair? So what then if Monica Lewinsky had engaged in oral hanky-panky with a sitting president, or if Kathleen Willey had her breast fondled by him in the Oval Office; it was their business and no one else's. Consensual sex was a private matter for everyone—including a president—and the rest of us had best refrain from peering into what amounted to his bedroom. Let Bill and Hillary sort things out between themselves, for whatever suited them should suit us all.

Activists in the media, however, took a very different tack. Those with a conservative bent were determined to uphold family values. They did not understand how the American public could so casually accept immorality in the highest office in the land. What sort of example was this to set for our children? Hadn't voters, they reasoned, rejected Gary Hart's candidacy for less flagrant conduct and hadn't the Congress ejected Robert Packwood for comparable excesses? Besides, Clinton's efforts to suppress knowledge of his behavior amounted to subornation of perjury and/or obstruction of justice. These, they insisted, were not only wrong, but high crimes and misdemeanors for which impeachment was the proper response. To do less was to place the republic in jeopardy and to allow the president to be above the law. As such, it was a direct threat to the integrity of our democracy.

Committed liberals, of course, took a different view. They too were appalled, but they alleged that a conservative conspiracy was undermining the nation. As far as they were concerned, Kenneth Starr, the special prosecutor in charge of the Whitewater case, had exceeded his authority and abused the judicial process. In his zeal, the privacy of a whole group of persons was being invaded and they were being forced to incur legal expenses in response to an act of petty vengeance. That a hatred of Bill and Hillary Clinton could eventuate in such an outrage was, to their minds, a bigger scandal than anything the couple had actually done and, therefore, was a more grievous challenge to our institutions.

For those with reasonably good memories, this contretemps had a hoary ring. Some twenty-five years earlier virtually the same arguments were put forward in the Watergate affair. At that time, the first reaction of many observers when they heard of the break-in at the Democratic party headquarters was likewise that "Everybody does it." Because other presidents too had engaged in political espionage, they did not consider this instance worth making a fuss over and hoped that the incident would disappear. At that time, it was liberal media types who became incensed. As evidence of Nixon's participation in a coverup accumulated, they expounded on how this was a threat to the republic and demanded legal remedies. His conservative defenders, in contrast, were outraged by this journalistic excess. They could not understand how self-appointed Nixon-haters could be allowed to interfere with executing the nation's business. As usual, it was the moderates who found themselves in the middle, less sure of what to do than their more ideal-driven contemporaries.

As these two incidents demonstrate, ideals have often been politicized in the United States. As a democracy, the nation often carried forward its affairs through the competing bands of ideologues that James Madison[1] referred to as "factions." Almost whenever a civic policy is put forward, or a public career defended, the arguments offered have an idealistic tinge, with the players on both sides representing themselves as paladins promoting a cause so just that it deserves the support of the entire society. This is so because democracies require the assent of the governed in order to function. Participants in the process thus find it expedient to argue that their goals are exceptionally pure. They will even invent an idealized issue when none is at hand, knowing full well that if the public can be persuaded of its merit, it will back its champions. Since moral ideals are by definition pure, when people are convinced that a particular objective fits this bill, they stumble over themselves to endorse it. In essence, potential leaders with their ambitions afire grab an ideological flag, whitewash it to resemble what they think people want (today often on the basis of polling data), then rush to the front of the parade where they wave it as vigorously as they can so as to attract as many adherents as possible.

Earlier we saw that stickball is a team sport. With two sides and multiple players on each, the object is for one to defeat the other. Generally, this is best accomplished through intrasquad cooperation, for while individual talents matter, so do team spirit and throwing the ball to the right base. If morality is, in fact, comparable to stickball, it too depends on a team effort. What is accepted as right is not merely a matter of cloistered judgments, but of coordinated actions and shared perceptions. Specifically, for a moral ideal to have currency, it must do so as the standard of a collectivity. This, of course, places a premium on assembling like-minded constituencies.

The politicization of ideals has a variety of consequences. One of them is that particular ideals must be plastic enough to meet the needs of a multiplicity of people. Unless they can be manipulated to appeal to a broad range of potential converts, few are likely to be impressed by them. A second consequence is that ideals must be extreme enough to peak the interest of the apathetic. If they are put forward tepidly, they tend to be overlooked in favor of more vivid presentations. Furthermore, with the objective being to recruit a sufficiently large number to prevail, the pressures on the uncommitted can be enormous. People are not only asked which side they are on; they are mercilessly badgered until they make the correct decision. To be undecided is usually equated with being on the wrong team, hence the moderate will be chided for having no convictions.

The result of all this is the mobilization of competing ideological movements. Two, or more, hostile camps emerge, with the dividing line between the "good" guys and the "bad" ones becoming ever more distinct. In such an environment, those who wish to remain uncommitted are out of luck. Their efforts to be reasonable are not applauded as prudent or well-balanced, but are attacked as disengaged, disingenuous, or depraved. This is especially so when single-issue groups, such as the gender radicals, are engaged, for they have no compunctions about whipsawing noncombatants until they acquiesce. Ideals, it seems, are not merely private matters between a person and his conscience, but public acts that are subject to public constraints. Although individuals for their own reasons may lean toward one objective over another, they rarely do so in isolation or without external influences. As a result, their choices hinge not only on their personal vulnerabilities or needs, but on the pressures to which they are exposed and the supports they can muster.

With more than an attachment to our private fantasies necessary for a particular vision to succeed, ideological maelstroms swirl around us all the time. As gregarious creatures attuned to the opinions and emotions of others, when these are intense, they often substitute for our personal commitments without our realizing it. In the end, those determined to remain aloof from the fray often feel disoriented, and even guilty, for trying to maintain their independence. Lacking the vivid standards of their more polarized peers, they can lose sight of what is at stake. Bereft of comparable idealistic guidance, blamed for failing to join the proper coalition, and perhaps feeling blameworthy for being wishy-washy, they are the Rodney Dangerfields of our moral terrain. Rather than being applauded for taking the time to evaluate a complicated reality, they are denied communal respect and are shoved to the margins. Worse still, without a compelling vision of their own with which to ward off such assaults, they may retreat into an impotent spectatorship, their own ambivalence leaving them vulnerable to manipulation by the less scrupulous. As Doris Kearns Goodwin[2] has reported, Lyndon Johnson—a man who should have known—was fond of observing that "What convinces is conviction." No wonder then that the moderates, less sure than the true believers that they hold the key to saving the world, tend to be less passionate and therefore less convincing to themselves and others.

Historically, the United States has been the battlefield for numerous idealistic movements.[3] From its origins as the home of groups seeking refuge to pursue their private agendas, it has sheltered the Massachusetts Pilgrims, the Maryland Catholics, the Pennsylvania Quakers, and the Rhode Island dissenters. It has similarly welcomed the Shakers, the Mennonites, the Hutterites, and ultimately even tolerated the Mormons. The country has also proven fertile ground for a plethora of both secular and religious revivals. To go back only two centuries, at the start of the 1800s it saw the Second Great Awakening, which was quickly supplanted by the Anti-Masonic frenzy, which in turn gave way to abolitionism, Know-Nothingism, the suffragette movement, and temperance agitation. This century has likewise witnessed Progressivism, Prohibition, the New Deal, American-Firstism, McCarthyism, Civil Rights, the War on Poverty, Feminism, Born-Again Christianity, and Political Correctness, to name a few.

Generally, when these "isms" fall, they fall of their own accord. Those not swept up in their enthusiasm may quietly bemoan their excesses, but lacking the political machinery of the activists, their influence is limited. More commonly, they are co-opted and absorbed by the extremists. Though their reservations frequently temper the fanaticism of the committed, they are as apt to be the ones unconsciously radicalized. Thus, when the avant garde decides to grow its hair long, the centrists are at first scandalized, but rather than make a fuss, they soon grow theirs moderately long—this compromise seeming to them the "sensible" choice. In the end, we get something comparable to what Patrick Moynihan[4] called "defining deviance down." The moderates simply grow accustomed to the excesses of the radicals and these begin to appear less extravagant.

Nowadays the two principal camps contesting our social ideals may roughly be labeled the "liberal" and the "conservative." Although, in the morality game, there are numerous sides, not just these two, they are the currently dominant alignments, frequently subsuming others by redefining them as within their own borders. Whether consciously or not, most people voluntarily identify with them—despite not fully accepting the tenets of either. Even those of us who covet our independence are affected by their dictates. Indeed, they set the terms of our political debates, often defining the very concepts in which the issues are discussed. In consequence, it often seems as if the more vocal partisans are the sole custodians of all the potential answers and that the rest of us must select from options they put forward, real autonomy having been proscribed as seditious.

CULTURE WARS

In recent years, the division between liberals and conservatives has become so fierce that their clashes have been likened to a "culture war." James Hunter[5] has gone so far as to assert that this conflict is nothing less than an effort to redefine America's central values. He has proposed that as we have entered the modern era, it proved necessary to reconsider the standards applied to the family, art, education, law, and politics; that at first industrialization, and later the advent of the information age, compelled people to rethink their beliefs. Issues such as abortion, homosexuality, and school prayer became flash-points over which hostile belligerents squared off and traded punches. In addition, with the nation becoming increasingly diverse, the old Judeo-Christian consensus began to crumble and a more secular perspective shouldered its way to the fore. With Hindus, Muslims, and atheists increasingly a part of the mix, the old verities no longer drew automatic assent and more pertinent replacements seemed mandatory.

This conservative-liberal divide has apparently polarized attitudes over how to solve our social problems, with an intractable debate between old-fashioned and progressive factions capturing the public imagination. Adherents of the former tend to cling to the counsel of the time-tested authorities, while those of the latter pursue what they perceive to be a more rationalistic modernism. In the area of the family, for instance, the battle has been joined over questions of sexuality and family solidarity—with the desirability of sexual freedom, the wisdom of divorce, and the nature of childrearing practices dividing the players and straining their good will. In public education, where government-supported schools have traditionally promoted "civic virtue,"[6] the problem seems to be in deciding what is virtuous. While everyone agrees that democracy must be preserved, the traditional Anglo-Saxon verities appear outdated to pluralists with roots in Southeastern Europe, Africa, and Asia. They want their children taught that their ancestral cultures also have worth. Meanwhile their adversaries were equally discomfited and fret that our common democratic heritage is under siege by newcomers who fail to appreciate its uniqueness. They wish to reinforce our mutual commitment to fairness by stressing the legacy derived from the British Isles. Similarly, in the arts, it is topics such as censorship that set pulses racing, while a church-state rivalry has excited arguments over how far First Amendment rights should extend. Sometimes these disagreements grow so fierce that each side advocates laws to constrain the other. Hunter has expressed confidence that these clashes will ultimately subside through mutual accommodation and assimilation, but to date this state of affairs has not yet arrived.

Martin Lipset,[7] it may be recalled, spoke of a shared *American Creed* that centered on liberty, equality, individualism, populism, and laissez-faire government, but this has apparently come to mean different things to different constituencies. To muddy the waters further, conservatives and liberals often adopt identical language, despite referring to divergent objectives. A simple illustration is the term "opportunity." When Newt Gingrich sought to advance the Republican Contract with America, he invoked the image of an "opportunity society" and argued that it was necessary to remove impediments to entrepreneurial expansion by decreasing the capital gains tax and reducing government regulation of small business. After this proposal began to generate public support, Bill Clinton speedily announced that his goal too was increased opportunity. For him, however, an opportunity society implied something decidedly different. His expressed desire was to fund additional training programs for blue collar workers, thereby enabling them to obtain previously unavailable employment.

In area upon area, liberals and conservatives disagree over what is important. Thus, although both favor rationality, they differ on what it means to be rational. Liberals, for instance, are outwardly on the side of science. They regularly endorse studies to discover the "root" causes of social problems and strongly support scientifically based secular education. Conservatives, in contrast, celebrate tradition, though they scarcely construe this as irrational. While they do approve of religion, they also support the established literary canon.[8] For them, valid lessons are embedded in ancient Greek philosophy, the plays of William Shakespeare, and the economics of Adam Smith. Indeed, they regard a lack of familiarity with these as a sign of cultural illiteracy. Moreover, though supposedly antiscientific, conservatives are often the primary sponsors of technological innovations. As the managers of modern corporations, they often rely on these to enhance their market penetration. Liberals, on the other hand, are apt to advocate a romantic return to a pristine nature unencumbered by all-terrain vehicles or metal cookstoves.

The two factions are further divided regarding the meaning of "equality." Both are stalwart advocates of Thomas Jefferson's ringing assertion that "All men are created equal," but perceive different implications in the phrase.[9] Conservatives tend to align themselves with Gingrich in acclaiming entrepreneurship. Their objective is an equal opportunity to enter the marketplace and to seek personal advantage. A fair chance at becoming successful is what they covet, not an equality of results. As long as the same rules are applied to all, they are satisfied. Liberals, however, recoil at this prospect. They consider such equivalence a fraudulent effort to steal the birthright of the less advantaged. Fair competition, in their view, exists only when everyone winds up with comparable rewards. When this does not happen, they assume that what has occurred is an abuse of power in which those on the top have utilized their position to manipulate the outcome in their favor.[10]

When it comes to the meaning of "democracy," the two factions similarly fail to achieve a meeting of minds. For liberals, democracy can be guaranteed only by a strong central government. In a nation that abides by the principle of "one man-one vote," they are persuaded that this will enable everyone, including the poor, to exercise control over their leaders. They also believe that a powerful federal establishment must ensure the rights of minorities, and, as importantly, protect them from exploitation; that, as a matter of fact, only a healthy, democratic, and centralized system has the clout to do so. Conservatives, in comparison, worry that a central authority potent enough to fulfill such desires is potent enough to quash them.[11] Democratic elections, they contend, cannot force bureaucrats to be accountable because most of what they do occurs outside the purview of those electing them. Conservatives would rather reserve guardianship of their collective fate to themselves and desire a radically decentralized society in which democracy is fostered by maximizing the decision-making capacity of every citizen. In their opinion, real democracy exists when individuals manage their own affairs, not when this task is delegated to "experts" residing a thousand miles away.

Even the significance of "freedom" has become a bone of contention. As might be expected, both sides glory in the fact that they dwell in a free country, with neither approving the installation of a monarchy or dictatorship. Yet most conservatives assume that freedom has its limits. In their estimation, liberty is not an absolute, but stops somewhere short of the tip of the other fellow's nose. They describe an overabundance of liberty as *license* that by its very nature obliterates freedom.[12] But more than this, they believe that for people to be truly free, they must voluntarily bind themselves to a sense of duty, for only a strong commitment not to interfere with the rights of others enables these to be exercised. Liberals, on the other hand, are more sanguine about the merits of unrestricted liberty and don't expect it to be abused. Since they believe that people are basically "nice,"[13] they are certain that if they are allowed to be themselves, they will also allow others to be themselves. For them, one of life's most profound truths is that niceness breeds niceness and that freedom breeds freedom. They find duty stuffy and constraining, whereas allowing one's inner child to sing is thought to guarantee a resplendent chorus dedicated to advancing everyone's individual self.

It should be apparent that much of the division between liberals and conservatives falls along the same fracture zone that separates Rousseau[14] from Hobbes.[15] Their enormously different conceptions of human nature lead to opposite conclusions regarding what makes life pleasant or civilization possible. As was explained earlier, Rousseau[16] believed in the inherent kindliness of human beings and their ability to thrive in unregulated cooperation. Hobbes, however, detected an unquenchable selfishness that required strong external boundaries. In a Rousseauian world rationality, equality, democracy, and freedom flow from wellsprings innate to every human being, whereas in a Hobbesian one people impetuously infringe upon the very circumstances that would allow them to be happy. In short, both perspectives perceive themselves as supporting a more satisfying mode of life; their quarrel concerns only the most effective mechanisms for attaining this. The differences, in sum, are about tactics, not goals.

Although each side tends to demonize the other, both encompass huge reserves of good will. Their failure to achieve a consensus regarding the best mode of social organization actually reflects the immense difficulty we all have in determining what is best. Whether or not they realize it, both are caught up in a middle-class revolution the likes of which has not previously occurred. If they disagree about where we should be headed, it is because we are all embarked upon a journey into uncharted territory. Paradoxically, despite their confident rhetoric, neither camp fully understands the consequences of its ideals, nor could it, for neither of them have ever been tested in operation.

Before moving on, it important to note that the radical activists are among the most diligent cultural warriors. The gender radicals, for example, have not been shy in offering recommendations on how to meet our impending challenges.[17] Thus among the ideals they promote are a streamlined military, a reorganized educational system, an altered job market, dramatic legal reforms, and a modified interpersonal etiquette—especially a sexual one. In the military, the goal has been to eliminate all gender specializations, with women free to engage in front-line combat and to fly jet interceptors. In school systems, they want special classrooms for girls, financing for team sports divided down the middle, and encouragement for girls to enter engineering programs. On the job front, they insist that these advances in education must come to fruition, with women smashing through the glass ceiling[18] and taking their rightful place as the chief operating officers of multinational corporations and as comparably paid and equally respected machinists on the factory floor. In the courts, besides increasing the number of female lawyers and judges, their primary objective is legal equity, with the same laws applying to all irrespective of sex. Finally, on the personal front, these gender idealists pursue such indelicate goals as encouraging women to assume the uppermost position in coitus and such sublime ones as outlawing all forms of sexual harassment.

A PATH NEVER TRAVELED

When, in class, I ask my college freshmen where the world is headed, a majority routinely assure me that this is the worst period in all of recorded history. With pollution, violence, and incivility rising on every side, they confidently predict that doom will soon overtake us. Knowing little about the past, they are horrified by the effects of automobile exhausts, while at the same time blithely unaware that animal-based transportation once left the streets strewn with manure. Likewise impressed by the prevalence of drive-by shootings, they are amazingly ignorant of the onetime ubiquity of private duels or the sanguinary aspects of ancient warfare. Though they may realize changes have taken place, they do not understand their source or appreciate that most of these have been for the better.

It has nonetheless become a cliché in modern circles that change is occurring more rapidly than ever. Most people similarly recognize that novelty can be difficult to assimilate. Still, they remain unfamiliar with the trends in which they are immersed. The most pervasive of these has undoubtedly been the growing dominance of the middle class. In terms of sheer numbers, U.S. census data[19] reveal that since the year 1900 the percentage of white collar workers has risen from 17% to more than 55% and that at the same time blue collar employment has fallen from a high of more than 40% to a current total of about 25%. More dramatic still has been the decline of farm labor from 37% to a meager 2%. As a consequence, there are now more white collar workers than blue collar ones. Hunter[20] is correct to have highlighted the implications of industrialization, but an

Chapter 9

increase in manufacturing output, and of information transfer, are only part of the picture. With market-based economies becoming ever more dominant, the breadth of their impact on our personal, as well as civic, conduct has expanded to an unprecedented degree.

Predictably, this middle-class explosion has left an indelible imprint on our social institutions, and our definition of social problems and, not unnaturally, has influenced the character of our ideals. To an extent many overlook, our aspirations have become middle-class aspirations. As those making an expanded proportion of society's decisions, members of this class have—like it or not—assumed a greater responsibility for leading us into virgin territory. As importantly, their determinations regarding how we should proceed are, in large part, grounded in their experience of a civilization more massive and complex than any that have preceded it. Never before have so many people been so dependent on strangers for their livelihood and security; never before have so many been exposed to the innumerable unpredictable quirks of a rapidly mutating technology. So despite the privileged position of the middle classes, how are they to decide which goals to endorse? How can they know which ones will work best for society?

For most people, their starting point in figuring things out is where they happen to find themselves. For members of the middle class this means the kind of work they do. Employed as managers and professionals, they ascertain on the job the desirability of making autonomous decisions, of getting along with co-workers from different backgrounds, and of directing the work of subordinates without resorting to violent sanctions. In particular, as Melvin Kohn[21] has demonstrated with regard to childrearing practices, they value self-direction. Having ascertained the desirability of independent decision making, they want their children to follow in their footsteps and to be capable of rational choice, even in conditions of uncertainty. They, more than members of the working classes, want their progeny to be curious, considerate, self-controlled, and happy, as opposed to obedient or neat and clean. Those lower in rank, by way of contrast, tend to demand conformity of their children, for that is what is demanded of them in the closely supervised, repetitive, and physically oriented jobs they occupy.

But an inclination toward self-direction does not, of itself, confer inspiration regarding ideals. It may be a stimulus to seeking solutions, but does not ipso facto supply their content. When making predictions about which objectives will work best in an inevitably obscure future, social leaders need theories in which they can believe and strategies in which they can repose confidence. In short, they need models from which to draw stimulation and comfort. Though few realize it, many of these are connected with the historical trends in which they are embedded. Contrary to conventional wisdom, when people decide what is optimum, they often do so in reaction to influences impinging upon them rather than from spontaneous preferences. Among the forces that have been most potent in this respect have been several that were highlighted by Gerhard Lenski[22] in a survey he did of social class transformations. Beginning with the era just before recorded history, he sought to establish the long-term patterns of social organization. Specifically, Lenski has argued that over the millennia there have been significant decreases in the incidence of interpersonal violence and in the degree of social distance between individuals, and a corresponding expansion in the amount of social rationality. How these tendencies are related to contemporary ideals will soon become evident.

To get some idea of what has occurred, we need to take a very long view. More than ten thousand years ago almost all human beings lived in hunter-gatherer communities.[23] In bands that rarely exceeded one hundred and fifty, they wandered the countryside in search of game, roots, and berries. This form of organization, however, was rapidly replaced by simple horticultural societies based on a digging stick technology. Despite the unsophisticated nature of this new system, it launched a revolution that had greater ramifications than our present industrial one. Because the more dependable food supply inherent in agriculture permitted larger scale groupings, people were able to live in villages that soon grew into towns, nations, and empires. The sedentary nature of these communities also facilitated the fabrication, and accumulation, of items of property such as clay pots and metal tools. Within short order, these were being traded, often over long distances. As transportation, primarily via ships, draft animals, and roads, metamorphosed to keep up with the demand, and as political institutions, in the form of kingdoms, multiethnic empires, and city-states, became more sophisticated, commerce became more stable and individuals wealthier. After many ups and downs, including the extensive downturn of early medieval Europe, social organization became sufficiently reliable to sustain the modern nation state with its industrial mode of production.[24] Truly massive manufacturing came into being only when businessmen felt secure enough to invest their money in large-scale enterprises and when mass transportation was efficient enough to enable the sale of large quantities of goods to customers residing hundreds of miles from their point of origin.[25]

In this grand march of history, the themes Lenski has identified are readily discernible. As his research reveals, the prevalence of physical violence, the degree of social distance, and the tendency toward rationality have varied in predictable ways. Thus, back in the days of the agricultural empires, violent behavior was omnipresent. To keep people who did not know each other together within the same huge political entity, it became necessary to intimidate them. Only then were they apt to hold a leader in sufficient awe. Moreover, with simultaneous advances in the technology of war, these repressive measures became drastic. Not only were people hacked apart in battle, but if a city stubbornly resisted subjugation, its conqueror might slaughter all the adult men, cut off their heads, and stack them in a pyramid by the main gate. Even within nations, the price for defying authority could be extreme. Those who have seen the movie *Braveheart* obtained some inkling of this. After finally capturing the Scottish rebel William Wallace,[26] King Edward I of England made an example of him in the manner of his times. As a warning to others not to follow the same path, Wallace was hanged by the neck until almost dead, then drawn by means of ropes until he again almost expired, then disemboweled, and finally cut into four quarters each of which was taken to a different part of the realm to be displayed on a pole before the assembled populace.

Contrary to popular belief, overt social violence has been on the decline for centuries. Despite up-ticks in street crime, or aberrations such as the Holocaust, physical injury is less universal than it once was. Indeed, the triumph of the marketplace has, in part, been predicated upon this development. People simply will not devote themselves to making, trading, and collecting personal property if they expect thieves to be lurking around every corner, destructive warfare to break out momentarily, or arbitrary confiscations to be the daily prerogative of a ruler. What has happened is that as societies have grown, the controls keeping them orderly have become more internalized. Instead of requiring the explicit commands of external governors, people have been socialized to follow rules to which they are personally committed.

Turning to changes in social distance, a similar progression is detectable. Though hunter-gatherer societies were remarkably egalitarian, once nation-states developed, kings and nobles were set apart from the rest. These hierarchical leaders resided in large private compounds; reserved the best clothing, jewelry, and edibles for themselves; and exercised the power of life and death over their subjects. Many never even interacted with those who came to be regarded as their inferiors. This extreme social distance was a fact of life in societies as diverse as ancient Egypt, the Roman Empire, and the *ancien regime* of early modern France.

Given the disparity of authority between the rulers and the ruled, it might be assumed that the privileges of the elite would have been perpetuated indefinitely. Yet, in recent centuries, democracy has been on the rise worldwide. One of the unanticipated side effects of industrialization has, in fact, been a dramatic increase in personal equality. When in the 1830s Alexis de Tocqueville[27] toured America, he was impressed with the familiarity with which even tradesman treated him. As a member of the minor French nobility, this would have been unthinkable in his homeland. He was also acutely aware that these attitudes extended within the family, where women and children were accorded more influence than in contemporary Europe. Though Marxists would disagree, this growing familiarity can be directly traced to the expansion of the marketplace and industrialization. As technology has grown progressively more complex, social organizations more elaborate, and marketing strategies more refined, the talents needed to manage them have expanded accordingly. Because no individual, or small group of individuals—not luxury-loving aristocrats, bloated capitalists, or Soviet apparatchiks—can handle this load without assistance, those who have been called on to assume this role have been none other than members of the middle class. Moreover, as the specialists who enable the system to operate, they must be properly motivated. Energetic and educated, they have demanded, and received, respect in the form of material compensation and political clout—hence the upsurge in democracy and equality.

Lastly, changes in rationality have emerged even though our human brains probably have not altered much in the past hundred thousand years. August Comte[28] interpreted this as a progression from the theological to the metaphysical and thence to the scientific, and plausibly attributed it to the march of civilization. A more illuminating explanation, however, must begin with the fact that hunter-gatherers did not have a huge store of information at their disposal. Their limited personal contacts, primarily with people of the same backgrounds, as well as their illiteracy, confined them to what they could remember and verbally share with their peers. Much of their wisdom was therefore encapsulated in the emotionally salient myths and rituals of their religion. Even after agriculture took root, because its members too were confronted with a myriad of uncertainties, like their predecessors, they relied on supernatural protectors to make sense of their circumstances. The main difference was that given their more advanced technologies, their belief systems were more elaborate and more consistently enforced by an entrenched priesthood.

The breakthrough to rationality eventually came through the growth of commerce. Literacy, for instance, evolved from a need to keep track of stored commodities and of mercantile transactions. Money itself did not arrive on the European scene until around 650 BC, but when it did, wrought dramatic changes. These advances expanded[29] still further when in the High Middle Ages businessmen acquired the mathematical tools to calculate their expenditures with some exactness.[30] It was not until this period that the invention of double-entry bookkeeping and letters of credit really enabled them to determine profitability and loss. This, in turn, so raised the prestige of calculation that it was emulated within the newly emerging domain of science. Indeed, the dilettantes who were to be its initial sponsors could not have made their discoveries had they not been able to use numbers to categorize natural events.

Also of inestimable importance to rationality was the development of printing, for it made it possible to record, and disseminate, immense stores of information. This was eventually to make mass education practical. Indeed, only after the triumph of this latter could rationality be regarded as the standard. The result was that Max Weber[31] could, at the beginning of this century, use the concept of rationality to explain how bureaucracies operate and, more recently, economists could speculate that rational choice-making undergirds all social interactions. It should, therefore, come as no surprise that those most responsible for, and those who benefited most from, this development are members of the middle class. As scientists, middle managers, professionals, educators, and consumers of education, they have been the engine propelling rationality forward.

Given these trends, there remains the question of how they are related to the decisions of the middle class to adopt specific ideals. The point of connection seems to be the process through which people determine what aspirations to embrace. Their ideals, whether of the right or left, are typically generated through a series of distinguishable stages, that, although they do not possess a geometric exactitude, follow a discernible logic. The first of these steps is marked by the presence of a social challenge. A shared problem, often a crisis, mobilizes the collective energies of a community and sustains its search for a viable answer. The collapse of traditional female roles in our mass-market society constitutes such a challenge, as does the difficulty encountered in integrating African-Americans into an open social class system. These perils can be real or perceived, but must be sufficiently unsettling for an heroic solution to feel imperative.

The next stage in creating a concrete ideal entails generating a vision. Those who feel uncomfortable need to invent, or discover, a credible model of what to do. Because this can be daunting when projecting into an unknown future, ideals tend to be constructed from familiar materials. People typically draw inspiration from previous experience. The archetypes they devise may seem fresh, but, in fact, generally have roots in the old and comfortable. The history of science is replete with examples of this phenomenon. In ancient Greece, for instance, when people were trying to understand how the heart worked, they compared it with a furnace.[32] It was not until early modern times, when efficient pumps were developed, that these became the blueprint for a theory about the circulation of blood. Similarly, the brain was long such a mystery that to the early Egyptians it appeared purposeless. Only our contemporary discovery of the computer has provided investigators with the confidence that a chemical/mechanical arrangement, rather than a spiritual one, can explain its functioning.

When looking at the history of idealism, a comparable use of analogies springs to view. Plato,[33] when he was seeking a plan for the reform of Athens, adopted Sparta as his prototype, whereas Margaret Mead[34] proffered a misunderstanding of Samoan culture as a template for the reorganization of Western society. Radical feminists too have reasoned by way of analogy. Their vision of gender equality obtained its inspiration, in part, from modern democratic nations. Were the practice of one man one vote not as commonplace as it is, gender equivalence would have been more difficult to imagine. Likewise, had not a Marxist world view preceded theirs, it is doubtful that they would have been as boldly utopian. Tutored, as they have been, in a political and academic environment in which a multitude of educated people have considered class-based exploitation to be a fact, transferring this to gender relations has felt natural.

Still, drawing a credible analogy is only part of elaborating an idealistic vision. Because what occurred in the past almost never exactly fits what must be done in the present, there is a need for extrapolation. The model must be extended into the new area and altered to conform with its requirements. Usually this entails a "purification rite." To become "ideal," a vision must be sanitized and the difficulties in its application ignored. As a result, rather than reporting the realities of its source, it is aggrandized and transformed into something that is the "best" or the "most." Purporting to be complete and faultless, as it will, the ideal cannot be contaminated, or diminished, by qualifications or by competing trends. More than enduring extrapolation, it will have been pushed toward the glowing endpoint of what seems to be a predetermined continuum. Idealists, after all, seek optimal solutions, not adequate ones. Once touched up and simplified, their visions are no longer encumbered by specifics that might dilute their promise and they now assume an untarnished luminosity that is neither challenged nor amended.

The upshot of this refurbishment is that instead of a single person being blinded by his idiosyncratic hopes, an entire population can sustain, and mutually verify, a common illusion. Religious fundamentalists, for instance, do more than find answers in the Bible. For them, it represents God's revealed word and hence is correct in all its particulars. Though scholars have detected numerous contradictions in its text,[35] true believers discount these. When told that the story of Noah, at various points, enumerates the animals loaded onto the ark differently or that Joshua's stopping the sun in the sky contradicts physical law, they are unimpressed. Since, for them, true means totally true, the Bible can be nothing less than a literal account of God's Will.

To sum up, constructing an ideal entails extending and purifying an objective appropriated from preexiting sources to make it seem the inevitable answer to a vexing problem. In contemporary America this often involves intensifying the three historical trends identified by Lenski and projecting their endpoints into a speculative future. The result is that decreases in social distance, diminutions in violence, and increases in rationality are pushed as far as they can go by radical feminists, radical civil rights activists, and radical medicalists alike. In the case of the feminists, they begin by converting equality into an absolute standard. Though they would be scandalized at the suggestion, in adopting androgyny as their unimpeachable goal, they move beyond democracy into the realm of the chimerical. Recent centuries do reveal a march toward decreasing social distance in politics, economics, and family relations, but they wish to travel past these to total equality in every regard. Actual advances in social mobility, legal equity, and participation in social decision-making leave them unimpressed. Only a complete absence of gender bias, with no relevant differences between men and women, meets their test of acceptability. Never mind that social hierarchies are universal, that gender-based divisions of labor are ubiquitous, or that millions of women desire a status distinct from men, they indefatigably assert that their benchmark must take precedence.

The gender radicals also wish to banish violence from relationships between the sexes. Although some gender frictions have always existed,[36] they expect the future to hold none. This may initially seem reasonable in that intimate violence has, for some time, been on the decline. It was, we can recall, not many years ago that the movies unabashedly showed John Wayne spanking his leading ladies and James Bond forcibly seducing his. In both cases, their conquests squealed with delight—much to the pleasure of approving audiences. Today this seems not only old fashioned, but almost like applauding rape. We have traveled so far that students at Antioch College[37] recently thought it reasonable to remove all coercion from dating relations by mandating that before a boy touches a girl, he must explicitly ask her permission, which must be explicitly given. Interestingly, for violence to be completely expunged from heterosexual relationships, their inherent passions and sexual tensions would need to be eliminated as well. This, of course, would imply a radical expansion of rationality. Since intimate relations are in large part irrational—being swept as they periodically are by surges of intense emotion—they would have to be dramatically calmed down.[38] In the world of triumphant feminist ideologues, old-fashioned love would, therefore, need to be replaced by more balanced calculations and personal attachments by the mandates of political correctness.

Some may find it surprising, but the radical civil rights agenda likewise involves extensive purification. Its emphasis on comprehensive racial equality seeks more than ordinary fairness. By insisting on exactly equivalent economic and political results, it asks for what has never been previously achieved. More than proposing a reduction in social distance, it would eradicate all distinctions by requiring the same outcomes for everyone. Similarly, its stress on the legal enforcement of minority rights partakes of the trend toward social rationality. First, in asserting that prejudice is decisive in maintaining racism, it, in effect, alleges that the senselessness of the bigots is responsible for continued injustices. Were their ignorance effaced by reasonable educational policies, a large proportion of these could theoretically be eliminated. Second, it assumes that rationalistic legislation is the sturdiest instrument for enforcing interpersonal virtue. Objective, and capable of universal application, it is presumed capable of evening out inequalities in birth and skin color. Unfortunately, this overestimates the efficacy of legal remedies.[39] In supposing them to be fundamentally rational, it leaves out their human element. In fact, because formal regulations can never anticipate all relevant consequences, and because their interpretation invariably depends on the interests of players, their infallibility exists only in the imagination of the uncritical and the naive.

But the process of creating an effective ideal is not yet finished. There is another step that must be completed, that is, the induction of the ideal into a group setting. Specifically, the extended and purified vision needs to be buffed up and purveyed to a collectivity that is prepared to be bedazzled by it. Despite the fact that extrapolating from earlier circumstances to a luminescent future is a universal human propensity, this is unlikely to happen without the participation of dedicated activists. These intermediaries serve as catalysts who integrate social forces and provide the impetus to make them effectual by inaugurating social movements and by providing them with their leadership. Hence it is that without a St. Paul[40] to tirelessly proselytize among the gentiles, there could not have been a Christian Church; without a Vladimir Lenin to goad reluctant Bolsheviks into action, there would have been no October Revolution; and without a Gloria Steinem to shape the editorial policy of a *Ms.* Magazine, feminism could not have spread as rapidly.

Sadly, most activists tend not to be agreeable people. Monomaniacal in orientation and ruthless in tactics, they appear angelic only from afar or through the eyes of the devout. For temperamental and personal reasons, they generally possess an intense interest in obtaining power and/or in effectuating a specific outcome. Often intent on obtaining revenge for real or imagined affronts, they may endeavor to persuade us that their personal enemies are also ours. As ax grinders,[41] they typically nurse their resentments through periods of hardship, until, when an opening occurs, they can spring into action. Like Adolf Hitler,[42] who survived the Beer Hall Putsch to take advantage of the disorders inherent in the Great Depression, they are poised to exploit whatever confusions arise. Where other more genteel souls modify their priorities as external circumstances shift, their lack of flexibility enables them to pursue a favored ideal, even as their adversaries are consumed by doubt.

Were they, however, to nurse their grudges in isolation, these messiahs could not succeed. Their private vendettas must be translated into concrete alliances to have an impact. It is the united strength of the coalitions they help fashion that enables their objectives to flourish. Although such movements may be sparked in many ways, without common ideals to animate them, they would possess neither hope nor direction. Knowing this, visionaries dedicate considerable energy to instilling shared convictions.[43] Usually they do not invent these, but like astute politicians, usurp the leadership of preexisting trends and through a combination of threats, guile, and propaganda induce others to rally around them. If they are lucky, these coalitions reach a critical mass and a bandwagon effect emerges in which the emotions and imaginations of the participants interact to reinforce each other. What seemed a feasible answer to specific individuals will now take on an aura of destiny. Sanctified by the contagion of a collective passion, the participants cease examining the ideal and begin insisting on absolute obedience to it. A reverse *the-emperor-has-no-clothes* syndrome then occurs and the crowd exults in a communal enthusiasm. Should a child now shout, "But he has nothing on!" unlike in the Anderson fairy tale, they would respond: "Oh yes he has!"

After a vision has achieved such currency, extremism is almost a foregone conclusion. And with little to check its advance, it eventually becomes dangerous. Often only a disastrous application of an ideal can persuade people to abandon it. Thus, millions of Germans relinquished their faith in Nazism[44] only after their nation lost a catastrophic war. As often happens in religious cults, what they had come to regard as holy was not logically investigated—for to do so would have seemed impious. Nor are true believers always dissuaded by calamity.[45] The walls of their cities may be collapsing, but the devout are sufficiently ingenious to find rationalizations for the debacle. When encouraged by like-minded others, their tenacity can be remarkable. The ultimate tragedy of unreflective idealism is, therefore, not that people try to solve problems in ways that can't work, but that they won't let go of them no matter what. As Richard Bernstein[46] explains in his *Dictatorship of Virtue*, theirs becomes a *fanaticism* wherein they redouble their efforts even as they are leading them to defeat.

SOCIAL RESPONSIBILITY

In the face of idealistic excess, and the social pressures that help sanctify it, how can conscientious persons retain their balance? The task is not simple. Given the persistence of the radicals, an independent judgment can be difficult to sustain. Yet if, as individuals, we have an obligation to be responsible to ourselves, we surely have one to uphold the lineaments of civil society.[47] Clearly, a lack of effort in rebuffing the blandishments of the throng is as potentially destructive as is succumbing to luminosity blindness. Perhaps more so. In a middle-class world, where each of us has more influence than ever before, there is a need for prudence in implementing visions that could have deleterious effects. Would-be leaders, who volunteer to be their brothers keepers,[48] ought at least pause to investigate the terrain before they blunder ahead.

One of the greatest hazards of contemporary idealism is our widespread desire for instant solutions. When confronted with perplexing problems, plans that advertise themselves as foolproof have an obvious appeal. Moral messiahs, because they are cognizant of the personal insecurities of their audiences, hasten to provide such assurances. To make matters worse, these visions are portrayed as so perfect that questioning them is represented as blasphemous. Yet they must be questioned. To not do so—to take an advocate's convictions at face value—is, to use an old-fashioned expression, to buy a pig in a poke. Worse than this, it is to purchase it on behalf of others whose permission one has not received.

When activists seek converts, they begin by exploiting the prima facie validity of their wares. As members of the same society as those they wish to influence, they can count upon a store of shared understandings to provide plausibility. Thus, radical feminists are aware that most Americans are ardent democrats. In equating androgyny with democracy, they therefore indulge in a bait and switch con game. First, they evoke emotional attachments to a familiar form of political organization, then they maneuver their targets into believing that an extreme brand of feminism is its equivalent. From the point of view of their victims, what is being recommended simply feels right. They may not understand why, but will give their assent on the assumption that they are endorsing the familiar and well-proven. A similar tactic is employed by radical medicalists. Because science today possesses a cachet few are bold enough to deny, their assertion of scientific grounds for being non-judgmental puts most of us on the defensive. Without access to data that might refute their theses, we simply rely on a long-established disposition to trust the experts.[49]

Perhaps the most dramatic example of this sort of manipulation was provided by Prohibition. Though based on neither science nor democracy, its enactment followed a century of religiously grounded agitation. The process of supplying its central ideal with an aura of authority began with the advent of industrialism. After factories packed with dangerous, surveillance-hungry machinery began to multiply, a call to control workplace drunkenness emerged.[50] At first, businessmen organized avowedly religious revivals to instill a desire for sobriety. When time demonstrated that these were insufficient, the effort was redirected toward constitutional reform. Few remember the emotional bandwagon that, in the wake of World War I, carried the Eighteenth Amendment to ratification, but it was all-consuming. The defects inherent in imposing abstinence on millions who did not want it—which within a decade became obvious—were invisible to voters enthralled by projections of heaven on earth. Their sincere Christian convictions were such that could not imagine how universal sobriety would do anything other than uplift the entire nation. Their religious faith having been transferred to a political agenda, it too seemed sacrosanct and beyond invalidation.

Social responsibility, however, entails an obligation to see beyond one's predilections. If ideals are treated as objects of veneration, a suspension of disbelief can leave one willing to accept the inherently shoddy.[51] Whatever the hyperbole to which idealists rise, there is a need to avoid plunking one's money down on the equivalent of home fitness equipment. Answers to the very real problems generated by a world in unprecedented flux cannot be guaranteed by mere attractiveness. Nor can a prepackaged loyalty to a political faith—whether liberal or conservative—obviate the need to investigate what works. Moral maturity is essential.[52] Those interested in hastening a better future must confront the unexpected and the unwelcome. Rather than uncritically latch onto the superficially authentic, they have to brave the real world with all its flaws, including the prospect that specific projections will not pan out.

Despite the tendency to regard ideals as absolutes, it is more prudent to treat them as hypotheses. Because they can be wrong, they must be tested, and, should they fail, be rejected. Ideals not subject to such disconfirmation can lead to disaster. The truth is that that which is assumed to be beyond error is sure to be controverted later on. What begin as small mistakes will accumulate until in the end the departure from reality is enormous. The appropriate attitude is therefore one of caution. Paradoxically, even the ostensibly perfect needs to be corrected. While visions of the sublime may beckon us to abandon our critical faculties, it is crucial to remain tentative, for an excessive of zeal can interfere with a timely application of the brakes. Despite the fact that some social theorists assure us we can define the world any way we desire, no matter how fervent the majority endorsing a particular goal, if it does not produce the goods, it cannot be satisfying.

Unfortunately the morality game is such that it encourages extremism. The informal rules at its core are invariably buttressed by commitments to idealized endpoints. Because both individually and collectively, its players desire what seems essential to human needs, they simplify and intensify what they pursue. Likewise, that which is deemed certain is not subjected to doubt; hence divergent views are not heeded. The result is that the latter tend to be dismissed, or, if threatening, to be attacked. Moral negotiations, therefore, have a way of escalating past the point of reason—with the ensuing good guy-bad guy struggle becoming extravagant. Ironically, democracy itself seems to invite excess—the bully pulpit of Teddy Roosevelt being none other than a moral pulpit. Because majority rule inevitably entails a need to assemble working majorities, vivid ideals present a beguiling tool for attracting the necessary followings. This is why utopian promises for solving shared problems are the currency of political campaigns. Rallying cries such as Herbert Hoover's "A chicken in every pot" or the Supreme Court's "Separate is inherently unequal," though artless, are assimilated into the world views of disparate constituencies from thence to be translated into concrete demands for school busing or increased educational funding.

Idealism, not to put too fine a point on the matter, can be overdone. If its seductive examples are too simplified, its negotiations too truculent, or its emotions too violent, the benefits it promises to bestow are quickly exhausted. Because moderation is as vital to genuine moral progress as is a dedication to pursuing positive transformations, soaring to impossible heights within one's imagination, though a marvelous spur to creativity, when unrestrained, can be lethal. Fortunately, middle-class status appears to confer a desire for discretion. Despite the temptations of extremism, as people rise within a democratic hierarchy, they seem to develop an abhorrence of radicalism. Though often castigated for their proclivity toward compromise and conformity, they prefer tolerance, pragmatism, and self-discipline. This may not be romantic, and is surely not millenary, but it is steady, safe, and profitable.

In the study of middle-class values alluded to in Chapter 2, Alan Wolfe[53] found that far from being hidebound ideologues, contemporary American suburbanites have a nuanced and broad-minded attitude toward values. Contrary to what the activists say, as he reports in *One Nation, After All*, they are not tied to a single idealist vision that they are determined to impose on others whatever the cost. On the contrary, "Moderation and tolerance—an appreciation of the modest virtues—are the bedrock moral principles of the American middle class... American society [in sum] is dominated by the ideas of the *reasonable* majority: people who believe themselves to be modest in their appetites, quiet in their beliefs, and restrained in their inclinations."

In two hundred interviews, in eight communities across the country, Wolfe discovered that even middle-class religious conservatives are accepting of other people's beliefs. Ironically, while many on the left perceive them to be unreconstructed right-wingers, they perceive themselves as a beleaguered minority trying to hold back a liberal tide. Much of their obstinacy—which taken too far can be hazardous—is actually an effort to defend commitments they correctly believe to be under siege. To Wolfe's surprise, he concluded that "Conservative Christians are often more willing to acknowledge the degree to which America has changed since the battles over fundamentalism earlier in this century than are those adherents to the American Civil Liberties Union who act as if religious intolerance, rather than nonjudgmentalism, is still the dominant tone of the country's religiosity."

As a resident of Cobb County, Georgia, one of the regions Wolfe studied, I too have been struck by this openness. When I arrived in the area almost a decade ago, it was with trepidation. A lifelong northerner, I had been weaned on horror stories regarding the bigotry of the Bible Belt and expected that once my neighbors discovered I was a New York Jew, they would burn a cross on my lawn. This unease was enhanced when, on my first visit to the area, the chair of my college's Political Science department drove me through "downtown" Kennesaw to point out the store where the local "wildman" always worn a pair of pistols on his hips in ostentatious compliance with the town's ordinance requiring every homeowner to possess a gun. Nor did it help when the county commissioners subsequently passed a resolution denying a local theater group taxpayer support because it had produced a supposedly homosexual-friendly play.

Yet all this was misleading. As my neighbors, colleagues, and students quickly taught me, they were normal middle-class Americans, who, in Wolfe's words, were "trying to be faithful to their own values, while to the largest extent possible, respectful and nonjudgmental of others." Even the fundamentalists I encountered came in a variety of flavors, with even the most ardently religious willing to allow me to be different. When they learned that I was an agnostic, they might squint at me quizzically, wondering how this was possible, but they never sought to be punitive. Indeed, most were relatively sophisticated college graduates and consumers of the national news media who were able to hold as subtle a conversation as might be found in any New York City drawing room.

But this sort of moderation can, as I have said, be difficult to maintain. The world is a frightening place over which none of us has total dominion. Lacking a complete understanding of what is happening around us, we sometimes allow idealistic fairy tales to cushion the potential blows. As our tastes in movies and novels confirm, we often disappear into syrupy reveries with happy endings. These comforting assurances provide a useful shield, but, lamentably, one that leaves us exposed to our own gullibility. The most serious danger members of the middle-class face is thus not so much a tendency toward radicalism, as a vulnerability to being exploited by those who portray the fantastic as real. Though sometimes quixotic at heart, left to their own devices, few middle-class moderns are extravagant in action. Rather, it is in being co-opted by unscrupulously deceptive moralists, and unconsciously doing their bidding, that the real hazard dwells.

Because it is hope responsive to reality, as opposed to fantasies grounded in innocence, that are socially beneficial, naiveté can be a calamity. Despite its proclamations of magnanimity, it celebrates a self-indulgent retreat from the material world. Preferable by far is the adult ability to tolerate uncertainty, conflict, and intense emotion. Only it can reveal that imperfection, ignorance, and unfairness are normal parts of living that, with time and effort, can be overcome—although only incompletely. As human beings living in the midst of other limited human beings, however sparkling the future constructed in our imaginations, the one in which we reside is sure to cause some pain, frustration, and disappointment. This is not to say that the world never gets better, merely that things improve gradually and often at the margins. In the end, ideals that promise a revolution tend to deliver less than do ameliorative strategies that concentrate on smaller, more tangible advances.

As the well-known proverb has it, good intentions pave the road to hell. Unaccompanied by courage, intelligence, and resilience, they usually run aground. To be efficacious, efforts at improvement must take a long and a broad view. For my own part, I am not sure which is worse: the small-minded bigot or the small-minded idealist. Both are cut from the same cloth. Despite their protestations to the contrary, the easy answers each seeks cannot work. Nevertheless, the alternative, a critical idealism, is not child's play. It depends on continuous learning and continuous growth—on a hard-headed realism, not a squishy romanticism. The reality we must all confront is that no matter how much we may want to save the world, there are limits beyond which we cannot go before falling off the edge. An inability to achieve the preconceptions we once thought essential is therefore not so much a sign of failure as of growing up.

Notes and References

Chapter 1. Idealism on Trial

1. For an overview of the welfare system see Cozic, C. (1997). *Welfare Reform.* San Diego, CA: Greenhaven Press. For an assessment of some of its difficulties see: Gordon, L. (1994). *Pittied But Not Entitled: Single Mothers and the History of Welfare.* New York: Free Press. One of the best critiques of the 60s is found in Magnet, M. (1993). *The Dream and the Nightmare: The Sixties Legacy to the Underclass.* New York: William Morrow, while a chilling review of the decade's darker side is on view in Collier, P. & Horowitz, D. (1996). *Destructive Generation: Second Thoughts About the '60s.* New York: The Free Press.
2. One of the pioneers of this treatment was Marie Nyswander, whose story is told in Hentoff, N. (1968). *A Doctor Among the Addicts.* New York: Rand McNally.
3. Goffman, E. (1961). *Asylums.* New York: Anchor Books.
4. Among the best depictions of these institutions are found in Scull, A. (1974). *Museums of Madness: The Social Organization of Insanity in Nineteenth Century England.* Princeton University Ph.D. and Scull, A. (1981). *Madhouses, Mad-Doctors, and Madmen: The Social History of Psychiatry in the Victorian Era.* London: The Athlone Press. A particularly biting examination of the concept behind these insitutions is provided by Szasz, T. (1961). *The Myth of Mental Illness: Foundations of a Theory of Personal Conduct.* New York: Dell.
5. For a review of deinstitutionalization see: Johnson, A. B. (1990). *Out of Bedlam: The Truth About Deinstitutionalization.* New York: Basic Books.
6. Laing, R. D. (1960). *The Divided Self.* London: Tavistock.
7. Two works on homelessness are: Roleff, T. (1996). *The Homeless.* San Diego, CA: Greenhaven Press; Rossi, P. (1989). *Down and Out in America.* Chicago: University of Chicago Press.
8. At the time, one of the more salient patient goals was "normalization." The rationale for this, vis-a-vis the retared was provied by: Wolfensberger, W., with Nirje, B., et al. (1972). *The Principle of Normalization in Human Services.* Toronto: National Institute on Mental Retardation.

233

9. For an overview of organizational theory see: Boleman, L. G. & Deal T. E. (1991). *Reframing Organizations: Artistry, Choice, and Leadership.* San Francisco: Jossey-Bass.

10. Will, G. (1978). *The Pursuit of Happiness and Other Sobering Thoughts.* New Yok: Harper & Row.

11. Adams, S. (1996). *The Dilbert Principle.* New York: HarperCollins.

12. A sampling of social problems texts is as followws: Petersen, P. D., Wunder, D. F. & Mueller, H. L. (1999). *Social Problems: Globalization in the 21st Century.* Upper Saddle River, NJ: Prentice-Hall. Mooney, L. A., Knox, D. & Schacht, C. (1997). *Understanding Social Problems.* Minneapolis, MN: West. Neubeck, K. J. & Neubeck, M. A. (1997). *Social Problems: A Critical Approach,* 4th Edition. New York: McGraw-Hill. Eitzen, D. S. & Zinn, M. B. *Social Problems,* 5th Edition. Boston: Allyn and Bacon.

13. Hobbes, T. (1956). *Leviathan; Part I.* Chicago: Henry Regnery.

14. Rousseau, Jean-Jacques [1762] (1913). *The Social Contract.* In G. D. H. Cole (Ed.), *The Social Contract and Discourses.* London: Dent.

15. Rousseau, Jean-Jacques [1762] (1979). *Emile.* Trans. A. Bloom. New York: Basic Books.

16. For an interesting biography see: Cranston, M. (1982). *Jean-Jacques.* New York: W.W. Norton.

17. How social work texts approach these matters is exemplified by: Zastrow, C. & Krist-Ashman, K. (1990). *Understanding Human Behavior and the Social Environment,* 2nd Edition. Chicago: Nelson-Hall. A clinical sociology approach is found in: Rebach, H. M. & Bruhn, J. G. (1991). *Handbook of Clinical Sociology.* New York: Plenum Press.

18. In: Sandburg, C. (1939). *Abraham Lincoln: The War Years.* New York: Harcourt, Brace.

19. Lipset, S. M. (1996). *American Exceptionalism: A Double-Edged Sword.* New York: W.W. Norton.

20. de Tocqueville, A. (1966). *Democracy in America.* Translated by George Lawrence. New York: Harper & Row.

21. For other views of America's value systen see: Bellah, R. N., Madsen, R., Sullivan, W. M., Swindler, A., & .Tipton, S. M. (1985). *Habits of the Heart: Individualism and Commitment in American Life.* Berkeley, CA: University of California Press; Hearn, F. (1997). *Moral Order and Social Disorder: The American Search for Civil Society.* New York: Aldine de Gruyter; Lasch, C. (1979). *The Culture of Narcissism: American Life in an Age of Diminishing Expectations.* New York: Warner Books; and Seligman, A. B. (1992). *The Idea of Civil Society.* Princeton, NJ: Princeton University Press.

22. Sun-tzu (6th Century BC) (1988). *The Art of War.* Translated by Thomas Cleary. Boston: Shambala.

23. Shaw, G. B. [1921] (1963). *Back to Methuselah.* In: Complete Plays, with Prefaces. New York: Dodd, Mead.

24. Epstein, C. F. (1970). *Woman's Place: Options and Limit: in Professional Careers.* Berkeley, CA: University of California Press.

25. See Boswell, J. (1969). *Boswell's Life of Johnson.* New York: Grolier.

26. An idea explicated by Sigmund Freud. In: Freud, S. (1953-1974). *The Standard Edition of the Complete Psychological Works of Sigmund Freud.* (Edited by J. Strachey). London: Hogarth Press and Institute for Psychoanalysis.

Chapter 2 In the Name of Morality

1. Fulghum, R. (1988). All I Really Need to Know I Learned in Kindergarten: Uncommon Thoughts on Common Things. New York: Villard Books.

2. The classical statement of the socially constructed nature of moral (and religious) rules is provided by: Durkheim, E. (1915). The Elementary Forms of Religious Life. New York: The Free Press. Also see: Durkheim, E. (1961). Moral Education. New York: The Free Press.

3. Perhaps the most influential recent champion of moral knowledge was: Moore, G. E. (1929). Principia Ethica. Cambridge: Cambridge University Press. Broader in influence and earlier in time was: Kant, I. (1949). Critique of Practical Reason. Chicago: University of Chicago Press.

4. For the clearest formulation of this concept see: Wilson, J. Q. (1993). The Moral Sense. New York: The Free Press.

5. Currently sliding from favor, but the strongest formulation of a moral judgment perspective was: Kohlberg. (1986). The Stages of Ethical Development. New York: Harper & Row. See also: Thomas, R. M. (1997). Moral Development Theories—Secular and Religious. Westport, CT: Greenwood Press: and Windmiller, M., Lambert, N. & Turiel, E., (Eds.) (1980). Moral Development and Socialization. Boston: Allyn and Bacon.

6. For a practitioner's view of evolutionary psychology see: Alexander, R. D. (1987). The Biology of Moral Systems. New York: Aldine. For a more popularized and comprehensive version see: Wright, R. (1994). The Moral Animal: Why We Are the Way We Are: The New Science of Evolutionary Psychology. New York: Pantheon Books.

7. Harris, W.H. & Levey, J. S. (Eds.) (1975). The New Columbia Encyclopedia: 4th Edition. New York: Columbia University Press.

8. Ballou, R. O. (Ed.) (1944). The World Bible. New York: The Viking Press.

9. Bennett, W. J. (Ed.) (1993). The Book of Virtues: A Treasury of Great Moral Stories. New York: Simon & Schuster.

10. For a general history of the movelemt consult: Martin, E. J. (1978). A History of the Iconoclastic Controversy. New York: AMS Press.

11. An extreme form of protestant iconoclasm is found among the Jehovah's Witnesses. They are so adamant that they refused to salute the American flag on the theory that it was a graven image. It took a ruling of the Supreme Court to grant them this right. See: Kors, A. C. & Silverglate, H. A. (1998). The Shadow University: The Betrayal of Liberty on America's Campuses. New York: The Free Press.

12. For a psychological analysis see: Lewis, M. & Saarni, C. (Eds.) (1993). Lying and Deception in Everyday Life. New York: Guilford Press.

13. For a history see: Gump, J. O. (1994). The Dust Rose Like Smoke: The Subjugation of the Zulu and the Sioux. Lincoln: The University of Nebraska Press.

14. An account of Truman's decision making process is found in: McCullough, D. (1992). Truman. New York: Simon & Schuster. For an overview see: Baker, P. R. (Ed.) (1968). The Atomic Bomb: The Great Decision. New York: Holt, Rinehart and Winston.

15. A good biography is available in: Lomask, M. (1982). Aaron Burr: The Conspiracy and Years of Exile 1805-1836. New York: Farrar, Straus, Giroux.

16. A charming satirical prespective on vegitarianism is included in: Ellenbogen, G. (Ed.) (1986). Oral Sadism and the Vegetarian Personality. New York: Brunner/Mazel.

17. For an introduction to Kevorkian's philosophy see: Betzold, M. (1993). Appointment with Dr. Death. Troy, Mich: Momentum Books.
18. See: Wright, A. (1964). Confucianism and Chinese Civilization. New York: Atheneum.
19. MacIntyre, A. (1981). After Virtue: A Study in Moral Theory. Notre Dame, IN: University of Notre Dame Press.
20. Gertrude Himmelfarb makes a similar point, contrasting Greek, Christian, and Victorian virtues. She also presents a nice thumbnail sketch of the evolution of moral thinking from "virtues" to "values." See: Himmelfarb, G. (1995). The De-Moralization of Society: From Victorian Virtues to Modern Values. New York: Alfred A. Knopf.
21. Franklin, B. (1950). The Autobiography of Benjamin Franklin. New York: Modern Library.
22. Bennett, W. J. (Ed.) (1993). The Book of Virtues: A Treasury of Great Moral Stories. New York: Simon & Schuster.
23. Greer, C. & Kohl, H. (1995). A Call to Character. New York: HarperCollins.
24. Included in: Bennett, op cit.
25. Included in: Ibid.
26. For the government's own assessment of this phenomenon and its need for protection see: U.S. General Accounting Office (1993). Whistleblower Protection. Washington, D.C.
27. Included in: Greer & Kohl, op cit.
28. For a sociological analysis of the functions of anger see: Fein, M. (1993). I.A.M.: A Common Sense Guide to Coping with Anger. Westport, CT: Praeger.
29. Lyman, S. M. (1989). The Seven Deadly Sins: Society and Evil. Dix Hills, NY: General Hall.
30. The groundbreaking analysis of science as a social process is: Kuhn, T. S. (1970). The Structure of Scientific Revolutions, 2nd Edition. Chicago: University of Chicago Press.
31. Among the exposes of sciences nonscientific ways are: Dewdney, A. K. (1997). Yes, We Have No Neutrons: An Eye-Opening Tour through the Twists and Turns of Bad Science. New York: John Wiley & Sons; Gable, J. & Sica, A. (Eds.) (1998). Ideologies and the Corruption of Thought. New Brunswick, NJ: Transaction; Hamilton, R. F. (1996). The Social Misconstruction of Reality: Validity and Verification in the Scholarly Community. New Haven: Yale University Press; and Cromer, A. (1997). Connected Knowledge: Science, Philosophy, and Education. New York: Oxford University Press.
32. For a history see: Payne, R. (1965). The Rise and Fall of Stalin. New York: Simon & Schuster.
33. Boas, F. (1928). Anthropology and Modern Life. New York: Dover.
34. A fascinating discussion of a variety of social practices is found in: Harris, M. (1974). Cows, Pigs, Wars, and Witches. New York: Random House.
35. The standard formulation of ethical relativism is by: Westermarck, E. (1960). Ethical Relativity. Paterson, NJ: Littlefield, Adams.
36. Second only in importance as a disciple of Boas was: Benedict, R. (1934). Patterns of Culture. Boston: Houghton Mifflin.
37. Mead, M. (1928). Coming of Age in Samoa. New York: William Morrow.
38. In his day Watson was the nation's psychological guru. See: Buckley, K. W. (1989). Mechanical Man: John Broadus Watson and the Beginnings of Behaviorism. New York: The Guilford Press. Among his most influential advice books was: Watson, J. B. (1928). Psychological Care of Infant and Child. New York: Norton.

39. Discussed later in Chapter 4, Russell was very much part of the same movement as Mead. See: Russell, B. (1929). Marriage and Morals. New York: H. Liveright.
40. Freeman, D. (1996). Margaret Mead and the Heretic: The Making and Unmaking of an Anthropological Myth. New York: Penguin Books.
41. Science keeps churning up moralized theories of how the world works. Among the more influential recent myths is that of self-esteem. It was supposed to be a sovereign cure for most of society's ills. See: Hewitt, J. P. (1998). The Myth of Self-Esteem: Finding Happiness and Solving Problems in America. New York: St. Martin's Press. Even more recent has been the exposure of Rigoberta Menchu. The recipient of a Nobel Prize in literature, she became an icon for politically correct academics until her story of being a poor Central American peasant was revealed as a fraud. See: Stoll, D. (1998). Rigoberta Menchu and the Story of All Poor Guatemalans. Boulder, CO: Westview Press. Menchu, R. 1984. I Rigoberta Menchu, an Indian Woman in Guatemala. Translated by Ann Wright. London Verso. Even the classic account of multiple personalities has been shown to have been grossly misleading. See: Schreiber, F. R. (1973). Sybil. Chicago: Regnery; Miller, M. & Kantrowitz. (1999). Unmasking Sybil. Newsweek, Jan. 25, pp.66-68.

Chapter 3. Messianic Stickball

1. Piaget, J. (1965). *The Moral Judgment of the Child.* New York: The Free Press.
2. de Waal, F. B. M. (1996). *Good Natured: The Origins of Right and Wrong in Humans and Other Animals.* Cambridge, MA: Harvard University Press.
3. My own account of morality as a social activity is found in: Fein, M. (1997). *Hardball Without an Umpire: The Sociology of Morality.* Westport, CT: Praeger.
4. Caplow, T. (1982). "Christmas Gifts and Kin Networks." *American Sociological Review,* 47, 382-392. Caplow, T., Howard, H. B, Chadwick, B. A. Hill, R., & Williamson, M. H. (1982). *Middletown Families: Fifty Years of Change and Continuity.* Minneapolis: University of Minnesota Press.
5. Howard, P. K. (1995). *The Death of Common Sense: How Law Is Suffocating America.* New York: Random House.
6. Bennett, W. J. (Ed.) (1993). *The Book of Virtues: A Treasury of Great Moral Stories.* New York: Simon & Schuster.
7. For an overview of the abortion controversy see: Cook, A. E., Jelen T. G. & Wilcox, C. (1992). *Between Two Absolutes: Public Opinion and the Politics of Abortion.* Boulder, CO: Westview Press.
8. Fein, M. (1997). *Hardball Without an Umpire: The Sociology of Morality.* Westport, CT: Praeger.
9. Roiphe, K. (1993). *The Morning After: Sex, Fear, and Feminism On Campus.* Boston: Little, Brown.
10. Brownmiller, S. (1975). *Against Our Will: Men, Women and Rape.* New York: Bantam.
11. MacKinnon, C. A. (1987). *Feminism Unmodified: Discourses on Life and Law.* Cambridge, MA: Harvard University Press.
12. When moral emotions become especially strong they can initiate social panics that have dire consequences. See: Goode, E. & Ben-Yehuda, N. (1994). *Moral Panics: The Social Construction of Deviance.* Cambridge: Blackwell.
13. Lemert, E. M. (1997). *The Trouble with Evil: Social Control at the Edge of Morality.* Albany, NY: State University of New York Press.

14. Faludi, S. (1991). *Backlash: The Undeclared War Against American Women*. New York: Crown.
15. French, M. (1992). *The War Against Women*. New York: Summit Books.
16. Heise, L. (1989). The global war against women. *The Washington Post*, April 9, pp. B1, B4.
17. Lemert, op cit.
18. For two versions of Wovoka's impact see: Hittman, M. (1997). *Wovoka and the Ghost Dance*. Lincoln: University of Nebraska Press; Gump, J. O. (1994). *The Dust Rose Like Smoke: The Subjugation of the Zulu and the Sioux*. Lincoln: The University of Nebraska Press.
19. Talmon, J. L. (1985). *Political Messianism: The Romantic Phase*. Boulder, CO: Westview Press.

Chapter 4. Dreams or Nightmares

1. For an extensive survey of utopianism see: Manuel, F. E. & Manuel F. P. (1979). *Utopian Thought in the Western World*. Cambridge, MA: Belknap Press.
2. See: Gorman, P. (1979). *Pythagoras: A Life*. London: Routledge and Keegan Paul.
3. For a survey of Plato's writings see: Edman, I. (Ed.) (1928). *The Works of Plato;* Jowett Translation. New York: Simon and Schuster.
4. Stone, I. F. (1988). *The Trial of Socrates*. Boston: Little, Brown.
5. Plato (1941). *The Republic;* Jowett translation. New York: The Modern Library.
6. The totalitarian aspects of left wing elitism are dissected in: Ellis, R. J. (1998). *The Dark Side of the Left: Illiberal Egalitarianism in America*. Lawrence, KS: University of Kansas Press.
7. This seems to be the same attitude as displayed in Proudhon and Rousseau. Both deride property as an artificial invention that discourages sharing. See: Proudhon, P. J. [1840] (1994). *What Is Property?* Edited and translated by Donald R. Kelly & Bonnie G. Smith. New York: Cambridge University Press; Rousseau, Jean-Jacques [1762] (1913). *The Social Contract*. In G. D. H. Cole (Ed.), *The Social Contract and Discourses*. London: Dent.
8. *Looking Backward*, one of America's most enduring utopian novels, is equally hard on the family, literally predicting its abandonment. See: Bellamy, E. (1982). *Looking Backward, 2000-1887*. New York: Penguin.
9. For a sympathetic description see: Spiro, M. E. (1958). *Children of the Kibbutz: A Study in Child Training and Personality*. Cambridge, MA: Harvard University Press.
10. Mead, M. (1928). *Coming of Age in Samoa*. New York: William Morrow.
11. Watson was extreme. Despite being a psychologist, he seems to have had an emotion phobia. See: Buckley, K. W. (1989). *Mechanical Man: John Broadus Watson and the Beginnings of Behaviorism*. New York: The Guilford Press.
12. And a very extensive genre it is: Manuel, F. E. & Manuel F. P. (1979). op cit.
13. To put More in context read: Ridley, J. (1982). *Statesman and Saint: Cardinal Wolsey, Sir Thomas More and the Politics of Henry VIII*. New York: Viking Press.
14. More, T. (1964). *Utopia*. Edited by Edward Surtz. New Haven: Yale University Press.
15. For an introduction to the convoluted ways of intellectuals see: Johnson, P. (1988). *Intellectuals*. New York: Harper & Row.
16. For this sad tale see: Erickson, C. (1978). *Bloody Mary*. New York: St. Martin's Press.

17. An up to date biography is: Schom, A. (1998). *Napoleon Bonaparte.* New York: HarperCollins.
18. A popular account of Hitler's life is found in: Toland, J. (1976). *Adolf Hitler.* Garden City, NY: Doubleday.
19. Hitler, A. (1972). *Mein Kampf.* Translated by Ralph Manheim. Boston: Houghton Mifflin.
20. See: Holwerda, D. E. (Ed.) (1976). *Exploring the Heritage of John Calvin.* Grand Rapids: Baker Book House.
21. A talented, but troubled man. See: Reimann, V. (1976). *Goebbels.* Translated by Stephan Wendt. Garden City, NY: Doubleday.
22. For a sympathetic chronicle of Mao's life, see: Terrill, R. (1980). *A Biography: Mao.* New York: Harper & Row.
23. See: Chandler, D. (1992). *Brother Number One: A Political Biography of Pol Pot.* Boulder, CO: Westview Press.
24. Among the chroniclers of the early church's veiws on sexuality are: Ranke-Heinemann, U. (1990). *Eunuchs for the Kingdom of Heaven: Women, Sexuality, and the Catholic Church.* New York: Doubleday; Meeks, W. A. (1993). *The Origins of Christian Morality: The First Two Centuries.* New Haven: Yale University Press; Straus, B. R. (1987). *The Catholic Church.* London: David & Charles.
25. Augustine, St. (1961). *The Confessions.* Translated by R. S. Pine-Coffin. Baltimore, MD: Penguin Books.
26. The following account of the Shakers, including its quotes, is drawn from: Desroche, H. (1971). *The American Shakers: From Neo-Christianty to Presocialism.* Amherst. MA: University of Massachuesetts Press; Horgan, E. R. (1982). *The Shaker Holy Land.* Harvard, MA: The Harvard Common Press.
27. Millay, N. (1956). *Edna St. Vincent Millay: The Collected Poems.* New York: Harper & Row.
28. A textured and supportive life of Freud is available in: Gay, P. (1988). *Freud: A Life for Our Time.* New York: W. W. Norton.
29. Serious in the extreme, Philip Rieff makes it plain that Freud was at heart a moralist. See: Rieff, P. (1961). *Freud: The Mind of a Moralist.* Garden City, NY: Doubleday Anchor.
30. Russell, B. (1951). *The Autobiography of Bertrand Russell.* Boston: Little, Brown.
31. Russell, B. (1929). *Marriage and Morals.* New York: H. Liveright.
32. Although contemporary textbooks on marriage and the family often ignore the evidence, the lack of commitment in trial marriages seems to doom them to greater dissolution. See: Glen, N. (1997). *Closed Hearts, Closed Minds: The Textbook Story of Marriage.* New York: Institute for American Values.
33. Hefner, H. (Ed.) (1974). *The Twentieth Anniversary Playboy Reader.* Chicago: Playboy Press.
34. The standard social work interpretation is that the historic distinction between the deserving and the undeserving poor is invalid. For dissenting views see: Gordon, L. (1994). *Pittied But Not Entitled: Single Mothers and the History of Welfare.* New York: Free Press; Olasky, M. (1992). *The Tragedy of American Compassion.* Washington, D.C.: Regnery.

Chapter 5. Extreme I: Radical Feminism

1. A sampling of Steinem's thinking is found in the following: Steinem, G. (1983). *Outrageous Acts and Everyday Rebellions.* New York: Holt, Rinehart and Winston; Steinem, G. (1992). *Revolution From Within: A Book of Self-Esteem.* Boston: Little, Brown.
2. The totalitarian aspects of radical feminism are revealed in: Ellis, R. J. (1998). *The Dark Side of the Left: Illiberal Egalitarianism in America.* Lawrence, KS: University of Kansas Press.
3. A more expansive tendency toward sexlessness is explored in: Winick, C. (1968). *The New People: Desexualization in American Life.* New York: Pegasus.
4. Among the more virulent feminist diatribes against the family, and incidentaly against children, has been that of Shulamith Firestone. She believes that the family needs to be smashed and its childbearing and childrearing functions diffused "to the society as a whole." See: Firestone, S. (1970). *The Dialect of Sex: The Case for a Feminist Revolution.* New York: Morrow. Andrea Dworkin is likewise anti-family, describing it as an "open grave" for women. See: Dworkin, A. (1989). *Letters from the War Zone: Writings 1976-1989.* New York: E.P. Dutton.
5. Probably the most comprehensive feminist analysis of sexuality is Andrea Dworkin's which is avowedly lesbian in its conclusions. See: Dworkin, A. (1987). *Intercourse.* New York: The Free Press.
6. See: Firestone, op cit. Also, as Carolyn Graglia records, the feminist icon Kate Millet was argued in favor of state-run nurseries for children. According to Millet "One of consertvatisms' favorite myths is that every woman is a mother." See: Millet, K. (1969). *Sexual Politics.* New York: Doubleday.
7. In her plea for gender justice, Susan Okin calls repeatedly for the "demolition," "abolition," and disappearance" of gender. Presumably this means that femininity must be eliminated. See: Okin, S. (1989). *Justice, Gender, and Family.* New York: Basic Books.
8. Limbaugh, R. (1994). *See, I Told You So.* New York, Pocket Books.
9. Graglia complains of such things as feminist "hubris" in their "arrogant" denunciations of motherhood, etc. See: Graglia, F. C. (1998). *Domestic Tranquility: A Brief Against Feminism.* Dallas, TX: Spence.
10. As Richard Ellis explains, feminism "was not born moderate and then radicalized by the 1960s. From its inception, the term 'feminism,' in the minds of both its proponents and oponents has been linked with radicalism and even socialism." See: Ellis, R. J. (1998). *The Dark Side of the Left: Illiberal Egalitarianism in America.* Lawrence, KS: University of Kansas Press. Marcia Cohen gives details about the specific allegiances of founders of the feminist movement. Cohen, M. (1987). *The Sisterhood.* New York: Simon & Schuster.
11. Bernard, J. (1982). *The Future of Marriage.* New Haven: Yale University Press.
12. De Beauvoir, S. (1978). *The Second Sex.* New York: Alfred A. Knopf.
13. Horowitz puts the lie to Friedan's pretense of merely being a distraught suburban housewife. His research reveals that she was a left-leaning reporter for union newspapers before her tour in suburbia. See: Horowitz, D. (1998). *Betty Friedan and the Making of "The Feminine Mystique."* Amherst, MA: University of Massachuesetts Press.
14. Jagger, A. M. (1988). *Feminist Politics and Human Nature.* Totowa, NJ: Rowman & Littlefield.

15. Engels, F. (1972). *The Origin of the Family, Private Property, and the State*. New York: International Publishers.
16. Morgan, L. H. (1975). *The League of the Iroquois*. Secaucus, NJ: Citadel Press.
17. Marx, K. (1967). *Capital*. Edited by Fredrich Engels. New York: International Publishing.
18. Heise, L. (1989). The Glogal War Against Women. *The Washington Post*, April 9, pp. B1, B4.
19. MacKinnon, C. A. (1987). *Feminism Unmodified: Discourses on Life and Law*. Cambridge, MA: Harvard University Press.
20. Proudhon, P.J. [1840] (1994). *What Is Property?* Edited and translated by Donald R. Kelly & Bonnie G. Smith. New York: Cambridge University Press.
21. Rousseau, Jean-Jacques [1762] (1913). *The Social Contract*. In G. D. H. Cole (Ed.), *The Social Contract and Discourses*. London: Dent.
22. One of the earliest and most obviously Marxist perscriptions for how to orgainize a consciouness raising session was that of Kathie Sarachild. See: Sarachild, K. (1968). Consciousness raising: a radical weapon. In: Redstockings of the Women's Liberation Movement. (1968). *The Feminist Revolution*. New York: Random House.
23. Marx, K. & Engels, F. (1948). *The Communist Manifesto*. New York: International Publishing.
24. One instance of unmistakably Marxist language and sentiments is that of Firestone. See: Firestone, S., op cit.
25. Jagger, A. M. (1988). *Feminist Politics and Human Nature*. Totowa, NJ: Rowman & Littlefield.
26. Lorber, J. (1994). *Paradoxes of Gender*. New Haven: Yale University Press.
27. Faludi, S. (1991). *Backlash: The Undeclared War Against American Women*. New York: Crown.
28. As a columnist for *U.S. News & World Report*, one of John Leo's favorite activities is chronicling the coercive absurdities of political correctness. See: Leo, J. (1994). *Two Steps Ahead of the Thought Police*. New York: Simon & Schuster.
29. The French Revolution provides the model for a revolutionary reign of terror. Schama, S. (1989). *Citizens: A Chronicle of the French Revolution*. New York: Alfred A. Knopf.
30. A popular account of relationship difficulties, Maggie Scarf's book on intimacy is one of the more human discussions of the subject. See: Scarf, M. (1987). *Intimate Partners: Patterns in Love and Marriage*. New York: Random House.
31. Friedan, B. (1963). *The Feminine Mystique*. New York: W. W. Norton.
32. For an extended presentation of this position see: Wolf, N. (1992). *The Beauty Myth: How Images of Beauty Are Used Against Women*. New York: Doubleday.
33. Veblen, T. [1899] (1967). *The Theory of the Leisure Class*. New York: Viking Penguin.
34. Ibsen, H. (1941). *The Best Known Works of Ibsen*. New York: Bartholomew House.
35. Often underestimated in its impact, the Industrial Revolution needs to be understood in its total dimensions for its effects to be fully apreciated. See: Thompson, A. (1975). *The Dynamics of the Industrial Revolution*. New York: St. Martin's Press.
36. Daniel Chirot does an excellent job of explaining how changes in technology can have a ripple effect on other social changes. See: Chirot, D. (1986). *Social Change in the Modern Era*. San Diego: Harcourt, Brace, Jovanovich.
37. Rhode, D. (1997). *Speaking of Sex: The Denial of Gender Inequality*. Cambridge, MA: Harvard University Press.

38. Psychologists and biologists can today document dozens of physiological differences. See: Moir, A. & Jessel, D. (1989). *Brain Sex: The Real Difference Between Men and Women*. New York: Dell/Laurel. In comparison, Money and Erhardt earlier found few biological disparities and attributed most gender differences to socialization. These latter are now under review and have not fared well. See: Money, J. & Ehrhardt, A. E. (1972). *Man and Woman, Boy and Girl: The Differentiation and Dimorphism of Gender Identity from Conception to Maturity*. Baltimore: Johns Hopkins University.

39. Parsons, T. & Bales, R. F. (1955). *Family, Socialization and Interaction Process*. New York: The Free Press.

40. Tannen, D. (1990). *You Just Don't Understand: Women and Men in Conversation*. New York: William Morrow.

41. For another study confirming similar conclusions see: Lever, J. (1976). Sex differences in the games children play. *Social Problems*, 23, 478-487.

42. Carol Gilligan's research emphasizes the cooperative impulses of women. See: Gilligan, C. (1982). *In a Different Voice*. Cambridge, MA: Harvard University Press.

43. More a theory than a confirmed fact, the glass ceiling was first popularized by: Millman, M. & Kanter, R. M. (1975). *Another Voice*. New York: Doubleday.

44. Maccoby, E. E. & Jacklin, C. N. (1974). *The Psychology of Sex Differences*. Stanford: Stanford University Press; Maccoby, E. E. (Ed.) (1966). *The Development of Sex Differences*. Stanford: Stanford University Press.

45. Steven Goldberg argues that differences in average levels of aggressiveness can alone account for the greater concentration of men in positions of authority. See: Goldberg, S. (1973). *The Inevitability of Patriarchy*. New York: William Morrow.

46. For a sociological overview of intimacy see: Davis, M. S. (1973). *Intimate Relations*. New York: The Free Press. The anthropologist Helen Fisher does an excellent job of presenting the biological underpinnings of heterosexual intimacy. See: Fisher, H. E. (1992). *Anatomy of Love: The Natural History of Monogamy, Adultry, and Divorce*. New York: W. W. Norton.

47. Lasch, C. (1979). *The Culture of Narcissism: American Life in an Age of Diminishing Expectations*. New York: Warner Books.

48. For an ethnography of contemporary America patterns of coupling see: Blumstein, P. & Schwartz, P. (1985). *American Couples: Money, Work, Sex*. New York: Pocket Books.

49. When personal attachments are torn asunder, a variety of untoward consequences can follow. One of these is depression. See: Brown, G. & Harris, T. (1978). *Social Origins of Depression*. New York: The Free Press. Another is violence. See: Gelles, R. J. & Straus, M. A. (1989). *Intimate Violence: The Causes and Consequences of Abuse in the American Family*. New York: Touchstone Books.

50. For a brief on the necessity of families see: Bane, M. J. (1976). *Here to Stay: American Families in the Twentieth Century*. New York: Basic Books.

51. For one of the more passionate defenses of men in marriage see: Gilder, G. (1986). *Men and Marriage*. Gretna, LA: Pelican.

52. One of the best documented analyses of this propensity on college campuses is found in: Kors, A. C. & Silverglate, H. A. (1998). *The Shadow University: The Betrayal of Liberty on America's Campuses*. New York: The Free Press.

53. Today it is easy for men to be accused of creating a hostile work environment for women. But this very vulnerablity may create a hostile work environment for them. For the campus version of this story see: Kors, A. C. & Silverglate, H. A., ibid.

54. For Clarence Thomas' perspective see: Thomas, C. (1992). *Confronting the Future*. Washington, D.C.: Regnery.

55. Popenoe, D. (1996). *Life Without Father: Compelling New Evidence that Fatherhood and Marriage Are Indespensible for the Good of Children and Society.* New York: The Free Press.

56. Among the negative consequences of increased fatherlessness cited by David Blankenhorn are greater youth violence, more sexual abuse of children, and more widespread childhood poverty. See: Blankenhorn, D. (1995). *Fatherless America: Confronting Our Most Urgent Social Problem.* New York: Basic Books. Carolyn Graglia enumerates the pathologies involved with divorce, teenage pregnancies, crime, and declining birth rates. Graglia, F. C. (1998). *Domestic Tranquility: A Brief Against Feminism.* Dallas, TX: Spence.

57. Coltrane, S. (1997). Scientific half-truths and postmodern parody in the family values debate. *Contemporary Sociology,* 26, 7-10.

58. Stacey, J. (1996). *In the Name of the Family: Rethinking Family Values in the Postmodern Age.* Boston, MA: Beacon Press.

59. Coltrane, S. (1996). *Family Man: Fatherhood, Housework, and Gender Equity.* New York: Oxford University Press.

60. Fox-Genovese, E. (1996). *Feminism Is Not the Story of My Life: How Today's Feminist Elite Has Lost Touch with the Real Concerns of Women.* New York: Doubleday.

61. Sommers, C. H. (1994). *Who Stole Feminism: How Women Have Betrayed Women.* New York: Simon & Schuster.

62. Graglia, F. C., op cit.

63. As Gertude Himmelfarb ruefully observes divorce rates and rates of illegitimacy have soared. Today approximately half of all marriages end in divorce, and whereas in Victorian times only about 3% of children were born out of wedlock, nowadays almost one third are. See: Himmelfarb, G. (1995). *The De-Moralization of Society: From Victorian Virtues to Modern Values.* New York: Alfred A. Knopf.

64. The evidence is overwhelming that in order to prosper children require stable parenting, and especially stable mothering. For one thing, they need attachments they can count on in order to feel personally safe. For documentation see: Fraiberg, S. (1977). *Every Child's Birthright: In Defense of Mothering.* New York: Basic Books; Bowlby, J. (1969). *Attachment.* New York: Basic Books; Kagan, J. (1984). *The Nature of the Child.* New York: Basic Books.

65. Coontz, S. (1992). *The Way We Never Were: American Families and the Nostalgia Trap.* New York: Basic Books. Coontz, S. 1995. The way we weren't: the myth and reality of the 'traditional" family. *National Forum: The Phi Beta Kappa Journal,* Summer.

66. For further details regarding contemporary marital fragility see: Himmelfarb, G., op cit.

67. Himmelfarb presents a nice overview of the sort of gender division of labor that existed in Victorian English households. She makes it plain that this did indeed reduce marital frictions, while at the same time, contrary to the feminists, did not introduce a tyrannical patriarchy. See: Himmelfarb, G., ibid.

68. For the statisitcs consult: Gelles, R. J and Straus, M. A. (1989). *Intimate Violence: The Causes and Consequences of Abuse in the American Family.* New York: Touchstone Books.

69. For a description of how marital partners negotiate their differences see: Schwartz, P. (1994). *Peer Marriage: How Love Between Equals Really Works.* New York: The Free Press.

70. Horowitz, D. (1997). *Radical Son: A Generational Odyssey.* New York: The Free Press.

71. Stein, A. (1997). *Sex and Sensibility: Stories of a Lesbian Generation.* Berkeley: University of California Press.
72. Cohen, M. (1987). *The Sisterhood.* New York: Simon & Schuster.
73. Studies of how feminism is presented in classrooms show that skepticism is actively discouraged. See: Musil, C. M. (1992). *The Courage to Question: Women's Studies and Student Learning.* Washington D.C.: Association of American Colleges.
74. Whittier, N. (1995). *Feminist Generations: The Persistence of the Radical Women's Movement.* Philadelphia: Temple University Press. For a depiction of the role of lesbian activists in the formation of the movement see: Ellis, R. J. (1998). *The Dark Side of the Left: Illiberal Egalitarianism in America.* Lawrence, KS: University of Kansas Press.

Chapter 6. Extreme II: Radical Civil Rights

1. Royko, M. (1999). *One More Time: The Best of Mike Royko.* Chicago: University of Chicago Press.
2. Mair, G. (1994). *Oprah Winfrey: The Real Story.* Secaucus, NJ: Carol.
3. Kaplan, J. & Bernays, A. (1997). *The Language of Names: What We Call Ourselves and Why It Matters.* New York: Simon & Schuster.
4. Pitts, L. (1996). What's in a name? A message. *Miami Herald*, Feb 8.
5. Cited in Kaplan, J. & Bernays, A., op cit.
6. Genovese, E. D. (1974). *Roll, Jordan, Roll.* New York: Pantheon.
7. Thomas, H. (1997). *The Slave Trade: The Story of the Atlantic Slave Trade: 1440-1870.* New York: Simon & Schuster.
8. Olmsted, F. L. (1969). *The Cotton Kingdom.* New York: Modern Library; Patterson, O. (1982). *Slavery and Social Death: A Comparative Study.* Cambridge, MA: Harvard University Press.
9. DuBois, W. E. B. [1903] (1990). *The Souls of Black Folk.* New York: Vintage Books.
10. The Thernstrom's recently published book attempted to demonstrate that despite their ongoing problems, blacks had made enormous strides in contemporary America. Thernstrom, S. & Thernstrom, A. (1997). *America in Black and White: One Nation, Indivisible.* New York: Simon & Schuster.
11. On college campuses a double standard has come into existence with black students accorded the right to criticize even their most experienced professors. See: Kors, A. C. & Silverglate, H. A. (1998). *The Shadow University: The Betrayal of Liberty on America's Campuses.* New York: The Free Press.
12. I was both relieved and alarmed to discover the extent of this chilling effect as elaborated upon by Kors, A. C. & Silverglate, H. A., op cit.
13. The extent of "high-minded," albeit foolish multiculturalism in classrooms is documented by: Bernstein, R. (1994). *Dictatorship of Virtue: Multiculturalism and the Battle for America's Future.* New York: Alfred A. Knopf.
14. Kinder, R. R. & Sanders L. M. (1996). *Divided by Color: Racial Politics and Demcratic Ideals.* Chicago: University of Chicago Press.
15. Many white fear the balkinization of their country. See: Schlesinger, A. M. (1992). *The Disuniting of America.* New York: W. W. Norton; Skrentny, J. L. (1996). *The Ironies of Affirmative Action: Politics, Culture, and Justice in America.* Chicago: University of Chicago Press.
16. Sowell, T. (1984). *Civil Rights: Rhetoric or Reality?* New York: William Morrow.
17. Merriam-Webster. (1992). Hiram Warren Johnson. *Dictionary of Quotations.* Springfield, MA.

18. Hacker, A. (1995). *Two Nations: Black and White, Separate, Hostile, Unequal.* New York: Ballantine Books.
19. All subsequent quotations from Wolfe can be found in: Wolfe, A. (1996). *Marginalized in the Middle.* Chicago: University of Chicago Press.
20. The cognitive aspects of stereotyping are more complex than usually allowed. See: Hirschfield, L. A. (1996). *Race in the Making: Cognition, Culture, and the Child's Construction of Human Kinds.* Cambridge, MA: MIT Press.
21. For an openly Marxist analysis of the same phenomenon, see: Carr, L. G. (1997). *"Color-Blind" Racism.* Thousand Oaks, CA: Sage. In Tuch et al. the same phenomenon is labeled "laissez-faire racism" and seems to refer to the proposition that those who do not ascribe to the activist race policies of the authors must in this very "passivity" be racist. See: Tuch, S. A. & Martin, J. K. (Eds.) (1997). *Racial Attitudes in the 1990s: Continuity and Change.* Westport, CT: Praeger. Amy Elizabeth Ansell takes a similar position, describing those with whose policies she disagrees, as exemplifying a "new racism." See: Ansell, A. E. (1997). *New Right, New Racism: Race and Reaction in the United States and Britain.* New York: New York University Press. See likewise: Waller, J. (1998). *Face to Face: The Changing State of Racism across America.* New York: Insight.
22. Allport, G. (1954). *The Nature of Prejudice.* Boston: Beacon Press.
23. The extent of black violence can be truly disconcerting. See: Oliver, W. (1994). *The Violent Social World of Black Men.* New York: Lexington Books.
24. Sniderman, P. M. & Piazza, T. (1993). *The Scar of Race.* Cambridge, MA: The Belknap Press of Harvard University Press.
25. Stahl, L. (1997). STRIVE. *Sixty Minutes,* CBS News.
26. Weber, M. (1958). *The Protestant Ethic and the Spirit of Capitalism.* New York: Charles Scribner's Sons.
27. DuBois, W. E. B. [1899] (1996). *The Philadelphia Negro: A Social Study.* Philadelphia: University of Pennsylvania Press.
28. Their conclusions may be controversial, but their basic numbers are not disputed, hence see: Herrnstein, R. J. & Murray, C. (1994). *The Bell Curve: The Reshaping of American Life by Differences in Intelligence.* New York: Basic Books.
29. Ellis shows Adams to be a more complex and sensitive human being than previously suspected. See: Ellis, J. J. (1993). *Passionate Sage: The Character and Legacy of John Adams.* New York: W. W. Norton.
30. By far the most persuasive account of how bias infects the work of even careful scientists and how heredity becomes over-represented in their findings is that of: Gould, S. J. (1981). *The Mismeasure of Man.* New York: W. W. Norton.
31. The trends in expressed attitudes are unequivocal. For instance, where once whites were almost unanimous in their disapprobation of interracial marriages, almost 90% now express their acceptance of these alliances. See: Sniderman, P. M. & Carmines, E. G. (1998). *Reaching Beyond Race.* Cambridge, MA: Harvard University Press; Schuman, H., Steeh, C., Bobo, L. & Kysman, M. (1997). *Racial Attitudes in America: Trends and Interpretations.* Revised Edition. Cambridge, MA: Harvard University Press.
32. Ignatiev, N. (1995). *How the Irish Became White.* New York: Routledge.
33. White ethics have made remarkable strides, so much so that today they are often lumped together as European-Americans. See: Alba, R. D. (1990). *Ethnic Identity: The Transformation of White America.* New Haven: Yale University Press.
34. A case study from Chicago is presented by: Cayton, H. R. & Drake, St. C. (1946). *Black Metropolis.* London: Jonathan Cape.

35. Usually oblivious to their own paternalism, even liberals can treat blacks like children who need protection. See: Sleeper, J. (1997). *Liberal Racism*. New York: Viking.
36. *Atlanta Journal Constitution* (1997). Race Advisory Board. Aug.10.
37. D'Souza, D. (1995). *The End of Racism: Principles for a Multiracial Society*. New York: The Free Press.
38. West, C. (1993). *Race Matters*. Boston: Beacon Press.
39. Billson, J. M. (1998). *Pathways to Manhood: Young Black Males Struggle for Identity*, 2nd Edition. New Brunswick, NJ: Transaction.
40. Steele, S. (1990). *The Content of Our Character: A New Vision of Race in America*. New York: St. Martin's Press.
41. Steele, S. (1998). *A Dream Deferred: The Second Betrayal of Black Freedom in America*. New York: HarperCollins.
42. Aronson, E. (1988). *The Social Animal*, 5th Edition. New York: W. H. Freeman.
43. Deutsch, M. & Collins, M. E. (1951). *Interracial Housing: A Psychological Evaluation of a Social Experiment*. Minneapolis: University of Minnesota Press.
44. In: Thernstrom, S. & Thernstrom, A. (1997). *America in Black and White: One Nation, Indivisible*. New York: Simon & Schuster.
45. Sniderman, P. M. & Carmines, E. G., op cit.
46. Sowell, T. (1981). *Ethnic America*. New York: Basic Books; Sowell, T. (1994). *Race and Culture: A World View*. New York: Basic Books; Sowell, T. (1996). *Migrations and Cultures: A World View*. New York: Basic Books.
47. Lee, S. (1991). *Five for Five: The Films of Spike Lee*. New York: Stewart, Tabori and Chang.
48. Oscar Lewis created the concept of, and documented, a "culture of poverty," especially among latinos. See: Lewis, O. (1961). *The Children of Sanchez*. New York: Random House; Lewis, O. (1966). *La Vida: A Puerto Rican Family in the Culture of Poverty*. New York: Random House.
49. Myrdal, G. (1944). *An American Dilemma: The Negroe Problem and American Democracy*. New York: Harper & Row.
50. Cited in: Franklin, D. L. (1997). *Ensuring Inequality: The Structural Transformation of the African-American Family*. New York: Oxford University Press.
51. West, C., op cit.
52. For the details of how debilitating slavery can be see: Patterson, O. (1982). *Slavery and Social Death: A Comparative Study*. Cambridge, MA: Harvard University Press.
53. Park, R. (1950). *Race and Culture*. Glencoe, IL: The Free Press.
54. Gambino, R. (1974). *Blood of My Blood*. New York: Anchor Books.
55. Zborowski, M. & Herzog, E. (1962). *Life Is with People: The Culture of the Shtetl*. New York: Schocken Books; Yaffe, J. (1968). *American Jews*. New York: Random House.
56. For an account of the mixing, and non-mixing, that occurred in New York City see: Glazer, N. & Moynihan, D. P. (1963). *Beyond the Melting Pot*. Cambridge, MA: MIT Press.
57. Butterfield, F. (1995). *All God's Chidren: The Bosket Family and the Tradition of Violence*. New York: Alfed A. Knopf.
58. Similar cases occurred in California vis-a-vis George Jackson and the Black Panthers. See: Collier, P. & Horowitz, D. (Eds.) (1997). *The Race Card: White Guilt, Black Resentment, and the Assault on Truth and Justice*. Rocklin, CA: Forum.
59. Dash, L. (1996). *Rosa Lee: A Mother and Her Family in Urban America*. New York: Basic Books.

60. Despite protestations of valuing education, reports from the frontline indicate very different attitudes between blacks and whites. See: Metz, M. H. (1978). *Classrooms and Corridors: The Crisis of Authority in Desgregated Secondary Schools*. Berkeley: University of California Press.

61. For what is probably the most influentuial cultural interpretation of the black family see: Frazier, E. F. [1939] (1960). *The Negro Family in the United States*. Chicago: University of Chicago Press.

62. For a denial of the connection, however, see: Guttman, H. G. (1977). *The Black Family in Slavery and Freedom, 1750-1925*. New York: Vintage Books.

63. DuBois, W. E. B. [1903] (1990). *The Souls of Black Folk*. New York: Vintage Books.

64. Franklin, D. L. (1997). *Ensuring Inequality: The Structural Transformation of the African-American Family*. New York: Oxford University Press.

65. DuBois, W. E. B., op cit.

66. Blassingame, J. W. (1979). *The Slave Community: Plantation Life in the Antebellum South*. New York: Oxford University Press.

67. Williams, J. (1998). *Thurgood Marshall: American Revolutionary*. New York: Times Books.

68. Douglass, F. [1945] (1968). *Narrative of the Life of Fredrick Douglass*. New York: Signet Books.

69. The plight of the black woman is elaborated upon in: Ladner, J. (1971). *Tommorow's Tomorrow: The Black Woman*. New York: Doubleday.

70. Moynihan, D. P. (1965). *The Negro Family: The Case for National Action*. Washington, D. C.: Department of Labor.

71. Franklin, D. L., op cit.

72. Kearns, D. (1976). *Lyndon Johnson and the American Dream*. New York: Harper & Row.

73. Franklin, D. L., op cit.

74. See: Patterson, O. (1997). *The Ordeal of Integration: Progress and Resentment in America's "Racial" Crisis*. Washington, D.C.: Civitas/Counterpoint.

75. Cruse, H. (1967). *The Crisis of the Negro Intellectual: A Historical Analysis of the Failure of Black Leadership*. New York: William Morrow.

76. Despite almost universal condemnation, hierarchy is a universal human phenomenon, found in every society and every era. See: Hurst, C. E. (1995). *Social Inequality: Forms, Causes, and Consequences*, 2nd Edition. Boston: Allyn and Bacon; Kerbo, H. R. (1996). *Social Stratification and Inequality*, 3rd Edition. New York: McGraw-Hill.

77. Gouldner, A. W. (1954). *Patterns of Industrial Bureaucracy: A Case Study of Modern Factory Administration*. New York: The Free Press.

78. Stephen Carter, a professor of law at Yale University, expresses his ambivalence at being helped to get into college because of his race. He is particularly concerned to defend his own abilities as responsible for his success. See: Carter, S. L. (1991). *Reflections of an Affirmative Action Baby*. New York: Basic Books.

79. Piven, F. F. & Cloward, R. A. (1977). *Poor People's Movement's: Why They Succeed, How They Fail*. New York: Vintage.

80. Among the works which enumerate the disabilites inherent in slavery and its sequels are: Dollard, J. (1937). *Caste and Class in a Southern Town*. New Haven: Yale University Press.; Frazier, E. F. (1957). *Black Bourgeosie*. New York: Free Press; Franklin, J. H. (1969). *From Slavery to Freedom*. New York: Vintage Books.

81. Fanon, F. (1967). *Black Skin, White Masks*. New York: Grove Press.

82. Cose, E. (1993). *The Rage of a Privledged Class*. New York: HarperCollins.

83. Kohn, M. (1969). *Class and Conformity: A Study in Values.* Homewood, IL: The Dorsey Press.

84. Jennifer Hochschild argues that as long as discrimination remains, the American Dream is denied to even middle class blacks. See: Hochschild, J. (1995). *Facing Up to the American Dream.* Princeton, NJ: Princeton University Press.

85. Majors, R. & Billson, J. M. (1993). *The Cool Pose: The Dilemma of Black Manhood in America.* New York: Simon & Schuster.

86. Anderson, E. (1990). *Streetwise: Race, Class and Change in an Urban Community.* Chicago: University of Chicago Press.

87. For an overview of the relation between blacks and the legal system see: Kennedy, R. (1997). *Race, Crime, and the Law.* New York: Random House. For a passionate defense of jury nullification see: Butler, P. (1995). Racially based jury nullification: black power in the criminal justice system." *Yale Law Review,* 105, 677.

88. Wilson, W. J. (1978). *The Declining Significance of Race: Blacks and Changing American Institutions.* Chicago: University of Chicago Press.

89. As an example, the long time advocate of integration, Christopher Jencks, has come to the anguished conclusion that policies he has advocated have not been particularly successful. See: Jencks, C. (1992). *Rethinking Social Policy: Race, Poverty and the Underclass.* Cambridge, MA: Harvard University Press.

Chapter 7. Extreme III: Radical Medicalism

1. Wilson, J. Q. (1997). *Moral Judgment.* New York: The Free Press.

2. Walker, L. E. (1979). *The Battered Woman.* New York: Harper & Row.

3. Greenberg, D. F. (1988). *The Construction of Homosexuality.* Chicago: The University of Chicago Press.

4. Hart, C. W. M. (1988). *The Tiwis of North Australia,* 3rd Edition. New York: Holt, Rinehart and Winston.

5. Adamson, H. E. (1978). *The Cheyennes: Indians of the Great Plains,* 2nd Edition. New York: Holt, Rinehart and Winston.

6. Meeks, W. A. (1993). *The Origins of Christian Morality: The First Two Centuries.* New Haven: Yale University Press.

7. Freud, S. (1953-1974). *The Standard Edition of the Complete Psychological Works of Sigmund Freud.* (Edited by J. Strachey). London: Hogarth Press and Institute for Psychoanalysis.

8. American Psychiatric Association Committee on Nomenclature and Statistics. (1968). *Diagnostic and Statistical Manual of Mental Disorders;* 2nd Edition. Washington, D. C.

9. American Psychiatric Association Task Force on Nomenclature and Statistics. (1980). *Diagnostic and Statistical Manual of Mental Disorders;* 3rd Edition. Washington, D. C.

10. The account that follows, including quotes, is from: Kirk, S. A. & Kutchins, H. (1992). *The Selling of DSM: The Rhetoric of Science in Psychiatry.* New York: Aldine de Gruyter.

11. For a more detailed discussion of how morality operates see: Fein, M. (1997). *Hardball Without an Umpire: The Sociology of Morality.* Westport, CT: Praeger.

12. Siegler, M. (1974). *Models of Madness, Models of Medicine.* New York: MacMillan.

13. In sociology, deviance refers to behaviors that break important norms in important ways. In many ways, what is deviant is used to define what is normal. See: Erikson, K. (1964). Notes on the sociology of deviance, In Becker, H., *The Other Side: Perspectives on Deviance.* New York: The Free Press.

14. For a sociological, and a medical, rendition of the medical explanation of deviant behaviors see: Eaton, W. W. (1986). *The Sociology of Mental Disorders*, 2nd Edition. Westport, CT: Praeger; Gove, W. (Ed.) 1982. *Deviance and Mental Illness*. Beverly Hills: Sage; Ausubel, D. (1967). Personality disorder is disease. In Scheff, T. (Ed.), *Mental Illness and Social Process*. New York: Harper & Row.

15. For an historical account of how "mental illness" was regarded see: Skultans, V. (1979). *English Madness: Ideas on Insanity 1580-1890*. London: Routledge & Kegan Paul.

16. Leifer, R. (1969). *In the Name of Mental Health*. New York: Science.

17. For a heavily physiological explanation of mental disorders see: Wender, P. H. & Klein, D. F. (1981). *Mind, Mood & Medicine: A Guide to the New Biopsychiatry*. New York: New American Library.

18. Sociologists have indeed studied the aspects, and functions, of this role. See: Parsons, T. (1964). *Social Structure and Personality*. New York: The Free Press of Glencoe.

19. For an unself-conscious handbook on violence as a medical problem see: Fenley, M. A. et al. (1993). *The Prevention of Youth Violence: A Framework for Community Action*. Atlanta: Centers for Disease Control and Prevention.

20. For some pros and cons on personal problems as disease entities see: Wing, J. K. (1978). *Reasoning about Madness*. Oxford: Oxford University Press.

21. Spitzer, R. & Williams, J. (1982). The definition and diagnosis of mental disorder. In Gove, W. (Ed.), *Deviance and Mental Illness*. Beverly Hills: Sage.

22. American Psychiatric Association Task Force on Nomenclature and Statistics. (1980). *Diagnostic and Statistical Manual of Mental Disorders;* 3rd Edition. Washington, D. C.

23. For a non-technical, but graphic, depiction of schizophrenia see: Schulz, C. G & Kilgalen, R. K. (1969). *Case Studies in Schizophrenia*. New York: Basic Books.

24. The disease "hysteria" was the precursor of the "histrionic" personality, but because the term referred to the woman's uterus as the cause of the condition, it was jettisoned in favor of a more gender neutral word. See: Veith, I. (1965). *Hysteria: The History of a Disease*. Chicago: University of Chicago Press.

25. From: Kirk, S. A. & Kutchins, H. A., op cit.

26. American Psychiatric Association; Task Force on DSM-IV. (1994). *Diagnostic and Statistical Manual of Mental Disorders;* 4th Edition. Washington, D. C.

27. For the case of psychoanalysis see: Fine, R. (1979). *A History of Psychoanalysis*. New York: Columbia University Press.

28. An example is: Alexander, F. & Selsnick, S. (1966). *The History of Psychiatry*. New York: Harper & Row.

29. Fraser, A. (1979). *King Charles II*. London: Weidenfeld & Nicholson.

30. Scull, A. (1974). *Museums of Madness: The Social Organization of Insanity in Nineteenth Century England*. Princeton University Ph.D.

31. Scull, A. (1989). *Social Order/Mental Disorder: Anglo-American Psychiatry in Historical Perspective*. Berkeley: University of California Press.

32. Scull, A., ibid.

33. Scull, A. (1981). *Madhouses, Mad-Doctors, and Madmen: The Social History of Psychiatry in the Victorian Era*. London: The Athlone Press.

34. The barbarity of some of these techniques is hard to fathom. Prefrontal lobotomies, for instance, entailed driving an ice-pick-like device into the brain and swishing it around in the manner of a windshield wiper. See: Valenstein, E. S. (1986). *Great and Desperate Cures: The Rise and Decline of Psychosurgery and Other Radical Treatments for Mental Illness*. New York: Basic Books.

35. Wilson, D. C. (1975). *Stranger and Traveler: The Story of Dorothea Dix, American Reformer*. Boston: Little, Brown.

36. Levi, H. E. (1949). *An Introduction to Legal Reasoning.* Chicago: University of Chicago Press.
37. Lombroso-Ferrero, G. (1972). *Criminal Man, According to the Classification of Cesare Lombroso.* Montclair, NJ: Patterson Smith.
38. Hume, D. [1739] (1961). *A Treatise on Human Nature.* New York: Dolphin Books.
39. Freud's "talking cure" was devised in conjunction with Joseph Breuer. See: Breuer, J. & Freud, S. (1957). *Studies on Hysteria.* New York: Basic Books.
40. Gay, P. (1988). *Freud: A Life for Our Time.* New York: W. W. Norton.
41. A brief review of sociological concepts, such as "role," can be found in: Wachniak et al. (1993). *Sociological Perspectives: A Resource Manual.* Kennesaw, GA: Kennesaw State University.
42. Examples of personal roles are: scapegoat, caretaker, family hero, family mascot and the family beauty. See: Fein, M. (1990). *Role Change: A Resocialization Perspective.* New York: Praeger.
43. How personal roles are used in family therapy is exemplified by: Minuchin, S. (1974). *Families and Family Therapy.* Cambridge, MA: Harvard University Press.
44. Fein, M., *Role Change*, op cit.
45. Nixon, R. (1962). *Six Crises.* New York: Doubleday.
46. Wills, G. (1969). *Nixon Agonistes: The Crisis of the Self-Made Man.* Boston: Houghton Mifflin.
47. Ambrose, S. E. (1987). *Nixon: The Education of a Politician 1913-1962.* New York: Simon & Schuster.
48. Temperament seems to be a fairly stable, and biologically inherited, aspect of personality. See: Chess, S. & Thomas, A. (1986). *Temperament in Clinical Practice.* New York: Guilford Press.
49. Kubler-Ross, E. (1969). *On Death and Dying.* New York: MacMillan.
50. The term "psychotherapy" does not have a precise meaning, but a widely admired discussion of it is found in: Frank, J. (1973). *Persuasion and Healing; A Comparative Study of Psychotherapy.* Baltimore: Johns Hopkins University Press.
51. An overview of various alternatives is available in: London, P. (1964). *The Modes and Morals of Psychotherapy.* New York: Holt, Rinehart and Winston. Also includes an exploration of the moral dimension of therapy.
52. John B. Watson's "behaviorism" was a radical attempt to eliminate superstition from psychology by virtually defining emotion out of existence. See: Watson, J. B. (1914). *Behavior: An Introduction to Comparative Psychology.* New York: Holt.
53. For an anthropological examination of this practice see: Lemert, E. M. (1997). *The Trouble with Evil: Social Control at the Edge of Morality.* Albany, NY: State University of New York Press.
54. Rousseau, Jean-Jacques [1762] (1913). *The Social Contract.* In G. D. H. Cole (Ed.), *The Social Contract and Discourses.* London: Dent.
55. In *Whose Keeper*, Alan Wolfe compares the relative importance of political, economic, and social factors in understanding how civil society works. Wolfe, A. (1989). *Whose Keeper? Social Science and Moral Obligation.* Berkeley, CA: University of California Press. For a more historical perspective see: Seligman, A. B. (1992). *The Idea of Civil Society.* Princeton, NJ: Princeton University Press.
56. Wilson, J. Q. (1997). *Moral Judgment.* New York: The Free Press.
57. Moore, M.S. (1984). *Law and Psychiatry.* Cambridge: Cambridge University Press.
58. Howard, P. K. (1995). *The Death of Common Sense: How Law Is Suffocating America.* New York: Random House.
59. American Psychiatric Association; Task Force on DSM-IV, op cit.

60. Emotions, such as anger, turn out to be social as well as personal phenomena. In their communication and motivation functions, they are interpersonal means of controlling behavior. See: Fein, M. (1993). *I.A.M.: A Common Sense Guide to Coping with Anger.* Westport, CT: Praeger.

61. For further details of the specific application of intense emotions to creating and sustaining moral principles see: Fein, M. (1997). *Hardball Without an Umpire: The Sociology of Morality.* Westport, CT: Praeger.

62. For one example of excuses see: Olson, W. K. (1997). *The Excuse Factory: How Today's Employment Laws Promote Mediocrity in the Workplace.* New York: The Free Press.

63. Austin, J. L. (1961). *Philosophical Papers.* Edited by J. O. Urmson & G. J. Warnock. Oxford: The Clarendon Press.

64. Scott, M. B. & Lyman S. (1968). Accounts. *American Sociological Review*, 33, 46-62.

65. Goffman, E. (1971). *Relations in Public.* New York: Basic Books.

66. For an overview of labeling theory as applied to mental illness see: Scheff, T. J. (1966). *Being Mentally Ill.* Chicago: Aldine.

67. Goffman, E. (1963). *Stigma.* Englewood Cliffs, NJ: Prentice-Hall.

68. Staddon, J. (1995). On responsibility and punishment." *The Atlantic Monthly*, February, 88-94.

69. Rogers, C. (1951). *Client Centered Therapy.* Boston: Houghton-Mifflin.

70. For an introduction to how Rogers believes people should treat one another see: Rogers, C. R. (1961). *On Becoming a Person: A Therapist's View of Psychotherapy.* Boston: Houghton-Mifflin.

71. For an account of medicine as a form of social control see: Horowitz, A. V. (1982). *The Social Control of Mental Illness.* New York: Academic Press.

72. Dr. Peter Kramer argues passionately that the latest psychotropic drugs can reformulate our personalities in almost mystical ways. See: Kramer, P. D. (1993). *Listening to Prozac: A Psychiatrist Explores Antidepressant Drugs and the Remaking of the Self.* New York: Viking.

73. For a discussion on why effective control of crime depends on morally credible control agents, see: Robinson, P. H. (1995). Moral credibility and crime. *Atlantic Monthly*, March, 72-78.

Chapter 8.   Luminosity Blindness

1. For an explanation of why this security is so vital see: Erikson, E. H. (1963). *Childhood and Society,* 2nd Edition. New York: W. W. Norton.

2. Twain, M. (1996). *Chapters from my Autobiography.* New York: Oxford University Press.

3. As Melville Dalton demonstrates, even organizational rewards are distributed in an informal, and sometimes irrational, manner. Dalton, M. (1959). *Men Who Manage.* New York: John Wiley & Sons.

4. Barnard, C. (1938). *The Function of the Executive.* Cambridge, MA: Harvard University Press.

5. See as noted perviously: Schulz, C. G & Kilgalen, R. K. (1969). *Case Studies in Schizophrenia.* New York: Basic Books.

6. Horowitz, D. (1997). *Radical Son: A Generational Odyssey.* New York: The Free Press.

7. Peck, M. S. (1978). *The Road Less Travelled.* New York: Simon & Schuster.

8. Wolfe, A. (1996). *Marginalized in the Middle*. Chicago: University of Chicago Press.
9. An example of how optimistic educational reformers can be is on display in: Holt, J. (1964). *How Children Fail*. New York: Dell.
10. The latest of a long line of community-oriented sociological reformers is: Etzioni, A. (1993). *The Spirit of Community: The Reinvention of American Society*. New York: Simon & Schuster.
11. Wolfe, A., op cit.
12. The popularizer of "unconditional love" was, of course, Carl Rogers. See: Rogers, C. (1951). *Client Centered Therapy*. Boston: Houghton-Mifflin.
13. For an example of good advice see: Scarf, M. (1987). *Intimate Partners: Patterns in Love and Marriage*. New York: Random House.
14. Symbols are so significant that in sociology an entire theory, namely symbolic interactionism, revolves around them. See: Mead, G. H. (1934). *Mind, Self, and Society*. Chicago: University of Chicago Press.
15. See: Brissett, D. & Edgley, C. (Eds.) (1990). *Life as Theater: A Dramaturgical Source Book*, 2nd Edition. New York: Aldine de Gruyter.
16. The romanticism of Jefferson's concept of "equality" is nicely exposed in Joseph Ellis' companion works on him and John Adams. Ellis, J. J. (1996). *American Sphinx: The Character of Thomas Jefferson*. New York: Alfred A. Knopf; Ellis, J. J. (1993). *Passionate Sage: The Character and Legacy of John Adams*. New York: W. W. Norton. How the founders, in general, understood the concept of equality is constructively analyzed, In: West, T. G. (1997). *Vindicating the Founders: Race, Sex, Class, and Justice in the Origins of America*. Lanham, MD: Rowman & Littlefield.
17. Browning, R. (1970). *Poetical Works, 1833-1864*. Edited by Ian Jack. New York: Oxford University Press.
18. Goffman, E. (1961). *Asylums*. New York: Anchor Books.
19. Barnard, C., op cit.
20. The imperative coordination, that is, the orders from superior to subordinate, we take for granted depends upon the existence of hierarchies. See: Dahrendorf, R. (1959). *Class and Class Conflict in an Industrial Society*. Stanford, CA: Stanford University Press.
21. Santayana, G. [1905-06] (1954). *The Life of Reason*. New York: Scribner.
22. For further atrocities see: Shirer, W. L. (1960). *The Rise and Fall of the Third Reich: A History of Nazi Germany*. New York: Simon & Schuster.
23. Olasky, M. (1992). *The Tragedy of American Compassion*. Washington, D.C.: Regnery.
24. More recently, in its reforms of the New York City welfare system, Mayor Guiliani's task force found that nearly 60% of applicants for assistance were not eligible, and nearly 50% did not even reside at the address given on their application. See: Zuckerman, M. B. (1995). Showing the way on welfare. *U.S. News & World Report*, May 22.
25. Rothwax, H. J. (1995). *Guilty: The Collapse of Criminal Justice*. New York: Random House.
26. A sample of the gushing journalism is found in: Donnelly, P. (1997). *Diana: A Tribute to the People's Princess*. Philadelphia: Courage Books.
27. The degree to which an idealistic person can suspend disbelief is painfully revealed in Miriam Williams excruciatingly honest retrospective of her years living in a Jesus cult. See: Williams, M. (1998). *Heaven's Harlots: My Fifteen Years as a Sacred Prostitute in the Children of God Cult*. New York: William Morrow.

Chapter 9. No Respect

1. Madison, J., Hamilton, A., & Jay, J. 1966. *The Federalist Papers.* Edited by W. Kendall and G. W. Carey. New Rochelle, NY: Arlington House.
2. Kearns, D. (1976). *Lyndon Johnson and the American Dream.* New York: Harper & Row.
3. For a synopsis of American history see: Johnson, P. (1997). *A History of the American People.* New York: HarperCollins.
4. Moynihan, D. P. (1993). Defining deviancy down. *American Scholar,* Summer.
5. Hunter, J. D. (1991). *Culture Wars: The Struggle to Define America.* New York: Basic Books.
6. A conservative review of the traditional virtues is found in: West, T. G. (1997). *Vindicating the Founders: Race, Sex, Class, and Justice in the Origins of America.* Lanham, MD: Rowman & Littlefield. A liberal interpretation of the same territory is found in: Loewen, J. (1995). *Lies My Teacher Told Me: Everything Your American History Textbook Got Wrong.* New York: The New Press.
7. Lipset, S. M. (1996). *American Exceptionalism: A Double-Edged Sword.* New York: W. W. Norton.
8. The passion of those didicated to this canon is nowhere better demonstrated than in: Ellis, J. M. (1997). *Literature Lost: Social Agendas and the Corruption of the Humanities.* New Haven: Yale University Press.
9. What equality meant to a well-meaning slave owner is explained in: Ellis, J. J. (1996). *American Sphinx: The Character of Thomas Jefferson.* New York: Alfred A. Knopf. And to a sturdy New England Yankee: Ellis, J. J. (1993). *Passionate Sage: The Character and Legacy of John Adams.* New York: W. W. Norton.
10. There is a contentious dispute between those who believe, like James Coleman, that education makes opportunity available to those prepared to take advantage of it and those like Samuel Bowles who are convinced that it is a con game designed to channel poor children into inferior occupations. See: Coleman, J. S. et al. (1966). *Equality of Educational Opportunity.* Washington, D.C.: U.S. Government Printing Office; Bowles, S. & Gintis, H. (1976). *Schooling in Capitalist America: Educational Reform and the Contradictions of Economic Life.* New York: Basic Books.
11. F. A. Hayek documented this propensity in the case of Nazi Germany, while Ludvig von Mises did so for socialism in general. See: Hayek, F. A. von (1944). *The Road to Serfdom.* With Forward by John Chamberlain. Chicago: University of Chicago Press; Von Mises, L. (1951). *Socialism: An Economic and Sociological Analysis.* Translated by J. Kahane. New Haven: Yale University Press.
12. The classic defense of liberty is that of John Stuart Mill. Mill, J. S. (1956). *On Liberty.* Edited by C. V. Shields. New York: Liberal Arts Press.
13. Thus Carl Roger believes that all people are basically trying to self-actualize and that with only a little support from their therapists they work diligently to solve their own problems. See: Rogers, C. R. (1961). *On Becoming a Person: A Therapist's View of Psychotherapy.* Boston: Houghton-Mifflin.
14. Rousseau, Jean-Jacques [1762] (1913). *The Social Contract.* In G. D. H. Cole (Ed.), *The Social Contract and Discourses.* London: Dent.
15. Hobbes, T. (1956). *Leviathan; Part I.* Chicago: Regnery.
16. Rousseau, Jean-Jacques [1762] (1979). *Emile.* Translated by A. Bloom. New York: Basic Books.
17. Among those who have offered "suggestions" are: Bernard, J. (1982). *The Future of Marriage.* New Haven: Yale University Press; Friedan, B. (1963). *The Feminine*

Mystique. New York: W. W. Norton; MacKinnon, C. A. (1987). *Feminism Unmodified: Discourses on Life and Law*. Cambridge, MA: Harvard University Press.

18. For an explanation of this concept by its originators see: Millman, M. & Kanter, R. M. (1975). *Another Voice*. New York: Doubleday.

19. Hurst, C. E. (1995). *Social Inequality: Forms, Causes, and Consequences*, 2nd Edition. Boston: Allyn and Bacon; Kerbo, H. R. (1996). *Social Stratification and Inequality*, 3rd Edition. New York: McGraw-Hill.

20. Hunter, J. D., op cit.

21. Kohn, M. (1969). *Class and Conformity: A Study in Values*. Homewood, IL: The Dorsey Press.

22. Lenski, G. (1966). *Power and Privledge: A Theory of Social Stratification*. New York: McGraw-Hill.

23. For a history see: Pfeiffer, J. E. (1977). *The Emergence of Society: A Prehistory of the Establishment*. New York: McGraw-Hill.

24. For a further history see: McNeill, W. H. (1963). *The Rise of the West: A History of the Human Community*. New York: Mentor; For a clarification of why trust is essential to large-scale industrial societies see: Fukuyama, F. (1995). *Trust: The Social Virtues and the Creation of Prosperity*. New York: The Free Press.

25. For details regarding the emergence of modern Europian society see: Braudel, F. (1979). *Civilization & Capitalism: 15th-18th Century*, Vols 1-3. Translated by Sian Reynolds. New York: Harper & Row.

26. Gray, D. J. (1991). *William Wallace: The King's Enemy*. New York: Barnes & Noble.

27. de Tocqueville, A. (1966). *Democracy in America*. Translated by George Lawrence. New York: Harper & Row.

28. In: Collins, R. & Makowsky, M. (1993). *The Discovery of Society*, 5th Edition. New York: McGraw-Hill.

29. For the significance of rationality for modern business consult: Chirot, D. (1986). *Social Change in the Modern Era*. San Diego: Harcourt, Brace, Jovanovich.

30. On the late emergence of double-entry bookkeeping, etc. see: Crosby, A. W. (1997). *The Measure of Reality*. New York: Cambridge University Press.

31. Gerth, H. H. & Mills, C. W. (Eds.) (1946). *From Max Weber: Essays in Sociology*. New York: Oxford University Press.

32. Miller, J. (1978). *The Body in Question*. New York: Vintage Books.

33. Plato (1941). *The Republic*. (Jowett translation) New York: The Modern Library.

34. Mead, M. (1928). *Coming of Age in Samoa*. New York: William Morrow.

35. For examples see: Friedman, R. E. (1987). *Who Wrote the Bible?* New York: Summit Books.

36. Zeldin, T. (1994). *An Intimate History of Humanity*. New York: HarperCollins.

37. Leo, J. (1994). *Two Steps Ahead of the Thought Police*. New York: Simon & Schuster.

38. For an ardent feminist's view of sexuality see: Dworkin, A. (1987). *Intercourse*. New York: The Free Press.

39. For an account of the limitations of laws see: Howard, P. K. (1995). *The Death of Common Sense: How Law Is Suffocating America*. New York: Random House.

40. Straus, B. R. (1987). *The Catholic Church*. London: David & Charles.

41. Ax grinders are those, who for personal reasons, are so dedicated to achieving a particular result that they spend most of their time sharpening their weapons. See in: Fein, M. (1997). *Hardball Without an Umpire: The Sociology of Morality*. Westport, CT: Praeger.

42. Toland, J. (1976). *Adolf Hitler*. Garden City, NY: Doubleday.

43. For an account of how ideologies operate see: Mannheim, K. (1936). *Ideology and Utopia.* New York: Harcourt, Brace, and World.
44. Shirer, W. L. (1960). *The Rise and Fall of the Third Reich: A History of Nazi Germany.* New York: Simon & Schuster.
45. Williams, M. (1998). *Heaven's Harlots: My Fifteen Years as a Sacred Prostitute in the Children of God Cult.* New York: William Morrow.
46. Bernstein, R. (1994). *Dictatorship of Virtue: Multiculturalism and the Battle for America's Future.* New York: Alfred A. Knopf; Santayana, G. [1905-06] (1954). *The Life of Reason, or the Phases of Human Progress.* Edited by Daniel Cory. New York: Scribner.
47. For the meaning of "civil society" see: Seligman, A. B. (1992). *The Idea of Civil Society.* Princeton, NJ: Princeton University Press: Hearn, F. (1997). *Moral Order and Social Disorder: The American Search for Civil Society.* New York: Aldine de Gruyter.
48. For a discussion of what we owe each other see: Wolfe, A. (1989). *Whose Keeper? Social Science and Moral Obligation.* Berkeley, CA: University of California Press.
49. In sociology, for instance, Max Weber's data on the Protestant Ethic was long taken for granted. But Eeven so venerable an expert as Weber may not be correct in all his particulars. See: Hamilton, R. F. (1996). *The Social Misconstruction of Reality: Validity and Verification in the Scholarly Community.* New Haven: Yale University Press.
50. The religious revivals of the Second Great Awakening received their impetus from the likes of flour mill operators who wanted their employees to come to work on time and not to fall into the machinery. See: Johnson, P. E. (1978). *A Shopkeeper's Millennium: Society and Revivals in Rochester New York 1815-1837.* New York: Hill and Wang.
51. The quality of American university education is currently laboring under the handicap of thousands of tenured professors dedicated more to political correctness than intellectual honesty. See: Kimball, R. (1990). *Tenured Radicals: How Politics has Corrupted our Higher Education.* New York: HarperCollins.
52. For my take on this question see: Fein, M., op cit.
53. Wolfe, A. (1998). *One Nation, After All.* New York: Viking.

Index